SEASONS OF THE HEART

Vel Hobbs

Copyright © 2008 by Vel Hobbs

SEASONS OF THE HEART
by Vel Hobbs

Printed in the United States of America

ISBN 978-1-60647-209-5

Scriptures taken from the Holy Bible, New International Version, Copyright © 1973, 1978, 1984. International Bible Society. Used by permission of Zondervan Bible Publisher.

www.xulonpress.com

To everything there is a season,
A time for every purpose under heaven;

A time to be born,
And a time to die;

A time to plant,
And a time to pluck up what is planted;

A time to kill,
And a time to heal;

A time to break down,
And a time to build up;

A time to weep,
And a time to laugh;

A time to mourn,
And a time to dance;

A time to cast away stones,
And a time to gather stones;

A time to embrace,
And a time to refrain from embracing;

A time to gain,
And a time to lose;

A time to keep,
And a time to throw away;

A time to tear,
And a time to sew;

A time to keep silent,
And a time to speak;

A time to love,
And a time to hate;

A time of war,
And a time of peace.

(Ecclesiastes 3: 1-8)

"A PASTOR'S HEART"

A pastor is a shepherd. The Greek word *poi men* occurs seventeen times in the New Testament, and of these seventeen times, this verse in Ephesians is the only place where it is translated *"pastor"*. The other sixteen times, it is translated *"shepherd"*. Paul is telling us in this Scripture that *the pastor is to be the shepherd of his flock – of his church.*

- **Ephesians 4:11 ... *"And he Himself gave some to be apostles, some prophets, some evangelists, and some pastors and teachers."***

- **Matthew 9:36 ... *"When Jesus saw the multitudes, He was moved with compassion on them, because they fainted, and were scattered abroad, as sheep having no shepherd."***

Jesus is the Chief Shepherd – the Chief Pastor. He saw the multitudes and was moved with compassion by their needs. The outlook that Jesus had should demonstrate the Pastor's Heart. When we look at the Ministry of Jesus while He was still upon this earth, we get a true picture of what it means to be a pastor – a shepherd.

The ministry of a pastor is to feed the flock with knowledge and with understanding, to feed the souls of all who come, and consistently do so out of love. A pastor's church is not to be nearly as much about the "building" as it is to be about the "body of believers" therein.

JESUS had a PASTOR'S HEART, and I want to make a SPECIAL DEDICATION of this book to some people in my life whom I truly feel are PASTORS with a genuine PASTOR'S HEART. I also want to honor some whom I believe are a few of the "UNSUNG HEROS" of our Christian Faith. Servants of our Lord who earn their bread by the sweat of their brow with hard labor and long toil, and yet they find the strength and compassion to reach out to others who are lost and/or hurting. Some have small congregations where they minister and teach those who come in without much thought for themselves and their personal needs. Others expend themselves quietly and with great perseverance to carry the Message of Jesus Christ and His Love into our jails, prisons, homeless shelters, abuse centers, drug rehabilitation centers, to the streets, nursing homes, orphanages, and other mission fields in the secular world where they find people who are desperate and seeking real answers for their life.

My dear friends and fellow servants of Christ Jesus ... no one else may know you, *or even share in your commit-ment to the call which God has placed upon your life*, but be encouraged in knowing that your sacrifices are not going unnoticed by your Heavenly Father and your Eternal Reward will be magnificent! Take comfort from these words ...

Matthew 25: 31–40 ... *"When the Son of Man comes in his glory, and all the angels with him, he will sit on his throne in heavenly glory. All the nations will be gathered before him, and he will separate the people one from another as a shepherd separates the sheep from the goats. He will put the sheep on the right and the goats on the left. Then the King will say to those on his right, 'Come, you who are* *blessed by my Father; take your inheritance, the kingdom prepared for you since the creation of the world. For I was hungry and you gave me something to eat, I was thirsty and you gave me something to drink, I was a stranger and you invited me in. I needed clothes and you clothed me, I was sick and you looked after me, I was in prison and you came to visit me.' Then the righteous will answer him, 'Lord, when did we see you hungry and feed you, or thirsty and give you something to drink? When did we see you a stranger and invite you in, or needing clothes and clothe you? When did we see you sick or in prison and go to visit you?' The King will reply, 'I tell you the truth, whatever you did for one of the least of these brothers of mine, you did for me.'"*

Luke 15: 3–7 ... *Then Jesus told them this parable: "Suppose one of you has a hundred sheep and loses one of them. Does he not leave the ninety-nine in the open country and go after the lost sheep until he finds it? And when he finds it, he joyfully puts it on his shoulders and goes home. Then he calls his friends and neighbors together and says, 'Rejoice with me; I have found my lost sheep.' I tell you that in the same way there will be more rejoicing in heaven over one sinner who repents than over ninety-nine righteous persons who do not need to repent."*

Please do not misunderstand what I am saying here. I firmly believe the Scriptures teach us that the *"laborers are worthy of their hire"*, and the pastors of our churches need to not only be lifted up in Christian Fellowship but to also have the financial support of their congregations. I am not saying that well-known pastors of large churches are not led of God to be used in reaching multitudes with the Message of the Gospel. God has a specific Call and a specific Purpose for each of His Children as they labor for His Kingdom. In whatever position in life that God has placed you ... that is your "mission field" and He will bless your labor.

But there are so many who make great personal sacrifices to follow the Call of God upon their lives, and yet they often remain unknown by others. To these "UNSUNG HEROS OF OUR CHRISTIAN FAITH" ... you have my deep gratitude and deep respect. THANK YOU & GOD BLESS YOU! Here are a few who have personally touched my life.

- **Pastor Wilbur Booth**: you never knew how much a confused teenager needed to sit under your teaching, to visit your home, and to see the Love of God lived out in a way that I was so hungry for. After leaving home, and turning away from God for so many years, the Truth of the Love of God lived daily by you and your wife, never completely left my heart. I always longed to KNOW JESUS the way that you did – now I do!

- **Pastor Terry Morris**: it was many years before I met another minister with the same "Pastor's Heart" that I had witnessed in Pastor Wilbur Booth. I met Pastor Terry Morris in late 2004. During the context of our first conversation, I asked Pastor Terry what his beliefs were – what denomination they were. I will never forget his answer, *"Well, I guess we would be called non-denominational. All I know is that we just love Jesus."* From the first time that I sat under Pastor Terry's preaching, I have continued to witness a true "Shepherd's Heart" within this man and his wife, Paula. Never grow discouraged because God is using you to touch lives in ways you will only know when this earthly journey has been completed.

- **Pastor Larry Stites**: by trade, Pastor Larry has a construction company, and he built the church he pastors with his own hands. Through Jesus Christ, Larry was set free from a life of sin and confusion. God planted a burning desire to share the Message of the Gospel deep within his heart. Larry is also my first cousin, so I know how very far God has brought him on his journey. I also know that he has encouraged and inspired many with his level of commitment and deep faith. I, too, have been encouraged and inspired by the ministry of this man.

- **Evangelist & Gospel Singer Jesse Turner**: having first met in 2001, Jesse and I have walked through some pretty stormy weather as friends and as "family" in Christ Jesus. We have also witnessed some wonderful times of Spiritual Refreshment and deep workings of the Holy Spirit in our respective lives and in the lives of others. Jesse ministers in song and in God's Word at churches throughout the country. But I am honoring him in the dedication of this book for his unselfish and tireless ministry into the prison systems for more than two decades. My friend, God has not forgotten your sacrifices and He is holding great rewards for you in His Kingdom.

- **Robert & Audrey DuBois @ Hope For All In Jesus Prison Outreach**: both are tireless in carrying God's Word with a real "heart" for the inmates into so many prison environments. Both are now in their seventies and have been in this ministry for twenty-six years. For more than a decade, Ms. Audrey as *"her girls"* lovingly call her, carries her ministry of encouragement every Friday night into the Women's Quarters of Montgomery County Jail ... in her wheelchair.

This lady has encouraged and inspired me over the past several years far more than even I can find the words to express.

- **The Father & The Son & The Holy Spirit**: thank you, **Father God**, for your mercy, your understanding, your forgiveness, your unconditional love, and for the PLAN that you have always had for my life. Thank you, **Lord Jesus,** for being willing to give your life for my sins, for taking the wounds for my healing, and for even now sitting at the **Right Hand of God our Father** in intercession for me. Thank you, **Holy Spirit**, for filling me with comfort, for intercession when I don't know what to pray, for conviction when I slip or fall, for direction as I seek the Will and the Purpose of God for my life. With special dedication to the **ONE & ONLY GOD** whom I love and serve.

You can contact me, *via mail and email,* by utilizing the information below:

MINISTRY OF NEW HOPE
Vel Hobbs
PO Box 1662
Conroe, Texas 77305
Email: minisryofnewhope@consolidated.net
Website: www.ministryofnewhope.com

TABLE OF CONTENTS

PREFACE

"TO EVERYTHING THERE IS A SEASON"

*L*ife *is all about seasons ... changes and transitions.* There is a time for everything. In **Ecclesiastes 3: 1-11**, Solomon reminds his readers that life continues to march on through a series of inevitable transitions. In one lifetime we each will pass through *seasons of change.* Most often we have no control over many of the *life changes* we face, but we will always have a *personal choice* when it comes to dealing with these changes. Those *choices* will continue to shape and to guide our everyday lives.

Most of us have no problem handling the good times, but how do we deal with overwhelming loss and struggle? How we *choose* to handle the difficult times will affect the quality of our lives, and the lives of those around us, for years to come – often for a lifetime.

If we can learn to pass through the *seasons of change* with a positive and healthy attitude, our lives can become stronger and better in so many ways. If we get stuck in a *season of negative and unhealthy emotions* and refuse to *choose to heal,* our lives will grow empty and bitter. Please understand that I am not just *mouthing textbook platitudes* here, I am speaking from personal experience. I, too, have suffered tremendous loss and have known unquenchable pain. I, too, have passed through some incredible *"Seasons Of The Heart"*.

Change is growth, and while a change may be extremely needed and worthwhile, true and lasting *change* never comes easy, and real *change* never comes without a price. In this book I want to talk about *"God Healing Our Land"* in a very personal context.

- **2 Chronicles 7:14 ... *"If my people who are called by my name, will humble themselves and pray and seek my face and turn from their wicked ways, then I will hear from heaven and will forgive their sin and will heal their land."***

To be very honest, I had never thought of this Scripture in a *"deeply personal way"* until I heard a sermon on this concept. This message not only stirred my heart, but it changed the course of my life forever. My prayer for you, *the readers of this book*, is that God will use the words contained within these pages to stir your heart and to help you to make *personal choices* that will change the overall quality of your lives forever.

As we read the words of Solomon in the **Book of Ecclesiastes** we see that the *seasons of inevitable transitions* we must pass through in our lives today have been experienced by people of all ages for all of time. There are times for birth, death, weeping, laughing, mourning, dancing, silence, speaking, and even for war and peace.

People cannot control many situations when it comes to *life transitions,* and human reactions to circumstances are natural. Sometimes laughter is the only response – Sometimes tears. Without God, powerful contrasts cause people pain and indicate meaninglessness in life. But with God, we do have the power to turn those *negatives* into *positives*.

Change can challenge and grow us. We can allow the *seasons of change* to transform us, or we can resist them, but we cannot stop them. To resist the *changes of life* will only complicate the process. *Life transitions* will bring about the *"Seasons Of The Heart"* ... *those important changes that occur throughout the life cycle from the cradle to the grave.* Resistance to change will inevitably retard and restrict the transforming power of life's transitions.

While some transitions come easy, others roll in like angry tidal waves – leaving total devastation in their path. Life transitions can be as simple as leaving a familiar place to begin a new life in a less familiar environment, or they can be as painful as having to learn to go on when one is diagnosed with an incurable disease, loss of employment and financial security, or the devastating loss of a very special loved one.

Life is a perpetual transition. We each have *choices* to make regarding the *changes* we will each face in our respective lives. We can *choose* to passively sit by while "nature takes its course", which will prove to be a self-defeating purpose. Or we can decide to be aggressively engaged in becoming the people God intended us to be by learning to navigate the passages and the transitions of our life.

There is a *rhythm of opposite seasons* recorded in **Ecclesiastes 3: 1-8.** Without opposites, how do we know the reality of any experience? And how can we comfort others unless or until we have walked through the fire of refinement or the valley of death ourselves? How would we know darkness without light? How would we appreciate health if we were never sick? How can we know the deep darkness of grief if we have never experienced the death of a loved one? How can we know the healing power of true joy and the restoration of laughter if we have never wept the bitter tears of despair?

Jesus came to this earth as both the Son of God and Son of Man in order to truly know all that we walk through with life transitions ... *"He Bore The Stripes For Our Total Healing"*. He is our comfort in times of despair, and He is our strength in times of weakness.

- **2 Corinthians 1: 3-7 ...** *"Praise be to the God and Father of our Lord Jesus Christ, the Father of compassion and the God of all comfort, who comforts us in all our troubles, so that we can comfort those in any trouble with the comfort we ourselves have received from God. For just as the sufferings of Christ flow over into our lives, so also through Christ our comfort overflows. If we are distressed, it is for your comfort and salvation; if we are comforted, it is for your comfort, which produces in you patient endurance of the same sufferings we suffer. And our hope for you is firm, because we know that just as you share in our sufferings, so also you share in our comfort."*

In **Ecclesiastes Chapter Three** we read, *"To everything there is a season ..."* Like the four seasons of our calendar year, certain *"Seasons Of The Heart"* are predictable, but many of them are not. None of us can predict our *seasons of weeping* or our *seasons of laughter* – our *seasons of life* or our *seasons of death*.

Life transitions can be both sad and joyful, as there is *"a time to mourn, and a time to dance"*. At the same time, a life transition can be full of hope and hopelessness. Life transitions signal both an ending and a beginning. Sometimes it is difficult to envision a *beginning* while experiencing the pain of loss that is part of an *ending*. We must give ourselves permission to grieve our endings, and to be encouraged by the hope of new beginnings.

Life's transitions are inevitable. Accepting this reality is the *first step* necessary to effectively handling life's transitions. We can avoid, or even prevent, some painful changes but *transitions* are ultimately a way of life for everyone. Accepting this truth enables us to embrace life with its *seasons* of growth and development. When we go through a *season* of deep grief or debilitating struggle, we can *choose* to remain angry, depressed, and hopeless. Or we can *choose* to allow the pain to forge a passage into a new, hopeful, and meaningful life … *that choice is ours to make!*

The *second step* to effectively handling life's passages is to allow change to work. When struggling with change, it is comforting to know that God is in control and is manipulating the situation for good. **Romans 8:28 …** *"And we know that all things work together for good to those who love God, to those who are called according to His purpose."* Because this is true, it is just good common sense to stop the resistance and to TRUST IN GOD! Our faith has truly kicked in when we are able to submit our life completely to God. **1 Peter 5: 6&7 …** *"Humble yourselves, therefore, under God's mighty hand, that He may lift you up in due time. Cast all your anxiety on Him because He cares for you."*

The *third step* to effectively handling life's passages is perseverance … the ability to hang in there during difficult circumstances. **Romans 5: 1-5 …** *"Therefore, since we have been justified through faith, we have peace with God through our Lord Jesus Christ, through whom we have gained access by faith into this grace in which we now stand. And we rejoice in the hope of the glory of God. Not only so, but we also rejoice in our sufferings, because we know that suffering produces perseverance; perseverance, character; and character, hope. And hope does not* *disappoint us because God has poured out His love into our hearts by the Holy Spirit whom He has given us."*

As Children of God we need to grow strong spiritual muscles. We need to grow deep spiritual roots in order for us to be able to endure the storms of life. **1 Peter 1: 6&7 ...** *"In this you greatly rejoice, though now for a while you may have had to suffer grief in all kinds of trials. These have come so that your faith – of greater worth than gold, which perishes even though refined by fire – may be proved genuine and may result in praise, glory and honor when Jesus Christ is revealed."*

Character can be cultivated as we persevere through the pain of change. As we pass through a painful season of life, God's Promises Give Hope. Hope when we are hopeless can come only through a personal relationship with Jesus Christ who gives us such promises as we find in **Jeremiah 29:11** *... For I know the plans I have for you," saith the Lord, "plans to prosper you and not to harm you, plans to give you hope and a future".* The "key" in this Scripture is to recognize that God knows the Plans that He has for our life, and to trust in Him and His Plans rather than trying to get Him to bless our plans whenever our plans may not be in accordance with His Will and His purpose for our life.

The *final step* to effectively handling life's passages is to wait for the Purposes of God to unfold. When a change is painful, we can always trust that God has a Purpose in it. We, *like nature*, require the *winter seasons* for renewal and for growth. It can be said of each new day ... *"we have not passed this way before"*. Every day brings new experiences and new challenges that stretch our faith in God. Without God, people are left to wonder what direction to take, or they wear themselves out with trying to understand the *"whys"* of life. With God, believers can know that every new day is in His Hands. He will guide us according to His Eternal Plan. As the Israelites followed the Ark in order to *"know the way"*, so we can look to God and to His Word in order to know the way that He wants us to go. When we have done all that we can do, it is time to ... *Stand Still and Let God Move.*

Life is filled with change. *We grow; we develop; we mature.* Some people go through many changes before becoming Christians. Others are fortunate enough to come to the Lord at a young age and experience their *life changes* with Him. Hopefully, the changes we experience will help us to grow and to mature. When we are open to God's Will, we never know the surprises that He may have in store for us. That's what the Good New of Jesus Christ does ... *it makes astounding changes in people's lives that could not happen in any other way.* Whenever Christ enters a life ... He Changes Things! For some, the change is more noticeable than for others. We need to let Christ work in our lives so that we can have a positive and a healing impact upon our world, and to live a fuller and more rewarding life for ourselves.

As joyous or as painful as they may be, we will all pass through life's transitions. If we have God in our lives, we can trust Him through the changes – *knowing that every day that passes brings us closer to our eternal destiny in the Presence of God Himself.*

As we read the observations of Solomon, we see nothing short of eternity can give true meaning to the *changes* and *transitions* of this life. **Ecclesiastes 3:11 ...** *"He has made everything beautiful in its time. Also He has put eternity in their hearts, except that no one can find out the work that God does from beginning to end."*

I, personally, have walked – even crawled – through so many of life's transitions. By the Grace and the Mercy of God, I have not only survived, but also ... *through a Personal Relationship with Jesus Christ* ... I have been delivered, healed and restored above all that I could ever have dreamed possible. I want to share the comfort that is found in God with others who are walking through their own fiery furnace of life's passages or are crawling through the deep darkness of the shadow of death.

My sole purpose for writing this book is to help and to encourage others. I want to give God all Honor, all Praise, and all Glory forever and forever. All that I am or may ever become, and all that I have accomplished or may ever achieve, is truly only because of Him. I am nothing within my own power, but ... *"I can do all things through Christ who strengthens me"* **(Philippians 4:13).**

I want to dedicate this book, *"Seasons Of The Heart"*, to the many Brothers & Sisters who have helped me to success-fully walk through some very tough and deeply painful life transitions, and to those who have taught me and have encour-aged me to deepen my spiritual walk and to strengthen my faith in Christ Jesus ... *"May God Hold You Close In The Palm Of His Hand"*.

Most of all I want to say ... Thank You, Father God, for never giving up on me; Thank You, Lord Jesus, for dying for my sins; and Thank You, Holy Spirit, for being my daily Guide and consistent Counselor through all seasons.

CHAPTER ONE

"A TIME TO HEAL"

What is *"to heal"*? According to Webster's New World Dictionary … to make sound, well, or healthy again; restore health *(heal the sick)*; to cure or get rid of *(a disease)*; to cause *(a wound, sore, etc.)* to become closed or scarred so as to restore a healthy condition; to free from grief, troubles, evil, etc.; to remedy or get rid of *(grief, troubles, etc.)*; to makeup *(breach, differences, etc.)*; reconcile. To become well or healthy again; be cured.

- **2 Chronicles 7:14 … *"If my people, who are called by my name, will humble themselves and pray and seek my face and turn from their wicked ways, then will I hear from heaven and will forgive their sin and will heal their land."***

Let's talk here about *emotional healing*. Some events in life cause pain that goes extremely deep with long-lasting effects to a person's overall well-being. This time of event is often called a *trauma*. While we normally know the cause of the *trauma*, there are times when a person can go through their entire life without being aware of what caused the original damage. Whatever happened to them could

have occurred at such a tender age, or have been so traumatic in substance, that the event may be blocked from their
conscious memory.

Remembered or not, trauma can influence our reactions
in certain unhealthy ways or can cause us to make unhealthy
decisions. Those whose *traumas* don't get healed may
grow up to damage themselves, others, and even there own
families.

What causes *trauma*? Most experts divide trauma into
two major categories ... *invasion trauma* and *abandonment
trauma*. Invasion trauma is when something happens to a
person that creates damage. *Abandonment trauma* is when
something did not happen to a person *(such as not feeling
loved, protected, or nurtured)* that creates damage. These
two kinds of trauma affect the four aspects of people's lives
... *emotional, physical, sexual, and spiritual.* First, let's look
at the aspects of *Invasion Trauma* ...

- *Emotional Invasion* occurs when people feel criticized, shamed, or blamed. This damage can be
  caused by either *verbal communication* or *nonverbal
  actions*. Sighs or facial expressions can express
  anger or displeasure and can be taken as criticism.
  God gave us our emotions, and we all need to learn
  how to express them in a healthy and non-threatened
  manner. However, people are often talked out of their
  feelings with statements such as, *"Big boys don't
  cry"*, or *"Christians shouldn't feel that way"*.

  Emotional invasion also occurs when an adult or
  authority figure reverses roles and expects a child to
  be the protector or the caregiver ... *a child is put in a
  position of giving emotional care instead of receiving
  it*. Children from an *emotionally invasive* background
  often spend their lifetime without recovery.

- *Physical Invasion* occurs when a person is physically abused. This form of *trauma* may create permanent physical damage. The emotional effect of this can also be experienced if a person lives in a home environment in which someone else is being physically harmed. This is especially true when a child assumes the role of trying to protect a parent or a sibling from the abuser.

  From my childhood, I have spent years in recovering not only from the personal abuse of my father, but also from *growing up way before my time* because I was always looking for ways to try to protect my mother from being hurt by Daddy. If you are in, or still suffering from an abusive childhood, you may want to get a copy of my book entitled, "A House Divided" that will take you on a true journey of someone "healing from abuse".

- *Sexual Invasion* occurs when a person is penetrated or touched in sexual areas outside of the mutual *"consenting"* relationship of marriage. This is a very broad definition because even consenting sexual relationships between people who are not married can have a traumatizing effect because it is outside of God's plan. *Sexual invasion* can also happen when people are teased or criticized about their bodies.

- *Spiritual Invasion* occurs when people are led to believe that they are unworthy of God's love and grace. Often rigid, fear-based religious teaching, *even if it is well-intended*, can have this effect. This results in shame that people often can't seem to shake.

  Religious confusion had me so filled with shame and fear I wanted no part of God. Even after I asked Jesus Christ into my life as my Lord and Savior, it was a long and difficult journey to become free of the damage deep within from *spiritual invasion* caused by *physical abuse* and *rigid legalistic doctrines.* Knowing that my Heavenly Father loves me unconditionally, knowing that Jesus loved me so much He chose to die for my sins, has enabled me to know and to love myself and others. God loves you, too, just as you are and longs to help you to become all that He created you to be in life.

We have listed some of the aspects of *Invasion Trauma,* so now let us look at some of the aspects of *Abandonment Trauma* ...

- *Emotional Abandonment* occurs when love, attention, care, nurturing, and affirmation are not given ... resulting in profound loneliness. When this type of *emotional abandonment* occurs during childhood, these adults often find it extremely difficult or virtually impossible to form healthy and lasting relationships. As a result, they spend their entire life in a state of perpetual loneliness and unhealthy relationships.
- *Physical Abandonment* occurs when people's basic needs for food, shelter, and clothing aren't met. People who aren't touched enough – *with hugs or cuddles* – will experience a form of *physical abandonment* called *"touch deprivation".* From personal experience I can tell you that this often leads to *self-denial* and *broken relationships.* It took me many years to allow myself to enjoy simple *acts of affection,* and even longer to admit that I actually yearned for them!
- *Sexual Abandonment* occurs when parents and other responsible adults don't educate children about their bodies and model healthy sexuality. Lack of correct information can have devastating long-term results.

26

- *Spiritual Abandonment* occurs when healthy spiritual teaching and role models are not available. Nothing can be more devastating on one's life than deeply inbred religious confusion or disillusionment. Any form of trauma that happens at the hands of a religious authority figure can create profound spiritual damage.

The above categories of *Invasion Trauma* and *Abandonment Trauma* can, and often do, overlap. Damage in one aspect of a person's life can have an effect in another aspect of that person's life.

Everyone needs healing because everyone is born into sin. In this *fallen world,* people face hurts, pain, sickness, difficulties, and traumas. People are broken by the sins of others, as well as by their own sins. Sin tears apart the fabric of relationships and mars the wholeness of intimacy. When broken people are alienated from themselves, others, and God ... evil infiltrates, dividing the parts and scattering them to increase the sense of alienation through felt distance and misunderstanding.

The result is not only profound inner emptiness, but also a tendency to fend for oneself while rejecting others' care and involvement ... *needing and trusting become too risky.* The more that one is broken and wounded ... *the more that one ventures down the spiral of isolation and independence from others.* These *"behaviors"* involve an interplay of arrogance *("I can do it on my own")* and self-righteousness *("Whatever went wrong, it's not my fault")* resulting in greater blindness and self-deception. Broken and wounded people need healing that comes from a renewed relationship with God and with others.

Symptoms of *unhealed trauma* can include anxiety and panic disorders, depression, anger, loneliness, attachment disorders, and addictions of all kinds. Panic, anxiety, flashbacks, and uncontrolled anger are sometimes labeled under the diagnosis of Post Traumatic Stress Disorder (PTDS). This can be a very serious and destructive condition. If you suffer from this disorder, please get some professional help as soon as possible. You can't do this all alone!

Trauma survivors may cope with the *remembered* or *not remembered* trauma in a variety of ways. Some, *almost unconsciously*, may seek to repeat the trauma in their adult lives while hoping for a different result or trying to be in control by becoming the perpetrator of the trauma on someone else. This is called *"trauma repetition"*. FOR EXAMPLE: *victims of abuse* often create relationships with people who treat them poorly, or they go the other direction entirely by avoiding any person or event that triggers memories of the abuse.

If you are a victim of childhood abuse that you, *as an adult,* are repeating – *either as the abused or the abuser* – please get professional help to stop the abuse! If you have children living in an abusive environment – *physical or emotional* – please take whatever steps are necessary to get them out of such an environment as quickly and as permanently as possible. DO YOU LOVE YOUR CHILDREN? If so, please don't be responsible for inflicting the *scars of an abusive childhood* upon your innocent children ... *scars they will, too, most likely carry for their lifetime and inflict upon their own children one day.*

The path to recovery includes a number of steps. Healing is a journey! There are a number of things that *trauma survivors* need on their *journey to recovery:*

- *Trauma Survivors* need to be educated about the nature of trauma. Any denial may need to be confronted. Sometimes it is helpful to do this in groups of other survivors.

- *Trauma Survivors* need comforting, acceptance, and nonjudgmental listeners who believe in them and offer them hope.
- *Trauma Survivors* need help in expressing their anger about what has happened to them. This includes their right to express anger at the person who hurt them. If it is potentially too dangerous to physically confront the perpetrator, write a letter – *that won't necessarily be sent* – but can be just as powerful in the process of releasing pent up emotions. Opportunities to be angry with God may also be needed. Helping someone to understand how God could let such awful things happen can be a very important part of the healing process.

Being a Christian does not guarantee a pain-free existence. In fact, our Faith may expose us to difficulties and struggles that we may not otherwise have experienced. Here are a few things that *"Believers"* need to know about life's traumas:

1. God has given people *"free-will"* and people are responsible for a great deal of human suffering.
2. Suffering is not always punishment. God does allow people to face the miserable consequences of their sinful choices, but it doesn't mean that every suffering person in the world is being punished. Sometimes God allows people to suffer in order to strengthen their resolve, to shake them out of their complacency, or to help them to empathize with other hurting people.
3. God does not leave our side when we suffer. He is the one friend whom we can trust to never leave us or forsake us.

4. God will reward us for the suffering that we endure for His sake *(suffering for His sake – not enduring abuse at the hands of a spouse or someone else).*

5. When we trust in God, we can change our perspective on life's traumas from *"Why me?"* to *"How can I grow from this and then use it to help someone else?"*

- *Trauma Survivors* need instruction in the process of grieving the losses that the trauma has caused in their lives. Help them to *grieve for a season* in order to heal, and help them to *release the grief* in order to not *grieve for a lifetime.*

- *Trauma Survivors* need to know that they didn't deserve their hurts and that they didn't cause them. They <u>are</u> the victims. They <u>are not</u> the perpetrators!

- *Trauma Survivors* need help in structuring boundaries so that they will not be harmed again by old, current, or new relationships.

- *Trauma Survivors* need to see the positive strengths that can result from the healing of their trauma ... *for themselves and for their loved ones.*

- *Trauma Survivors* need to be able, eventually, to forgive. Forgiveness is the ultimate spiritual, *thus emotional and personal,* victory!

If you are working with *trauma survivors,* be aware that doing so can bring up one's own issues of trauma. If facing your own trauma interferes with the work you are doing to help someone else, back away and refer the person to someone else. We each need to get our own hurts healed in order to make us more effective in helping others to heal.

Let the healing begin! Thanksgiving Day 2001 ... what a day it started out to be for me. I felt so alone on a day that is set aside as a Day of Celebrating and Sharing with family and friends. A day set aside each year, *here in our country*, for us to Count our Blessings ... giving thanks for all that we have been blessed with over the past year. But I have to admit that as the days were counting down to this specific Thanksgiving Day, I was feeling a lot of things. Not too many of my emotions, however, were of gratitude or thanks giving! Instead, I was all caught up in my losses and was feeling pretty sorry for myself. I bet some of you know exactly what I mean. You have either been there, or are there right now!

I had read and heard the Scripture about *God Healing Our Land* many times, but never in quite the personal way that I heard a Minister in Missouri preach about it this particular Thanksgiving Season. This man was Pastor Larry Stites of Blessed Hope Church in Goodman, Missouri. I want to share with you just a little of his message. It made a real difference within my heart that day, and I pray that it will do the same for you.

Brother Larry acknowledged that we, *as Children of God*, need to be in continual prayer and intercession for our country and its leaders. It is even more imperative now than ever for us to be on our knees before God ... seeking new hope and healing for our nation. We need to be praying for our President, *(our First Lady – His Wife & Helpmate)*, our Military Leaders, our Spiritual Leaders, and all other Figures of Authority as they make decisions and take actions that will have tremendous bearing on the direction of the United States and the free world as we know it. But what about a closer to home, *deeply personal,* "LAND" that God wants to heal and to restore ... the very "HEART" of His people *(body, mind, & soul)*?

JESUS CHRIST did not come with a life-shortening suggestion, but with a life-saving power. His highest wish is for us to prosper and have health in both soul and body.

31

- **3 John 2 ... *"Beloved, I wish above all things that thou mayest prosper and be in health, even as thy soul prospereth."***

The story of Jesus is the story of deliverance. In the power of His pure and healthy being and in the strength of an undivided personality ... *the Master of men came into this world to bring release to mankind from their fears and frustrations – from their spiritual, physical, and mental illnesses – to make us whole men and women.*

- **1 Corinthians 14:33 ... *"For God is not a God of disorder (or confusion) but of peace."***

How can we have real peace in our nation when so many people are torn apart within their very being by strife, disappointment, disillusionment, and fear? If we, *as Children of God*, can not trust in Him enough to allow Him to bring healing and peace to our hearts, to take away the fear from our minds, how can we possibly trust Him enough to stand in FAITH for Him to deliver us from our enemies – *as a nation* – and to *"heal our land"*?

We must turn to God, *as individuals*, and seek deliverance from our respective destructive fears. We need God's healing within the very *"personal land of our lives"* first. Only then, will we truly walk in FAITH *versus* FEAR. Can we truly share a *Message of God's Deliverance and Healing* with anyone while we continue to live with our hearts frozen by fear; our lives void of deep and lasting relationships ... controlled by the *"what if's"* and *"if onlies"* that are often a result of our *life's transitions* or as the result of *personal trauma*? How can we possibly trust the well-being of our families or our nation into the Hands of God while at the same time we are afraid to trust the well-being of *"our heart – our land"* into His Hands?

32

Difficult experiences come in many degrees. A *trauma* would be considered a situation far beyond control, one that shakes a person to the core. A *trauma* can lead to mental disorders or even to suicide. Recovery is often slow, and flashbacks are common. As difficult as traumatic experiences are, however, they can also lead a person to God.

Traumatic experiences can drive people away from God or to Him. In both cases, a person may ask, *"Why would God do this to me?"* Those who turn from God ask this question in anger and accusation ... *that was me for many years.* Those who turn toward God ask the same question in order to learn His lesson for their lives, to seek the total comfort that only He can give, and to know how to use their experiences to help someone else ... *that has been me since I invited Jesus Christ into my life as my Lord & Savior, and "My Bestest Friend".* When traumatic experiences come ... *run to God – don't run away from God.*

Being a Christian does not guarantee a pain-free existence. In fact, our Faith exposes us to difficulties and struggles that we may not otherwise have experienced. As Believers in Jesus Christ, here are some things we need to know about the *traumas* we face and the *life changes* we each must walk through.

- God will never leave our side throughout the season of suffering. **Psalm 23: 4-6** ... *"Yea, though I walk through the valley of the shadow of death, I will fear no evil; for you are with me; Your rod and Your staff, they comfort me. You prepare a table before me in the presence of my enemies; you anoint my head with oil; my cup runs over. Surely goodness and mercy shall follow me all the days of my life; and I will dwell in the house of the Lord forever."*

- God will reward us for the suffering we endure for His sake. **Matthew 5:10 ...** *"Blessed are those who are persecuted for righteousness' sake, for theirs is the kingdom of heaven."*
- Suffering is not always punishment. God does allow people to face the miserable consequences of their sinful choices in order for them to turn from making the same choices in their future, thus, enabling them to help others make better choices in their own lives. Please do not think that every suffering person is doing so as a result of sin.

  While God gave us free will, *and we each will live with the consequences of our choices*, there are often other factors involved in our suffering. Satan's ultimate goal is to deceive and to destroy mankind's trust in the goodness and mercy of God, and often the actions of other people or an act of nature can land us in the middle of great suffering.

  Sometimes God allows people to suffer in order to strengthen their resolve, to shake them out of their complacency, or to help them empathize with other suffering people. We have all at one time or another in the midst of a person struggle had someone say to us, *"I know how you feel"*. Our first human reaction to that person is to ask, *"How can you know how I feel <u>unless</u> you have lived through what I am going through"?*

- **2 Corinthians 1: 3-7 ...** *"Praise be to the God and Father of our Lord Jesus Christ, the Father of compassion and the God of all comfort, who comforts us in all our troubles, so that we can comfort those in any trouble with the comfort we ourselves have received from God. For just as the sufferings of Christ flow over into our lives, so also* *through Christ our comfort overflows. If we are distressed; it is for your comfort and salvation; if we are comforted, it is for your comfort, which produces in you patient endurance of the same sufferings we suffer. And our hope for you is firm, because we know that just as you share in our sufferings, so also you share in our comfort."*

When we trust in God, we can change our perspective on *life's traumas* from *"why me?"* to *"how can I grow from this?"* When we choose to make Jesus Christ the Lord and Savior of our life, He becomes our Healer & Deliverer, and our very *"Bestest Friend"*. A *Friend* who will never leave us or forsake us, never deserts us, and never betrays the trust that we place in Him.

The healing that Jesus brings is more than spiritual, more than mental, and more than physical. It is all of those, and more! His healing is to make us whole; *healthy in Spirit, mind, body, in our relationships with others, in our attitudes, in our habits, and in our way of life for all the days of our life.*

Jesus is a COMPLETE DELIVERER from the hurts and ills of life. Jesus is my Lord and Savior – my Healer and Deliverer – my very Bestest Friend! My prayer for you is this ... by the time you finish reading this book that you will choose to invite Jesus Christ to become Your Bestest Friend as well.

- 1ˢᵗ **John 4:18 ...** *"There is no fear in love. But perfect love drives out fear, because fear has to do with punishment. The one who fears is not made perfect in love."*

- 3ʳᵈ **John 1:2 ...** *"Beloved, I wish above all things that thou may prosper and be in good health, even as thy soul prospers."*

- **John 3: 16&17** ... *"For God so loved the world that He gave His only begotten Son, that whoever believes in Him should not perish but have everlasting life. For God did not send His Son into the world to condemn the world, but that the world through Him might be saved."*

Jesus heals through wounds. The prophet Isaiah foresaw this when he wrote of Jesus in **Isaiah 53:5** ... *"He was wounded for our transgressions. He was bruised for our iniquities; the chastisement for our peace was upon Him, and by His stripes we are healed"*. Peter understood this as he also wrote in **1 Peter 2:24 that Jesus** *"bore our sins in His own body on the tree, that we, having died to our sins, might live for righteousness – by whose stripes (we) were healed"*. People are reconciled to God through Jesus' suffering. Because of this we have the possibility of seeing that which was once divided and scattered brought back together and healed.

So how do we move beyond the very human emotion of fear in order to open our hearts and our lives to all of the many blessings that our Heavenly Father wants to give us? How do we position ourselves to be the recipients of His supernatural deliverance, healing, and restoration? How do we allow God to walk us through the *seasons of transitions and change* in a positive and healthy way? How do we learn to grow into stronger and healthier people as a result of our time spent in the *Winter Season Of The Heart?*

We grow and we change by choosing to have *FAITH* in the *"Author and Finisher of Faith – Jesus Christ"*. Jesus was both ... *The Son of God and Son of Man.* He was born into this world as a tiny *"human"* baby, He grew up as a boy in the home of a carpenter, and He faced the same tests and temptations that we all face as we move through this life. *WHY?* So that He would understand our human needs

36

and weaknesses and would know how to comfort us in our deepest sorrow, meet us at our deepest point-of-need, restore to us all that Satan steals from us, heal us of our most devastating illness, and to be the *"KEY" to* unlock the door of our *"Prison of Fear"* to lead us forth in triumph and victory!

- **Hebrews 12: 2&3 ...** *"Let us fix our eyes on Jesus; the author and perfecter of our faith, who for the joy set before Him endured the cross, scorning its shame, and sat down at the right hand of the throne of God. Consider Him who endured such opposition from sinful man, so that you will not grow weary and lose heart."*

- **Hebrews 11:1 ...** *"Now faith is being sure of what we hope for and certain of what we do not see."*

When people accept *Christ's Sacrifice* on their behalf, when they embrace His broken body, their hearts are opened to recovery through a *Personal Relationship With Him.* The mystery of the love of Christ towards us compels us to face the depths of our brokenness and alienation. God's kindness breaks people's hearts over their sins, irresistibly draws their souls to His provision, and helps them to seek healing and recovery.

The journey to recovery is not a simple one. This journey takes time, it takes strength, it takes determination, and it takes faith ... *Faith in SOMEONE much stronger and wiser than the wisest of us.* And recovery takes our admitting that we can't do it all alone ... *we all need help now and then.*

In order to heal people's lives, God must perform major surgery. In the process of healing them, He exposes the sinfulness that Jesus died on the Cross to free us from. The process of healing and recovery is not easy, nor is it going to happen overnight. Deep wounds will take time to heal. Most often our greatest pain, *and our darkest sins,* is imbedded deep within the very fiber of our being. The healing process means *"going under the knife of the Master Surgeon"* to allow Him to get to the root cause of our sickness ... *be it a destructive addiction, abuse, discouragement, depression, grief, anger, bitterness, unforgiveness, loneliness, fear, or whatever it is that is draining the very life from us on a daily basis.*

Only when we can begin to understand and to accept the unconditional love of our Heavenly Father and begin to KNOW that He wants to heal us – *to set us free from whatever prison that is holding us* – only then will we be able to begin the process of recovery.

If you remember nothing else, remember this proven fact ... *when we can't do it alone, we can always trust in the mercy and the help of God.* And what God does for us is never for our sakes alone. Through our suffering, *and our recovery,* we may bring hope and help to others who are suffering in the same way. We can point them to the Greatest Healer of all ... JESUS CHRIST! Through our wounds, *and our journey of recovery,* we are in a position to invite others to make an appointment with the Great Physician Himself.

I want to walk with you through valleys of depression, guilt, fear, unforgiveness, anger, bitterness, betrayal, grief, death, discouragement, depression, and sin. Why would I want to revisit the pain of my own *"valleys"* or once again to take a walk through my own *"fiery furnaces"*? In order to help you in the same way that others cared enough to help me at times when I felt no hope was left.

Let me start by sharing with you one very solid truth that I had to learn the hard way. While we have a Heavenly Father who loves His Children, a Lord and Savior in Jesus Christ who chose to die in order that we might have an abundant life, *for by His wounds we were (and still are) healed,* we also have an adamant enemy in Satan whose greatest desire is to deceive and to destroy God's Ultimate Creation ... all mankind. If you have never trusted anyone, you will never experience true recovery until you can learn to trust and to ask for help. So, why not start with your Creator - your Heavenly Father. He is as close as your next breath ... *ready and willing to help you!*

How do I know that God truly loves us and wants us to heal? I would NOT be here today if I hadn't finally cried out for His help. I have suffered tremendous and devastating personal, professional, and emotional losses in my life. I have walked through the valley of disappointment, betrayal, and loss. I have struggled with the confusion of *"why"*? I do know how it feels to hurt, to trust – only to lose, and to hurt again. But today I choose to focus instead on the many *blessings* of my life, and to treasure the *lessons* learned through the pain.

Many times over the past twenty-one years I have been comforted and sustained by these words from **1 Corinthians Chapter Ten ...** *God promises that He will never let us be tested or tempted beyond that which we can bear. He will always make a way of escape – that we might be able to bear it.* So whatever *season of pain or struggle* you may be going through, God will bring you through to the other side if you will just ask Him and trust in His love.

If you are interested in knowing how the love of God has brought me from the very pits of hell on earth to be all that I am today, you can read my story in my book, "A House Divided". My story is far too in-depth to go into here, but the love and mercy of God brought me through pain and darkness that words are inadequate to express. Just believe that when I talk to you about abuse, death, desperation, confusion, illness, betrayal, fear, unforgiveness, grief, and overwhelming pain ... I can talk to you for real because I, *too*, have been there.

I cried out to God in desperation in 1987. That very day I began my journey out of the darkness and pain into the light and restoration of the love of Christ Jesus ... My Bestest Friend! I won't lie to you and tell you that my journey has been an easy one. In fact, often it was all I could do to find the strength to *"tie a knot in the end of the rope and hang on"* by sheer faith.

But no matter how hard it got, I have never walked one single step of this journey alone since that day in 1987 when I asked Jesus to come into my heart and to *please change me and to change my life.* I had finally reached a point where I could go no further on my own, and I had no one to turn to or no place to run to. I had nothing to lose by deciding to *"Try Jesus".* How about you ... are you at that place in your own life yet?

CHAPTER TWO

"CHOOSING TO FORGIVE"

This book is being written with the hope and with the prayer that each reader will ask God to enable them to recognize and to realize the many ways that our "heart" can become sick by our attitudes and our choices during our journey through the various *"Seasons Of The Heart"*.

While each of us will walk through our own personal seasons of both pain and great joy, there is *one absolute certainty* that will have an indescribable and irrefutable effect upon the final condition of each heart. The *one absolute certainty* that we, as individuals, can and do control is the *choice to forgive* or *to not forgive*.

The bitter roots of unforgiveness, *no matter how justifiable we may feel they are*, can and will destroy the peace of our heart and impart unbelievable and often irrevocable harm upon us in relationships, career, ministry, and in our physical health. We need to truly understand the choices we make when it comes to forgiveness as there will be long-term consequences of our choices. So, what does it mean *to forgive?*

"Forgive" from Webster's New World Dictionary: *to give up resentment against or the desire to punish; stop being angry with; pardon; to give up all claim to punish or*

exact penalty for (an offense); overlook; to cancel or remit (a debt); to show forgiveness – absolve.

It is awkward and painful when we have to confront a person who has wronged us horribly. It is one thing to talk abstractly about forgiveness ... *it is another matter altogether to actually have to forgive.* That kind of *"forgiveness"* is the true test of the Power of the Gospel.

In order for *"the land of our heart"* to be truly delivered and healed, we must *choose to forgive* those who have hurt us, forgive ourselves, and sometimes even forgive God for allowing some things that have happened in our lives or in the lives of those whom we love.

You don't have to try and hide your anger at God from God because He already knows what is in your heart, and He loves you anyway. God longs for you to come clean with Him so that He can deliver you from your bitterness and hurt. God wants to truly heal you and to restore you ... *emotionally, mentally, physically, financially, professionally, and spiritually.*

There can be such horrendous acts done against us by those whom we know, trust, and often even love that it is humanly impossible to forgive the person(s) responsible ... *acts of such ultimate betrayal and manipulation that the results of such acts can be total devastation and absolute destruction of the very fiber of our beings.* Whenever we are faced with circumstances that make it humanly impossible for us to forgive, we can turn to God for a Supernatural Power of Forgiveness and Healing to our emotions. Then, and only then, will we be able to receive the peace of absolute forgiveness, and to *"plant the seed of forgiveness"* into another's life.

- **Joseph's Forgiveness (Genesis 45:5) ... *"And now, do not be distressed and do not be angry with your-***

selves for selling me here, because it was to save lives that God sent me ahead of you."

The Power to Forgive comes as a Divine Gift. We choose to forgive, but God empowers our forgiveness. The desire for vengeance can be so overpowering that without God's intervention, genuine forgiveness rarely takes place. God enabled Joseph to choose forgiveness when his brothers deserved retribution. God used that willingness to assure the survival of the very brothers who had conspired to end Joseph's life. When the famine brought Joseph's brothers back into his life, they had no idea they were at the mercy of the brother they had betrayed. When Joseph finally revealed his identity, his brothers were terrified. They knew what they deserved. But instead of revenge, Joseph offered forgiveness and mercy ... *thanking God who worked out everything for His Glory.*

Joseph demonstrated the *cost of forgiveness*. We forgive, not by making the offense unimportant, but by loving the offender. For we need God's help. By making the choice to forgive those who have harmed us, with God's help, we will reap the *fruits of genuine forgiveness ... forgiveness for our own mistakes and misguided actions, mercy, compassion, empathy, and inner peace.*

- **Luke 6: 27&28 ...** *"But I tell you who hear me: Love your enemies, do good to those who hate you, bless those who curse you, pray for those who mistreat you."* When wronged, a human reaction often is to hate the person who wronged us and to plot ways to get even. **But Jesus said,** *"Love your enemies, do good to those who hate you and pray for those who spitefully use you."*

Such words turned many away from Christ then, and still do today. Loving one's enemies does not mean having affectionate feelings for them. Instead, it requires a decision to act in love toward them no matter how we feel. We need to pray and ask Christ to take our hurt and bitterness, and then to replace those feelings with His love.

Before I had personally experienced the *costs of forgiveness* versus the *fruits of forgiveness*, I had a hard time associating the Biblical Context of Forgiveness with Real World Forgiveness! But God, *in His Unconditional Love for us*, knows we have to genuinely forgive in order for us to truly heal within – enabling us to move forward with a positive and productive life. Whenever it seems to be humanly impossible to forgive, ask God to let His Forgiveness flow through you to the other person until you can genuinely forgive them. HE WILL DO SO! He has done so for me in seemingly impossible situations.

I spent the early years of my childhood in a home where abuse was prevalent ... *physical, emotional, sexual, and even spiritual abuse.* Survival depended upon my ability to hide my pain, swallow my tears, and close my heart against all genuine emotions. As a result, I entered adulthood locked inside my own personal prison of empty emotional isolation. I guarded my emotions against any close association with anyone who could cause me pain. I avoided personal commitment at all costs.

In striving to *insulate* myself from further hurt and betrayal, I was *isolating* myself from experiencing life to its fullest depths and loftiest heights. The only *"key"* to unlock the door of this prison was *Jesus Christ* ... my Lord and Savior, my Life Preserver, and my Bestest Friend. Through Him, I learned to forgive, to let go, to trust, to feel and to love. Because of His mercy, love, and forgiveness ... *I learned mercy, love, and forgiveness for the perpetrators of the abuse in my childhood.* Through the Love of God and

His Supernatural Healing and Restoration of my heart and emotions, I can now reach out to others who are struggling with the need to forgive and to be forgiven.

- **Luke 6: 37&38 ...***"Do not judge, and you will not be judged. Do not condemn, and you will not be condemned. Forgive, and you will be forgiven. Give, and it will be given to you. A good measure, pressed down, shaken together and running over, will be poured into your lap. For with the measure you use, it will be measured to you."*

The words *"give, and it will be given to you"* follow Jesus' words urging His followers not to judge or condemn others, but rather to forgive. People who have gracious and compassionate spirits, *refusing to judge and condemn*, will find gracious attitudes and compassion returned to them. People who forgive easily will find that they are forgiven their own offenses. The measure with which we give determines the measure with which we receive.

- **Luke 7:47 ...** *"Therefore, I tell you, her many sins have been forgiven – for she loved much. But he who has been forgiven little loves little."*

As humans, we are enormously complicated creatures. We feel injuries not only in our bodies but also in our emotions. And sometimes deep wounds in our inner selves fester for years, causing us to reach out and hurt anyone who comes near us. Or they cause us to withdraw within ourselves and we become unable to experience and/or to share genuine emotions with anyone.

Again and again our human nature wants to *"teach people a lesson"* or to make things worse for them than they made it for us. We see revenge as a way of getting back – of making ourselves whole again. But revenge never works! God, our loving Heavenly Father, knows that unforgiveness never works. **Jesus offers a solution that is radical ...** *forgive, and ye shall be forgiven.* When we make the choice to forgive, *we place ourselves in the position to be forgiven,* and all of us need to be forgiven sometimes.

To receive a blow and to refuse to pass it on is an act that requires extraordinary generosity. For most people, it does not come naturally. In our human self, we are too hard and resistant to be able to absorb the effect of an injury before we pass it on. We must become softer, gentler, more loving people ... *receiving a blow but unable by the fabric of our lives to transmit the force of it onto another.* Love and forgiveness are the special vocation of a true Christian. When we exercise love and forgiveness, we are able to find healing for our own wounds and offer balm for the healing of others.

When I was in my early thirties, I found myself caught up in a life-threatening web of fraud and deception that resulted in the sudden violent deaths of my husband and only child. For almost a decade I lived with fear and self-preservation as my only constant companions. In order to protect the lives of others who were close to me - *friends and family members* - I was also forced to live a life of total isolation for over three years. When I learned "who" was responsible for the devastation of my life and the deaths of my husband and daughter, I was overwhelmed with distress, filled with bitter anger, and raging with a need to retaliate.

On September 15th, 1989, I was finally free of all the repercussions and danger ... free to start over – free to build a new life for myself. On October 1st, 1989, I started a new job in Houston, Texas and struggled to put the pieces of my life back together. I desperately wanted to put the past behind me, and I ached to reclaim my life. But I couldn't ...

not until I learned how to forgive, to let go, and to heal from the wounds of my past.

When God showed me that I had to forgive the people who were literally responsible for the deaths of my husband and daughter ... *it was humanly impossible to do so.* My family had been the innocent victims of a cold and murderous game – a game played out by powerful individuals in order to control me and to make me cooperate in their illegal activities. How could anyone, *including God*, ask me to forgive such cold and malicious brutality? But God, *in His infinite wisdom and abundant love*, knew that I had to forgive in order to truly heal.

I struggled with unforgiveness – *fighting God* – for many months. Try as hard as I could, *within my human self*, I could not conjure up anything resembling forgiveness toward these people; especially the two prominent people responsible ... the man who had ordered the "contract" to be put upon my life, and the man who was assigned to actually carry out the act.

The longer I struggled with this *spirit of unforgiveness*, the more I came to know that I had to somehow learn to face and to forgive these two men if I were ever to be free of fear, and to have real peace within.

When I finally realized my need to forgive, *knowing it was not humanly possible to do so,* I turned to God for His Supernatural Intervention. Through the Holy Spirit, and the teachings of Dr. Oral Roberts, I was shown how to pray about all of this. I started by telling God that I knew I needed to forgive those responsible for the horrendous acts that had been done against my family and against myself. I wanted to forgive them and to let it all go ... *the bitter anger and the destructive vengeance I felt.* I wanted to forgive ... *so that I could be free of the negative devastating emotions.* I wanted emotional and spiritual healing.

I started asking God to forgive through me. As God's forgiveness flowed through me towards those who had brought such destruction and pain into my life, I felt a warm cleansing begin within my heart, within my spirit, and within my mind. Through the healing power of God, I soon found that I had actually forgiven the human selves of those responsible, and I truly began to pray for Salvation for their souls.

But God didn't stop there; the hardest steps of all lay in front of me ... *I now had to tell both of the men that I knew were directly responsible that I was aware of what they had done, and that I had forgiven them.* I wrote a detailed letter to the individual who was initially responsible for the deaths, telling him that I now had knowledge of all that had happened over the years and that I had forgiven him for his actions in all that had happened. I never heard anything back from him, but – *through my obeying God* – I was finally free of him and his actions. The individual who actually carried through with committing these acts of death was a very different story. God sent me into the Federal Penitentiary to tell this man that with the help and healing of my Heavenly Father, I had forgiven him for the part that he had played in the deaths of my husband and daughter.

As I sat there across the table from the man who was bragging about not only taking the lives of my loved ones, but also the lives of several others, I wanted to go across that table, grab him by the throat, and literally strangle the breath of life from him. I had prayed all the way on the drive from Houston to that prison in Oklahoma that God would take control of me, and of the entire situation, once I was face-to-face with this man. Now as I sat there and watched him brag of the awful deeds he had done to my family and to others, I could only rely upon prayer and the help of God to get me through this *"mission of forgiveness"*.

It took a long time, *seemingly hours*, for genuine forgiveness to flow freely from my heart to this man ... *forgiveness he chose to reject and to mock.* But as for me, *once genuine forgiveness was born within my heart and was freely given to this man,* waves of release from fear and the joy of inner peace washed over me. I walked away from that prison free and emotionally whole for the first time in many years ... *reaping the "fruits" of genuine forgiveness.*

I have to talk for a moment of a *physical healing in my body* as a result of my *choice to forgive* these men. If you are interested in knowing how this illness attacked my body and set up residence in my right foot, I urge you to read my book entitled, "Deceptive Seduction". This book tells of the deadly deception being perpetrated through the teachings of the New Age Movement and Satanism. All I want to share of that time in my life here is how my *choice of forgiving* freed me from one last illness and set me free.

For more than a year, *once I was free of the past,* my right foot remained swollen and very painful. It was always swollen too much to even think of putting on a shoe ... red, and very hot to the touch. I had to keep my shoeless foot propped up on a box under my desk at the office, and the constant throbbing pain made sleep at night very difficult. Doctors could find nothing wrong with my foot or with my overall health to account for this swelling, the redness, or the constant throbbing pain.

So I took the problem to Jesus, as I know that *"nothing is impossible with God"*, and I wanted deliverance and healing. Yet, in spite of my prayers and my faith, deliverance and healing did not come. Then I began to ask God to show me if there was anything within my heart or my life that was standing between me and His answers to my prayers ... His answers to my very real need. I had done all that I knew to do to get to the bottom of what was causing this problem with my foot, and nothing had helped. I needed Jesus Christ to step onto the scene and to heal me once and for all. You see, I truly believe that *"By His Stripes I Am Healed!"*

On night, *after months of suffering*, I cried out to God to show me if anything was standing between me and His healing of my foot. He then showed me, beyond any shadow of doubt, that I had a choice to make ... *a choice to truly forgive OR to not forgive*. That *choice* led me to that prison in Oklahoma.

When I left that prison, *although I was free from fear of this man and his associates*, my foot was no different. When I finally got back to Houston and went to bed that night, my foot was still swollen – red – hot – hurting. But when I woke up the next morning, my foot was absolutely normal once again ... no swelling, no redness, and no throbbing pain! It has been many years now since God helped me in my *choice to forgive* ... years of continuing health and lack of swelling or pain in my foot. When you understand the *"fruits of forgiveness"* versus the *"costs of forgiveness"*, you will find that it becomes far less difficult to *choose to forgive*.

Unforgiveness breeds hate, and the *Spirit of Hate* is a very ugly and destructive demon to live with. The ex-wife of this man in prison went with me into that prison on her own *"mission of forgiveness"*. She had lived with him for over fifteen years prior to divorcing him when he was arrested for brutally raping her nineteen-year old daughter-in-law at gunpoint. While her daughter-in-law was at the hospital being treated for the rape, this woman also learned that while he was her husband, this man had been sexually and emotionally abusing her young daughter for several years.

Only later did this lady *(who had become my close friend)* learn that her husband was also involved with the Mafia ... often operating as a *"hit man"* for *"contract elimination"* of people who either got *"out of line"* or simply *"got in the way"*. This *"fact"* she and I were told by a FBI Agent while sitting in his office at the FBI Headquarters in Oklahoma City. Her husband was the man who held the *"contract"* upon my own life that had resulted in the deaths of my husband and daughter.

Jackie had years of abusive behavior to forgive this man for. He, *while living with her family as her husband and step-father to her children,* had emotionally and mentally beaten down this lady until she was a mere whisper of the woman she has become since God freed her from him. Through the strength she received from God, *in spite of being almost paralyzed with fear of the repercussions of turning him over to authorities for the rape and the sexual abuse,* Jackie found the courage to bring charges against her husband and had the strength to carry through.

This same faith and determination to free herself and her children from this destructive and dangerous environment enabled Jackie to find the strength to get a divorce and to move forward with their lives. Over the years since, I have watched Jackie overcome many tough obstacles on her *journey to recovery* from her past. She is truly an amazing woman!

During the most devastating period of her life, Jackie had given her life over to God, and was redeemed and set free through the cleansing Blood of Jesus Christ the Son of God. The same Jesus who became her Savior and Redeemer, her Healer and Deliverer, is the same Jesus who has restored her in every aspect of her life ... *in spite of her past associations or fears.*

Shortly after her ex-husband was put into prison, Jackie had a complete nervous breakdown. In order to keep her out of the State Mental Institution in Iowa, I brought her to my home in Houston and cared for her until she recovered. During this period of recovery, Jackie began to grow stronger in the Lord and stronger within herself. But she was still carrying a *"Burden of Hate"* that was only allowing her to get so far in her release of the past ... *stopping her from total healing.*

51

The *Spirit of God* started dealing with Jackie about this hate ... *instructing her that she needed deliverance from the hate, and telling her that she must learn to forgive this man for all that he had done.* She struggled with God over this matter for many months – *caught in a trap of bitterness and inability to forgive* – that was keeping her from totally letting go of the past or from being able to totally move into a healthy future.

One day she could go no further. She knew she had to make the *choice to forgive.* But in order for her to be able to genuinely forgive, she knew that first she must first let go of the hate, and she also knew that only through the Power of God's Love would she be able to do so. That day she made the *choice* to be set free of the years of deep hatred for this man because of what he had perpetrated upon her and her children ... *that day Jackie made the choice to forgive what in man's eyes was unforgivable.*

Together, *Jackie and I,* united in the Name of Jesus Christ of Nazareth, took hold of God's Promise in His Word ... **"resist Satan and he must flee from you".** As we stood against the demonic force of hatred deep within my friend, the actual *Spirit of Hate* came out of her mouth and formed into the most hideous looking creature that stood at her side. Jackie actually saw this *demon* that stood about three feet in height. We continued to resist Satan with the Word of God in the mighty Name of Jesus, and within a few minutes the creature evaporated and melted away – never to return.

Once Jackie was free of the *Spirit of Hate,* she was able to make the trip to the prison with me to offer her own forgiveness – through the Power of God – to this man. He mocked her to her face, *as he had mocked me,* and threw our forgiveness back into our face. However, because we had obeyed God, we have reaped tremendous *"fruits"* from our act of *"genuine forgiveness".*

52

We both walked away from the prison that day knowing we had left behind all fear and devastation from our past. Today Jackie is a strong and healthy woman ... *physically, emotionally, and spiritually.* She married my big brother, Carl, in 1996 and became also my "sister" ... *both by law and in the Lord!* When Carl went home to be with his Sweet Jesus in January of 2005, the Power and the Love of Jesus once again lifted Jackie up with healing and restoration.

GOD IS GOOD! His command for us to *"forgive others"* is so that we can be free and restored once again. Besides, no matter what anyone ever does to us, we will never be asked to forgive as much as the Son of God has already forgiven us because of His Love for us.

- **Matthew 18: 21-35 ...** *Then Peter came to Jesus and asked, "Lord, how many times shall I forgive my brother when he sins against me? Up to seven times?" Jesus answered, "I tell you, not seven times, but seventy times seven. Therefore, the kingdom of heaven is like a king who wanted to settle accounts with his servants. As he began the settlement, a man who owed him ten thousand talents (that is, millions of dollars) was brought to him. Since he was not able to pay, the master ordered that he and his wife and his children and all that he had be sold to repay the debt. The servant fell on his knees before him. 'Be patient with me,' he begged, 'and I will repay the debt.' The servant's master took pity on him, canceled his debt and let him go. But when that servant went out, he found one of his fellow servants who owed him a hundred denarii's (that is, a few dollars). He grabbed him and began to choke him. 'Pay back what you owe me!' he demanded. His fellow servant fell to his knees and begged him, 'Be patient with me, and I will pay you back.' But* *he refused. Instead, he went off and had the man thrown into prison until he could pay the debt. When the other servants saw what had happened, they were greatly distressed and went and told their master everything that had happened. Then the master called the servant in. 'You wicked servant,' he said, 'I cancelled all that debt of yours because you begged me to. Shouldn't you have had mercy on your fellow servant just as I had on you?' In anger his master turned him over to the jailers to be tortured, until he should pay back all he owed. This is how my Heavenly Father will treat each of you unless you forgive your brother from the heart."*

Don't' Keep Count! "I'm sorry." "I forgive you." These words are often spoken, but what do they really mean? Does the other person have to keep on forgiving? Peter asked if forgiving a person seven times was enough. Jesus answered that seven times was not enough. Instead, Peter should forgive *"seventy times seven"* times. The point ... *Don't keep count – just keep on forgiving.*

Why did Jesus tell this parable about a man who, *after receiving great forgiveness for a large debt he owed to someone*, refused to forgive a person who owed him a small debt? Jesus was illustrating that we sinners have been graciously forgiven by God, *and are being forgiven daily*, over and over again. We should be just as gracious in forgiving others. To refuse to forgive others shows that we have not understood how much God has forgiven us.

What is <u>unforgiveness</u> ... *unforgiveness is a set of delayed emotions that consists of resentment, bitterness, hatred, hostility, anger, and fear.* These emotions arise in a person because of a transgression that has wounded them psychologically or physically. Unforgiveness consumes the heart like a cancer. The wounded person responds with hot emotions of anger and the fear of being wounded again. The emotions of anger and fear are <u>not</u> unforgiveness, but when these emotions are continually replayed mentally ... *the resulting delayed emotions <u>are</u> unforgiveness.*

What is <u>forgiveness</u> ... *forgiveness is more than relinquishing judgment to God or simply accepting the hurt and letting it pass.* True forgiveness occurs when those cold emotions of unforgiveness are changed to warm, loving, compassionate, caring, altruistic emotions resulting from a heartfelt transformation. *Forgiveness is both an act and a process* – it can be compared to canceling a debt. Forgiveness is not the same as reconciliation ... *it takes two to reconcile – it takes only one to forgive.*

God's forgiveness of humans and our forgiveness of one another are different – although related. Both involve an altruistic, emotional response by the forgiver toward another who needs forgiveness, but there's a difference in the one doing the forgiving. God has an infinite perspective on us, but we do not have that same perspective on others. God knows our hearts and our motives, so He can legitimately demand our repentance prior to forgiving. Humans, however, cannot demand repentance before granting forgiveness. In the Bible ... *Jesus ties together God's forgiveness of us with our forgiveness of others.*

Forgiveness is often thought of as a Christian Duty, but forgiveness can rarely be achieved when practiced as a duty. The positive, loving emotions of forgiveness that replace the delayed emotions of unforgiveness rarely flow from willful duty ... *they flow from a heart that is transformed by having experienced God's love and forgiveness.*

In genuine forgiveness, we need to experience empathy for the person who has harmed us, humility about our own sinfulness, and gratitude over having received forgiveness ourselves from God and from others. Experiencing forgiving emotions is not easy and requires time. We must, *as indi-*

viduals, decide whether we can experience the emotions that lead to the *changed heart of forgiveness.* Forgiveness cannot be summoned at will. When we are asked to forgive, it will take time to experience the new emotions. Talking about the transgression and the need for forgiveness will often be helpful in experiencing and granting forgiveness.

- *Recall The Hurt:* to heal, you must not deny that you have been hurt or offended, but you should not recall the hurt in whiny victimization or as finger-pointing blame. Instead, you should recall the hurt calmly and try to remember objectively what happened.
- *Empathize:* to empathize with the person who hurt you means attempting to understand what the transgressor might have been going through. Try to feel with the person who caused the hurt.
- *Give An Altruistic Gift Of Forgiveness:* try to recall a time when you harmed someone who later forgave you. Then you can more easily envision yourself giving that gift of forgiveness back to another, and *... we need to remember how our Heavenly Father continues to forgive us.*
- *Commit Publicly To Forgive:* this will help you to solidify the act of forgiveness. While you can truly forgive a person in your heart, you might doubt that forgiveness if you recall the incident and experience again some of the hot emotions. That's why it is important to publicly commit in some way to forgive *... speaking aloud or writing down your forgiveness, by telling a trusted friend, or by writing a follow-up letter to the person who harmed you – even if possible personal danger keeps you from mailing the letter, writing it will be very "freeing" for you.*
- *Hold On To Forgiveness:* when you doubt whether the forgiveness was real, you can hold on to the

forgiveness by remembering that there is a difference between remembering the event and experiencing the cold emotions.

- *Ask God for His Supernatural Intervention and Help:* for those times when forgiveness is humanly impossible due to the gravity of the transgression, remember you do not have to forgive all on your own.

Let us look beyond the material and temporal ... *for there are spiritual rewards.* The greatest of these is the opportunity of obtaining a hearing when we witness to our Faith in Christ. When we speak of God's guidance in our life, and *it has apparently gotten us somewhere,* our witness will be all the more credible to the man or woman who, *without the Spirit of God,* does not accept the things that comes from the Spirit of God. Some people will only heed those whom they view as *"having been there".*

God Has Expectations Of Us. When we are given a Directive from God, He fully expects us to follow through on it. His Directive is for us to forgive others as He has forgiven us offers no exceptions to His Rules!

- **Mark 11: 24-26 ...** *"Therefore I tell you, whatever you ask for in prayer, believe that you have received it, and it will be yours. And when you stand praying, if you hold anything against anyone, forgive him, so that your Father in heaven may forgive you for your sins."*

- **Romans 14: 10-12 ...** *You, then, why do you judge your brother? Or why do you look down on your brother? For we will all stand before God's judgment seat. It is written, "As surely as I live, says the Lord, every knee will bow before me; every tongue will confess to God."*

So then, each of us will give an account of himself *(or herself)* to God. The sobering words of these verses describe a day when each individual will stand alone before God Almighty to *"give account"*. At that moment there will be no excuses, no hidden agendas, and no chance to lie and get away with it. *Each person is ultimately accountable to God – not to others*. The context of these verses speaks of the diversity in the Christian fellowship, encouraging Believers to allow for differences of opinion in matters that do not conflict with God's Word. Elsewhere Paul encourages Believers to **"Work out your own salvation with fear and trembling" ... Philippians 2:12b**

We soon find it all but impossible to live the Christian life within our own strength and goodness. It is through God's strength that we know courage, and through His power that we know goodness. When we realize this, surrender becomes our priority because surrendering to Him means growth and progress. And there is no greater surrender, *when seeking to unite our will with God's Will,* than a genuine act of forgiveness towards someone who has hurt us.

We must each seek to grow in our Faith, *on our own*, before God. Accountability to others can help this process, but ultimately we each will be accountable to God for how we have lived. Follow God's Word because it is a sure and trustworthy guide.

I can assure you, from personal experience, that there is no act as freeing to one's heart and life as the act of *"Choosing To Forgive"*. If you are struggling with unforgiveness towards someone, with the help of Jesus, are you ready to let it go? If you truly want to forgive, please let me pray with you now ...

Our Heavenly Father, in your infinite wisdom and mercy, please search our hearts. Show us those areas deep within where seeds of bitterness, anger, resentment, and unforgiveness still linger. We believe that with your help, in the mighty

Name of Jesus, we can be set free to forgive and to be healed and restored. We ask for your forgiveness, Father God, and we now choose to forgive those who have hurt us. Father, we ask You to enable us through Christ Jesus to also forgive ourselves and to be restored. Thank you for Your help in our act of choosing to forgive and to be forgiven. Amen

If you have sincerely, *from your heart*, prayed this prayer ... *God has forgiven you.* He will enable you to live each day *"choosing to forgive"* others. You can move forward in freedom and be blessed with renewed emotional, physical, relational, and spiritual health.

CHAPTER THREE

"SEASONS OF DISACOURAGEMENT"

"*Discouragement Is A Tool Of Satan*" … the story is told that Satan was "*going out of business*". All of *his tools* were being offered for sale. They were attractively displayed on a table. What an army there was … *hatred, envy, jealousy, deceit!* One harmless-looking tool, much worn, was priced much higher than the rest. "*What is that tool?*" someone asked. "*Discouragement*" was the reply. "*Why is it so expensive?*" was the obvious question, considering the much worn state of the tool. Satan answered, "*Because it is more useful to me than any of the others.*"

Don't allow Satan to use your *discouragement* to destroy your *Faith* in your Heavenly Father. You will find that *discouragement* turns to *encouragement* when we look away from our circumstances and focus our eyes on the Lord. God never promised we would never have storms in our life … *He did promise to always bring us safely through the storms to the other side.*

- **Joshua 1:9** ... *"Do not be terrified; do not be discouraged, for the Lord will be with you wherever you go."*

- **John 14:27** ... *"Peace I leave with you; my peace I give you. I do not give to you as the world gives. Do not let your hearts be troubled and do not be afraid."*

As our Heavenly Father restores us spiritually, our soul prospers by the growing wisdom that leads to greater understanding. This builds our Faith in God to reach the level of *complete surrender of our life* into *His all-knowing care and unconditional love,* which brings us to *total peace with God* in our everyday life.

God desires to restore for us all the areas of our life that Satan has attacked and destroyed. He wishes, *above all things,* for us to reach out to Him by Faith and claim *His total restoration.* God wants only the best for us ... *His Children!* Satan wants us to be in continual pain so that he can use it to weaken and to discourage us from our belief in the goodness and love of our Savior. God takes, *if we will ask Him,* our human weakness and uses it to make us stronger. Likewise, God wants to take our discouragements, and turn them into joy.

What happens when people are discouraged? Some decide to give up. Others look to place blame. *Still others use discouragement as a slingshot to propel them to new heights. Discouragement* can cause *depression* with an inability for the person to act, and we will discuss *depression* in the following chapter of this book. But discouragement can also motivate a person and give them renewed determination. We can let discouragement cause us to find a way to solve the problem. We can pray, plan, and then move forward knowing that God goes with us.

David **(Psalm** **42):** **"Tears",** **"Cast** **Down",** **"Disquieted".** David ... *the great king of Israel, conquering hero, and slayer of Goliath* – uttered these unsettling words. Evidently this man, *who as a boy equipped with just a sling and his faith had conquered a giant,* also faced times of anxiety and fear. Throughout the **Psalms,** he laments people's wickedness and violence and entreats God to deliver him and his nation from evil. David wrote of *feeling alone and forgotten by God.* **I will say to God, my Rock, *"Why have you forgotten me? Why do I go mourning because of the oppression of the enemy?"***

David was discouraged because he had been exiled by a jealous king and so was unable to worship in the tabernacle. His soul was *"cast down"* and *"disquieted".* Such depressed feelings cause some people to turn away from God. Others allow those disquieted, depressed feelings to make them hope in God. During such times, *living by faith* takes on new meaning. Discouraged people must learn *to trust* what they cannot feel or see; knowing that ... *"the Lord will command His lovingkindness in the daytime, and in the night His song shall be with them".*

One of David's great contributions is the record in the **Psalms** of his response to his fears and anxieties. Instead of turning away from God ... *David grabbed more tightly onto Him.* Will our distress drive us to despair and discouragement ... *or to God?* May we, like David, find strength in the Lord our God?

- **Psalm 94:19 ... *"When anxiety was great within me, your consolation brought joy to my soul."***

- **Psalm 34:4 ... *"I sought the Lord, and he answered me; he delivered me from all my fears."***

David described his fears – *he didn't dismiss or deny them* – and then he turned them over to God. He replaced those thoughts by recalling *God's goodness, power,* and *faithful intervention* in his life. Doing so moved David to break out in praise and thankfulness ... *celebrating life and worshipping the God who had never forsaken him.*

- **Psalm 27:1 ... *"The Lord is my light and my salvation – whom shall I fear?"***

- **Psalm 42:11 ... *"Why are you downcast, O my soul? Why so disturbed within me? Put your hope in God, for I will yet praise him, My Savior and My God."***

Discouragement often occurs when people try to shoulder their own worries, cares, and fears only to begin to collapse under the weight. Discouragement is not a godly attitude because it reveals an unwillingness to trust God. Discouragement can be dealt a deathblow, however, when we constantly cast all our cares upon God because HE truly cares for us.

Casting our cares on God takes a great amount of *trust* and *humility*. We need to give Him all our cares, and not just the ones we think are big enough or important enough. God will even shoulder the cares that we have brought upon ourselves. His shoulders are big enough to carry all of our fears, worries, and troubles. When we give our cares to God, we can even brush off our discouragement and get back to work ... *we have much to do for God!*

Life is filled with problems, challenges, and disappointments. Things happen that foil our best-laid plans. Often we find ourselves let down and discouraged. Everyone knows about the unexpected *"suddenlies"* that come just when we thought everything was smoothly flowing along. We can all look back over our past and commiserate over the *"if onlies"*. And what about the *"what if's"* ... our emotions can really have a hey-day with that one! Sometimes, it is so bad that we just want to give up. *Discouragement sets in and says, "Why bother? Nobody cares anyhow."*

Despite the circumstances, discouragement doesn't have to overwhelm us. We can learn from it, benefit from it, and overcome it. When we are discouraged, our faith is often put to the test. It is time for us to reassess our goals and to reevaluate our responses. In some cases we will find that there were circumstances, or the actions of other people, that were beyond our control. These things need not overwhelm us ... *God is also God of the unexpected.* He sees those things before we do and *chooses to use them* to shape our personal and spiritual lives to our own good.

- **Romans 8:28 ...** *"We know that all things work together for good to those who love Christ, to those who are called according to His purpose."*

My childhood was one of bitter disappointments, confusion, fear, rejection, and the deep pain of abuse. I have gagged when forced to swallow the bitter dregs of betrayal. I have walked through the dark valley of disillusionment. I know discouragement ... *we have met face-to-face on more than one occasion.* I know how it feels to keep reaching deep inside to find the strength to just hold on for a little while longer until, *hopefully*, things will turn around. I have struggled with the confusion of *"why"*. I, *too*, do know how it feels to hurt, *to trust – only to lose*, and to hurt again. I, *too*, have endured the deep pain of excruciating loneliness. I have suffered tremendous and devastating personal, professional, and emotional losses in my life. For years my *"heart"* was torn with *thorns of anger, resentment, bitterness, frustration, discouragement, and unforgiveness.* But today I choose to focus instead on the many *BLESSINGS* of my life, and to honor the *LESSONS* learned from the pain.

My daughter, Susan, was born against all medical odds, after two life-threatening miscarriages. Since I was a little girl, I had longed for a child of my own ... *a daughter whom I could love and care for.* Then when I was old enough to pursue this dream, *"suddenly"* the medical experts were telling me my odds of ever carrying a fetus to term were slim to none. *"What if"* ... I did manage to give birth, would my child be all right? *"If only"* ... I didn't have physical problems that appeared to make my dream of being a mother impossible. I was so disappointed and deeply discouraged.

I had a choice to make ... *did I have the faith it would take to pursue my dream of motherhood?* On January 21st, 1970, God blessed me with a beautiful little girl! She was healthy, smart, and so very precious. She gave my life new meaning, and she became my reason for living.

On May 28th, 1984, my daughter's life was over - *snuffed out in one cruel instant.* I attended the funeral of my only child on my thirty-fourth birthday. My life-long dream of being a mother and of one day becoming a grandmother was ended forever ... *a complete hysterectomy in 1978, at twenty-eight years of age, making it impossible for me to have another child.*

The loss of my child was so overwhelming and so utterly devastating that it almost cost me my own life ... *but for the Grace and Divine Intervention of God.* While I continue to miss my little girl, *especially on special holidays,* I am so thankful for the *"gift"* of hearing my own child's first cry, seeing her first smile, hearing her say *"Mama"* for the very first time, watching her grow and change, being so proud of her independent spirit and her many accomplishments in such a short time of being on this earth.

For a brief time, I was a parent – *a mother* – so in spite of the pain of losing her, how can I not be thankful that God loved me so much that He shared Susan with me for fourteen unbelievable and unforgettable years? Following the miscarriages, *"what if"* I had been afraid to open my heart to try again? I would never have known the love or the joy that being a mother brings. Thank God, I was strong enough to look beyond the *discouragement* of the *"what if's"*, the *"if onlies"*, and the fear of the possible *"suddenlies"* that are a part of this life.

Discouragement ought to be our first indication that it is time to pray. We need to call on God to help us understand His Guidance in the midst of our circumstances. There are three underlying causes for discouragement:

1. Lack of confidence in God.
2. Lack of confidence in ourselves.
3. Lack of direction for the future.

Joshua faced these same challenges when he led the children of Israel into the Promised Land. As God told Joshua, He also promises us now as His Children:

- **Joshua 1: 5-9** ... *"No one will be able to stand up against you all the days of your life. As I was with Moses, so will I be with you; I will never leave you nor forsake you. Be strong and courageous, because you will lead these people to inherit the land I swore to their forefathers to give them. Be strong and very courageous. Be careful to obey all the law my servant Moses gave you; do not turn from it to the right or to the left, that you may be successful wherever you go. Do not let this Book of the Law depart from your mouth; meditate on it day and night, so that you may be careful to do everything written in it. Then you will be prosperous and successful. Have I not commanded you? Be strong and coura-*

geous. Do not be terrified; do not be discouraged, for the Lord your God will be with you wherever you go."

Once we really believe that God loves us and cares about us, we can begin to have confidence in *His Plan* for our lives. The *key* is lining up our lives and our prayers with the wise and certain promises of *God's Word*. When we quote the promises of God back to Him in our prayers, *we are agreeing with what God has already promised* and *reordering our lives accordingly.* In Jesus Christ, we can ...

- RIDE OUT THE STORM: we must not get beaten down by the storms of life and give up too soon. We must not quit.
- REALIZE THAT GOD USES ORDINARY PEOPLE: we don't have to be spiritual giants. God uses ordinary people to accomplish extraordinary things for Him every single day.

    1 Corinthians 1: 26-31 ... *"Brothers, think of what you were when you were called. Not many of you were wise by human standards; not many were influential; not many were of noble birth. But God chose the foolish things of the world to shame the wise; God chose the weak things of the world to shame the strong. He chose the lowly things of this world and the despised things – and the things that are not – to nullify the things that are, so that no one may boast before him. It is because of him that you are in Christ Jesus, who has become for us wisdom from God – that is, our righteousness, holiness, and redemption. Therefore, as it is written, let him who boasts boast in the Lord.'"*

- DON'T BE DEFEATED BY THE NEGATIVES: we must keep our focus on Christ and the wonderful possibilities in our lives. Listening to the *"negative voices"* will only discourage us.
- FOCUS ON CHRIST: it helps to envision what He can do for us and what we can do for Him. No life is meaningless if Christ is at the center of it.
- REMEMBER THAT WE ARE SPECIAL: God uniquely created us and designed us to serve Him. No one else can do what we can do for Him. We are uniquely gifted to minister to people no one else will ever meet or touch. We must not give up just because there are challenges and obstacles.
- FOCUS ON BEHAVIOR: we must do what is right no matter how we feel. We should make sure our behavior determines our feelings rather than allowing our feelings to determine our behavior. This sets us free to be creative, confident, and committed.
- BE PERSISTENT: we actualize the impossible when we honor God with our faith. There is an interesting story in the Bible about a persistent widow who insisted that a judge give her legal protection. The judge finally granted her request because she wouldn't give up.

Luke 18: 1-8 ... *Then Jesus told his disciples a parable to show them that they should always pray and not give up. He said, "In a certain town there was a judge who neither feared God nor cared about men. And there was a widow in that town who kept coming to him with the plea, 'Grant me justice against my adversary.' For some time he refused. But finally he said to himself, 'Even though I don't fear God or care about men, yet because this widow keeps bothering me, I will see that she get justice,* *so that she won't eventually wear me out with her coming!' And the Lord said, 'Listen to what the unjust judge says. And will not God bring about justice for his chosen ones, who cry out to him day and night? Will he keep putting them off? I tell you, he will see that they get justice, and quickly. However, when the Son of Man comes, will he find faith on the earth?"*

The *answer to discouragement* is getting our focus off of ourselves and our limited resources and to *begin focusing on the unlimited power of God.* He can do for us what we cannot do for ourselves. Even in the face of life's greatest challenges ... *His Grace Is Sufficient!* When we give our discouragement to God, He can encourage and draw us ever closer to Him.

- **Psalm 27:14 ... *"Wait for the Lord; be strong and take heart and wait for the Lord."***

- **Psalm 37: 3-5 & 23-25 ... *"Trust in the Lord and do good; dwell in the land and enjoy safe pasture. Delight yourself in the Lord and he will give you the desires of your heart. Commit your way to the Lord; trust in him and he will do this. If the Lord delights in a man's way, he makes his steps firm; though he stumble, he will not fall, for the Lord upholds him with his hand. I was young and now I am old, yet I have never seen the righteous forsaken or their children begging bread."***

"Desires Of Your Heart"? If you have truly committed your life and your future into God's Hands, *every aspect of it,* and if you have chosen to truly trust in Him and in *"the plans that He has for your life",* then you need to under-

70

stand this simple truth … *God knew us before we were in our mother's womb.* God knows the *beginning* and the *end* of our individual life, and ALL that lies in between … WE DON'T! So, *surrendering to your trust in God and His Plans for your life,* ask Him to remove the *"desires of your heart"* that are not of Him and to fill your heart with the *"desires"* that He knows is best for you.

Commit To God: the Amplified Bible *pictures us committing our load to God by "rolling it onto Him".* What are we to commit – *to trust –* to God?

- OURSELVES: **Psalm 22:8** … *"He trusts in the Lord; let the Lord rescue him. Let him deliver him, since he delights in him."*
- OUR BURDEN: **Psalm 55:22** … *"Cast your cares on the Lord and he will sustain you; he will never let the righteous fall."*
- OUR SOULS: **1 Peter 4:19** … *"So then, those who suffer according to God's will should commit themselves to their faithful Creator and continue to do good."*
- OUR WAY: **Psalm 37:5** … *"Commit your way to the Lord; trust in him."*
- OUR CAUSE: **1 Peter 2:23** … *"When they hurled their insults at him, he did not retaliate; when he suffered, he made no threats. Instead, he entrusted himself to him who judges justly."*
- OUR WORKS: **Proverbs 16:3** … *"Commit to the Lord whatever you do, and your plans will succeed."*

Jesus warned His followers that living as a Christian in the world would not be easy. Hardships, troubles, even persecutions would come. Some tribulations are part of living in a fallen world and happen to everyone – *others occur as Satan assaults people's faith.* Believers are to be prepared for these tribulations – *but not overwhelmed or discouraged by them.* The world gives tribulation – JESUS GIVES PEACE! We can *"be of good cheer"* because we know that Jesus has overcome the world ... *Christ has already won the ultimate victory over Satan, sin, and evil.*

- **John 16:33 ...** *"I have told you these things, so that in me you may have peace. In this world you will have trouble. But take heart! I have overcome the world."*

- **Isaiah 59:1 ...** *"Behold, the Lord's hand is not shortened, that it cannot save; nor his ear heavy, that it cannot hear."*

- **Isaiah 58:11 ...** *"The Lord will guide you always; he will satisfy your needs in a sun-scorched land and will strengthen your frame. You will be like a well-watered garden, like a spring whose waters never fail."*

I, *too*, have known painful relationships and failed marriages. I have lived with the utter devastation left by a bitter divorce, and the total shock of learning certain undeniable truths that annulled a marriage which I believed would last for a lifetime. Watching the *Death of a Marriage* is on of the hardest trials one can ever experience ... *dreams disappear, plans evaporate, trust becomes mistrust, respect turns into disillusionment, and hope becomes fear that can leave a scar so deep we may never heal.*

But we do have a choice. *We can allow our hurts to fade, to open our hearts to the healing balm of the love of our Heavenly Father, to look beyond the discouragement, and to move through the fear in order to allow ourselves to live and to love again.* Or we can *choose* to dwell in our own *"Season of Discouragement"* ... living – *no existing* – with the paralyzing fear of the *"what if's"*.

Life on this earth will carry its share of *disillusionments, losses,* and *discouragement* for everyone. It is how we *choose* to deal with them that will determine the quality of the rest of our lives. There is another important factor to remember ... *how we choose to handle the discouragements of our own lives will determine how effective we will be in reaching out to help others deal with the discouragements of their lives.*

I, *too,* have lived through the fear of suddenly being diagnosed with an incurable and debilitating illness ... *the gut-wrenching horror of watching one's body and/or mind succumb to a disease (or accident) over which we have no control.* I know the devastation of *suddenly* having one's spouse ripped from their life without warning ... *leaving our heart with a gaping hole so big the screaming winds of pain take our breath away.* On three separate occasions, *through no choice of my own,* I have come face-to-face with the total loss of employment, money, and all of my possessions. All three times ... *I had to stand as a woman alone* – with only my *Faith in God* and *Perseverance* to pull me through.

In spite of all my personal losses and deep pain ... Jesus Christ, *my very bestest friend,* has walked through the *"Valley Of The Shadow Of Death"* with me – delivering me with new faith, new direction, and complete trust in *His Plans* for my life. I pray daily that God will enable me to use my experiences to help someone else who is also struggling and/or hurting.

By the *Grace of God* I am free to move onward, forward, and upward with all areas of my life. I am free to live again – to love again. Free from the *"suddenlies",* the *"if onlies",* and the *"what if's".* I have learned to turn to Jesus in my *"Seasons of Discouragement".*

- **Jeremiah 29:11 ...** *"For I know the plans I have for you," declares the Lord, "Plans to prosper you and not to harm you, plans to give you hope and a future."*

My friends, there will always be *seasons of discouragement* with no earthly guarantee of any given outcome. But there is one sure guarantee that we do have ... *we can have a Friend in Jesus who will never leave us or forsake us. A Friend who sticketh closer than a brother. A Heavenly Father who will never let us be tested or tempted beyond what we can bear ... but will always provide a way of escape.* Faith with Perseverance ... *these are the keys to overcoming discouragement.*

- **James 5:11 ...** *"You have heard of Job's perseverance and have seen what the Lord finally brought about. The Lord is full of compassion and mercy."*

One sure way for believers to deal with negative emotions, *such as discouragement*, is to get their eyes off their own troubles, and to extend a *"helping hand"* to someone else because there are hurting people everywhere who need the healing touch of God's servants.

- **Galatians 6:9 ...** *"Let us not grow weary in doing good, for at the proper time we will reap a harvest if we do not give up."*

Paul encourages believers to *"not grow weary while doing good."* Continuing to do good and never seeing a harvest can be discouraging and frustrating. At times, loving words fall on deaf ears and hard work on thankless hearts. But no work for God is ever wasted ... *"In due season we shall reap if we do not lose heart".* We will reap a *harvest of blessings* as the Holy Spirit works in our lives. We must never allow *discouragement* to make us grow idle because our good works are valuable to God.

How do we move beyond our very human emotions in order to open our hearts and lives to all the many Blessings that our Heavenly Father wants to give to us? By having *FAITH* in the *"Author and Finisher of Faith" ... Jesus Christ – Our Lord and Savior.*

Jesus was born as *The Son of God* and *Son of Man.* He was born into this world as a tiny *"human"* baby. He grew up as a boy in the home of a carpenter, and He faced the same tests and temptations that we all face as we move through this life. *"WHY?"* So that HE would know how to comfort us in our deepest sorrow, meet us at our deepest point-of-need, restore to us all that Satan steals from us, heal us of our most devastating illness, and to be the *"KEY"* that can unlock the door of our own *"Personal Prison"* to lead us forth in triumphant victory!

- **Hebrew 12: 2-3 ...** *"Let us fix our eyes on Jesus; the author and perfecter of our faith, who for the joy set before him endured the cross, scorning its shame, and sat down at the right hand of the throne of God. Consider him who endured such opposition from sinful man, so that you will not grow weary and lose heart."*

Stay strong in Christ and don't allow discouragement to take the heart from you because God's Word gives us a promise ... *"weeping may endure for the night – but joy will come with the morning".* I would like to share something that I found to be quite enlightening and encouraging. I have no idea where this originated from, but I have no doubt that it was inspired by God to bring understanding and encouragement during confusing and/discouraging times.

A man was sleeping at night in his cabin when suddenly his room filled with light, and the Savior appeared. The Lord told the man He had work for him to do, and showed him a large rock in front of his cabin. The Lord explained that the man was to push against the rock with all his might. This the man did, day after day. For many years he toiled from sun up to sun down, his shoulders set squarely against the cold, massive surface of the unmoving rock, pushing with all his might. Each night the man returned to his cabin, sore and worn out, feeling that his whole day had been spent in vain.

Since the man was showing signs of *discouragement*, the Adversary *(Satan)* decided to enter into the picture by placing thoughts into the man's weary mind ... *"You have been pushing against that rock for along time, and it hasn't budged. Why kill yourself over this? You are never going to move it."* Thus, *Satan* was giving the man the impression that the task was impossible and that he was a failure. These thoughts *discouraged* and *disheartened* the man. *"Why kill myself over this?"* he thought. *"I'll just put in my time, giving just the minimum effort; and that will be good enough."* And that is what he planned to do, until one day he decided to make it a matter of prayer and take his troubled thoughts to the Lord.

"Lord," he said, *"I have labored long and hard in Your service, putting all my strength to do that which You have asked. Yet, after all this time, I have not even budged that rock by half a millimeter. What is wrong? Why am I failing?"* The Lord responded compassionately, *"My friend, when I asked you to serve Me and you accepted, I told you that your task was to push against that rock with all your strength, which you have done. Never once did I mention to you that I expected you to move it. Your task was to push. And now you come to Me with your strength spent, thinking that you have*

failed. But is that really so? Look at yourself. Your arms are strong and muscled, your back is sinewy and brown, your hands are calloused from constant pressure, and your legs have become massive and hard. Through opposition you have grown much, and your abilities now surpass that which you used to have. Yet you haven't moved the rock. But your calling was to be obedient and to push and to exercise your faith and trust in My wisdom. This you have done. I, my friend, will move the rock."

At times, when we hear a Word from God, we tend to use our own intellect to decipher what He wants, when actually what God wants is simple obedience and faith in Him. By all means, exercise the faith that moves mountains, but know that it is still God who moves the mountains.

When everything seems to go wrong ... just P.U.S.H.

When the job gets you down ... just P.U.S.H.

When people don't act the way you think they should ... just P.U.S.H.

When your money looks "gone" and the bills are due ... just P.U.S.H.

When people don't understand you ... just P.U.S.H.

P.U.S.H. ... Pray Until Something Happens!

CHAPTER FOUR

"VALLEY OF DEPRESSION"

The previous Chapter was dealing with *seasons of discouragement* ... do not confuse *discouragement* with *clinical depression*. At times everybody feels sad, down, and blue. In **Ecclesiastes 3:4**, Solomon wrote of *"a time to weep"* and *"a time to mourn"*. The writer of Hebrews assured believers they would have times of need in their lives.

- **Hebrews 4:16 ...** *"Let us come boldly to the throne of grace, that we may obtain mercy and find grace to help in time of need."*

While ongoing discouragement, left untreated, can lead to depression ... *depression is a deeper level of emotional turmoil that can affect many people in many ways.* According to research, nearly *one* in *five* people will experience significant and persistent *levels of depression* in their lifetime.

Significant and persistent depression causes people to miss more work than diabetes and heart disease, as well as being a major risk factor after heart attacks, strokes, long illness, and even sometimes after giving birth. Depression affects individuals, families, co-workers, and others who are in regular contact with the depressed person. Clearly, depression is a serious concern for many people. I would like to share some *true stories* of a few people whom I have personally known and have dealt with who suffered from depression.

- **Jackie:** years of physical, mental, and emotional abuse had driven this woman into such a deep depression *(and denial)* that she became unable to do even the simplest everyday chore or to make an everyday decision. She couldn't hold down a job, she couldn't give of herself emotionally to meet the emotional needs of her children; barely finding the strength to meet their physical needs on a daily basis, and she could only respond in fear and total submission to her abuser *(at that time this man was her husband)*. Jackie's fears and depression led her to an emotional breakdown. It took a lot of time, in-depth counseling, hard work, and a whole lot of faith in the love of her Heavenly Father, but Jackie walked out of her *Valley of Depression* several years ago and is a much stronger, healthier woman today.

- **Carl:** my big brother and Jackie's third husband ... *whom God brought into her life after she committed her life to Jesus Christ and was free of depression.* Carl is with his Sweet Jesus now, but for years he struggled with discouragement, pain, depression, and alcoholism. When Carl had his first leg amputated, he wouldn't take any medication to help his body and his mind to deal with the loss, the anger, and the deep discouragement. Unfortunately, *with the best of intentions,* several of the people whom Carl trusted to encourage him spiritually ... *drove him deeper into confusion, guilt, fear, and depression by attacking the level of his personal faith in the* *desire and the ability of Jesus Christ to physically heal him.*

As a result, he suffered *severe depression* for a very long time. Several months before he passed away, Carl had to have his second leg removed. This time, *still walking by faith*, he realized that God often uses medications, doctors, and counselors in His Healing Process ... *he accepted the help he needed to heal and never spent one day in depression.* With Jackie's love and with his newfound faith in his Savior, Jesus Christ, my brother walked away from alcoholism, and much later he also walked out of his long *Valley of Depression.*

- **Jessie:** a very dear friend of mine and a truly committed Minister of Song and the Gospel to so many ... including so many who are in prison. I met Jesse in 2001, at a time when he was going through some very heavy emotional and financial losses in his personal life that had also taken a toll on his ministry. Just when it seemed that things had finally been resolved and he could move forward in his personal life and in his ministry, Jesse was diagnosed with a very critical illness of cancer. God intervened, and Jesse came through the surgery with flying colors and is still cancer-free today.

  However, a few weeks after surgery, Jesse became so *depressed* that it became almost impossible for him to function. At first, he didn't realize that he was *suffering from depression.* But he listened to his daughters and to me, *as a counselor and his trusted friend,* and went to see his doctor. To make a long story short, Jesse learned that as a result of his illness he needed temporary medication and a different type of diet to level out the chemical imbalance in his body. Today, Jesse shares his *story of deliverance* not only from the cancer ... he tells others of his own walk through and out of the *Valley of Depression.*

- **Sammie:** what can I say about this man except to tell you that he is one of the kindest, gentlest, and most compassionate men that I have ever known? He loves with an unconditional love and has such a deep faith in God and love for our Lord. But, *according to him*, this has not always been the case.

  When I first met Sammie in March of 2003 ... *he was lost in a very dark and desperate depression where he struggled night and day against guilt, fear, low self-esteem, confusion, and thoughts of suicide.* Long before I met Sammie, he had overcome alcoholism and had committed his life to God. And, *after several months of counseling and deep prayer*, he came to accept the possibility that his depression could be a genetic and/or medically-based problem ... *understanding that depression can have many root causes – not rooted in sin.* Sammie got the medical help he needed to walk out of his *Valley of Depression.* It is truly amazing to watch the changes in his overall attitude, his level of self-esteem, and his daily life today. Sammie, *like all of us*, finds that God is still *"working"* on him today!

- **Vel Hobbs:** prior to living through the feeling of betrayal, confusion, and deep discouragement of the past ten months ... *my understanding of depression came from learned knowledge and from helping others work through their depression – now I understand the paralyzing pain of depression from being there myself.* Now I understand why people who are suffering from depression often have no idea *"why"* they feel the way they do nor do they understand *"what"* drives them to act in ways they really don't want to behave.

Thank God, *with a gradual understanding of my emotional discouragement that had somewhere along the way turned into a feeling of hopelessness*, I am walking out of my own personal *Valley of Depression* today. Recovery for me has become a process of healthier dietary and daily living habits, seeking Christian Counseling for myself, being able to come to terms with the fact that I was suffering from depression in the first place, and acknowledging that I needed help from God and others to recover.

If you are lost in your own *deep dark valley of depression*, please don't give up. There is truly a way out, and it is not by ending your own life – in a misguided hope – of ending the pain. And don't let the *misguided religious doctrines of good people* convince you that your *depression* is an *absolute result* of *sin* or *unforgiveness* in your heart. As there are *many factors* that contribute to *depression,* there are *many avenues* that God may use to lead you out of your personal *Valley of Depression.*

Although environmental issues can add to depression, actually a number of *medical factors* are involved, including thyroid abnormalities, female hormone fluctuations, and diabetes. Nutritional shortages leading to B-12 or iron deficiencies can cause depression. Patients with a recent history of stroke or heart attack are at high risk for depression. Following childbirth or surgery, many suffer from depression. Common prescription drugs such as anti-hypertensives or oral contraceptives, and recreational drugs such as alcohol or cocaine, can cause significant levels of depression. Abnormalities in the brain's management of hormones such as serotonin and nor epinephrine can also bring on overwhelming feelings of doom and gloom ... *depression.*

Understanding the existence of the *physical components* that can cause *depression* can help to put the *disorder* in context and give us an idea of how truly widespread depression is. Life has highs and lows, and as in a mountain range, the lows often come right after the highs. We may scale the heights of Spiritual Victory only to soon find ourselves in the *Dark Valley of Depression.* Depression has an insidious way of draining energy, twisting values, and assaulting one's Faith. Depression can affect anyone ... *many of the great characters of the Bible shared the lonely path through the valley of depression.*

<u>King David</u> wrote of his depression caused by unconfessed sin, leading to a groaning in his soul and a loss of strength *(Psalm 38).* God used depression as a signal to get <u>Nehemiah's </u>attention to do His Work *(Nehemiah 1:2).* <u>Job</u> experienced financial, personal, and relational losses that led him to curse the day he was born *(Job 1-3).* <u>Elijah</u> was so depressed after a great victory that he wanted to die *(1 Kings 19:4).*

Elijah stands out as one of Israel's greatest prophets. He exuded great courage in the face of evil, fearlessly confronting King Ahab and the false prophets of Baal. Yet when Queen Jezebel threatened to kill him, Elijah ran for his life and lapsed into *deep depression.* He prayed to God to let him die. He lost his appetite. His thinking was disturbed. He withdrew from everyone. During this *dark period ...* he curled up under a tree – wanting to die. Elijah's painful experience teaches us that even the most courageous and Spiritually Mature Believer can struggle with *depression!* Stop judging yourself and stop listening to the well-meaning judgment of others, and ... *seek the help you need to understand and to be set free of your depression.*

Elijah acted courageously, *yet when Jezebel threatened him,* alone and afraid ... Elijah couldn't take it anymore. Elijah knew God intimately and served Him faithfully, yet ... *he felt all alone and very depressed.* When Jezebel threatened him, Elijah reacted in fear. Fear is prevalent in many kinds of depression ... *anxiety and depression coexists in 70% of those who are diagnosed with depression.*

How did God respond to Elijah's fear and depression? *God responded with mercy.* God did not castigate or condemn Elijah for his condition ... *the response that many depressed Christians receives from others and expect to receive from God.* Instead, God provided rest and food and then encouraged Elijah to "go" and continue his ministry. How God responded to Elijah's depression should, *Biblically*, give us the right principles for helping a person who is depressed.

- *Encourage the person to take care of himself or herself physically* ... starting with a thorough medical check-up to determine if there are medical reasons for the depression.
- *Encourage action, but keep it simple* ... proper food and exercise with sufficient rest and sleep. Medication, if required, to level any chemical imbalance to enable the depressed person to return to the point where they can begin to think rationally once more and to find the strength and the faith to move forward and onward with their life. Encourage counseling, as no one can do it all alone.
- *Encourage the person to be goal-directed and then be very supportive of every accomplishment* ... set small goals in the beginning such as seeking medical help and counseling, and then begin to set and work towards some realistic life goals. Depressed people are filled with fear, uncertainty, and low self-esteem. Don't enable them to stay in depression by giving false praise, but do heartily applaud each and every accomplishment of their journey – no matter how small and insignificant it may appear. Remind them over and over that they matter, that they are loved,

and that there truly is life worth living after the valley of depression.

- *Address the depressed person's distorted way of thinking* ... they are not the only person on earth struggling with this disorder – others have overcome depression and are living full and complete lives. Encourage them to begin to reach out to help others. Helping others is a common and effective antidote to the disabling self-absorption and social withdrawal of depression.

What did Elijah learn from his time in the *Valley of Depression?* What can we learn from this Bible story? We serve a God who had miraculously delivered fire from heaven, and yet He is a God who still speaks in *"a still small voice"*. While God works in national revival, He is also at work in individual lives. God performs great miracles. More often, however, He is quietly at work in the souls and in the hurts of His people.

While certain forms of depression should be professionally treated, many *depressed feelings* are part of life's ups and downs. It helps to keep our perspective so we are not surprised at the down times. Like Elijah, we should listen for God's *"still small voice"* to comfort us. Through all of life we, *with Elijah*, can depend on one never failing truth ... *God will never leave us or forsake us.* Even in the depths of depression, God shows a loving concern and a way out.

Serious depression can present itself in a number of ways. While I hold a Degree of Associate of Theology in Christian Counseling and am a Board Certified Biblical Counselor through the International Board of Christian Counselors, I am not trained or knowledgeable in what medical treatment is needed to treat *major depression*. When I am talking, or am involved in general counseling with someone who shows signs of depression, I urge them to talk to their medical doctor and to seek whatever avenue of medical help they may need to deal with this problem ... *depression can be a very serious illness with very serious results, including suicide or attempted suicide, if left untreated.*

Here are some symptoms of serious depression: the person may feel stricken physically and feel their life has no meaning or purpose, there may be loss of appetite or an enormous increase of food intake by the individual, a major weight gain or a major weight loss, eating disorders may surface, frequent crying spells without apparent reason, inability to sleep or sleeping all of the time, isolation, deep feelings of low self-esteem, feelings of rejection, paranoia, etc.

While each of us experience some of these symptoms at some point in our lives, it is normally for only a short period of time as a temporary result of some type of setback in our lives, and we find a way to deal with it so that we can move on with our lives. However, when the above symptoms are experienced in a dramatic and disabling fashion for weeks or months at a timed, it is called *"major depression"*. When these symptoms are low-grade and chronic, it is called *"dysthymic disorder"*.

Depression can also alternate in a pattern of mood swings ... with a person feeling irritable and then euphoric, having insomnia, or being agitated. This could be a signal that the person is suffering from *"bipolar disorder"* or *"manic depressive illness"*. I hope that I have said enough here to discourage untrained professionals from trying to diagnose and/or treat depression.

Elijah demonstrated both healthy and unhealthy responses to depression. After the great victory on Mount Carmel, his life was threatened and he became afraid. *He focused on the situation instead of on God.* During a sequence of events, he sank deeper and deeper into a depressed state. His fear became so intense that he eventually ran away, isolated himself, and prayed that he would die.

But God responded to Elijah's depression in a very healthy way. Let's take a look at how He cared for Elijah and have the same compassion when we deal with a person suffering from depression. How did God respond to Elijah in his time of need?

- God sent an angel to remind Elijah that he was not alone.
- God encouraged Elijah, *not once – but twice*, to regain his strength by eating, drinking, and resting.
- Then, *after Elijah had been fed and was rested*, God led him back into ministry. He gave him a reason and a purpose for his life.

In times of trouble and difficulty, people long for comfort and understanding. As God's Hands and God's Heart in the world around us, let us strive to remember the *"God Of All Comfort"* gave needed comfort and encouragement. God never wastes a wound. Through our own sufferings, *and from studying the sufferings of great Bible Characters*, we learn the ability to empathize with others who suffer as we learn firsthand the comforting Power of a loving God. Then we can come alongside the sufferer ... *understanding how they feel and knowing what they need.* We can also assure them of God's comfort, for we have experienced His Mercy and His Comfort ourselves. God comforts us so that ***"we may be able to comfort those who are in any trouble with the comfort which we ourselves are comforted by God"***.

The line between discouragement *versus* depression isn't always clear, but here are some of the symptoms doctors look for in depression: *persistent feelings of sadness or gloom, loss of interest in things you enjoy, change in appetite or weight, sleeping too much or too little, difficulty concentrating, and irritability.* If any of these problems are interfering with your daily living – don't be afraid to seek help.

The story of Elijah reminds us of the importance of having a strong Personal Relationship with God. But I also want to stress the fact that while God can *supernaturally* heal any illness or disorder, *including depression,* He often uses other ways of delivering us. God often uses people to help sick people with their God-Given abilities, knowledge, and training. God often uses physicians, medicines, and treatment in *deliverance from depression.*

If you are suffering from diabetes, heart trouble, or a number of other life-draining diseases ... *is it a sin to seek medical help?* If you are suffering from depression ... *is it a sin to seek medical help?* Based on the Word of God, I don't believe that seeking medical help is a sin in either case.

Long before I was a committed Child of God, I literally came to the brink of ending my own life just to end the unbearable pain. I had learned at a very early age to *"be strong"* ... to feel that if we are *"strong enough"*, we can work our way through anything – no matter what life, or others, may throw our way. I had little patience or tolerance for what I perceived to be *"emotional weakness"* in others. HOW WRONG I WAS!

In the first place, *as my own personal means to survive,* I had shut down my emotions at a very early age. I had shut down those *"emotions of the heart"* that nurture love, compassion, and empathy for others. I had years of anger from which I drew strength, and also a strong driving force within me that was constantly pushing me to succeed and to *protect myself* from any more emotional pain – *no matter what the cost.*

When my husband was killed in 1982, I hid my pain and anger – returning to work the day after his funeral – never turning to anyone to help me through my time of loss. My doctor, *who was also a personal friend,* gave me some pills to enable me to sleep so that my emotions, *as well as my physical body,* could recover from the loss and the deep pain of grief. I set the bottle of pills in the medicine cabinet because I truly believed that I was far too strong to need pills to cope with my husband dying. Never mind the fact that for the first few months following his sudden death, *a fact that I never shared with family or friends who could have helped me*, I would often find myself alone in my Ford truck barreling down some deserted country road at speeds well beyond the limit of safe driving. *I was tough – I got through it by myself.* WRONG!

Nineteen short months later *my reason for living* was brutally ripped from my life. My fourteen-year old daughter, *Susan*, was dead without warning. Again, *being tough*, I thought that I could get through this loss on my own. The day after Susan's funeral I returned to work, *and on the surface*, I appeared to be getting on with my life. Once again, I wouldn't let my doctor/friend help me. Once again, I wouldn't allow myself to share my pain with friends or family. And when someone kindly suggested that I talk with a Grief Counselor, I became extremely angry and threw her well-meaning advice back in her face.

I couldn't sleep. When I would try to sleep, the horrible *dream* would come again to taunt me and to haunt me – *even in my waking hours*. I would see Susan on one side of a very tall fence that was made of very sharp slivers of unbreakable glass. I was on the opposite side of that fence and could find no way through the fence or over the fence to where my daughter was. Susan would begin crying, *"Mama, please help me"*, as she drifted farther and farther away from me until she was totally out of my sight … *yet her plea for her Mama to help her lingered in my ears twenty-four hours a day seven days a week.*

One Saturday afternoon, while my ex-husband was there on his way through Oklahoma, I thought maybe I could sleep for a little while since he was in the house. I lay down on my bed. As I began to drift into sleep … *the horrible haunting dream emerged yet once again.* All of a sudden it was as though I left my body lying on the bed, but was also floating over the bed watching everything that happened.

I saw myself get up and go into the bathroom. I took the full bottle of sleeping pills from the medicine cabinet and carried it with a glass of water back into my bedroom. I poured all of the pills into my hand and laid them neatly on the nightstand. I took out all of my valuables – *jewelry, the titles to my house and car, the money I had in my purse, and the bank books from my saving and checking accounts* – and placed them neatly across the top of the dresser. Then I took a piece of typing paper and neatly cut it into strips. On those strips of paper I wrote the name of each person whom I wanted to have my things.

Once I had attached the strips of paper to the respective items, I picked up the sleeping pills and the glass of water from the nightstand. At the moment I started to pour the pills from my hand into my mouth ... the *'me"* floating above rejoined the *"me"* lying on the bed. In that split second I realized that I was about to *take my own life.* Strong and tough Vel was about to *commit suicide,* an act that I had always felt only very weak people would ever do.

My ex-husband had been sitting at my dining-room table working on a Government Bid for a Food Service Contract at a Military Base, and he thought that I was finally sleeping. As I ran into the dining-room, he jumped out of his chair so fast and hard that it turned completely over. My *appearance* scared him that much. I was literally as white as a sheet and I had large drops of sweat pouring out of my entire body. He rushed me to the hospital where my doctor/friend met us. And there I learned a very interesting fact about our emotional and physical health.

The doctor explained to me that *our mind and emotions* are very much a critical part of our entire human make-up. That *my mind and my emotions* had been subjected to so much loss and pain within my life to that point, *without being given the help or the time needed to heal,* that it had affected my physical health as well. Added to the *emotional suffering* the *physical lack of sleep, rest, and proper nutrition* ... my *mind and emotions* could no longer go on – they had *simply shut down* in a desperate struggle to survive at all. I wasn't contemplating suicide in order to kill myself – I just couldn't handle the pain any longer. Then the doctor told me that he had been expecting this very moment for months ... *either to dealing with me as a patient suffering from a major emotional breakdown OR to be attending my funeral.*

I got the medication and the counseling I needed to make it through the grief, and my life continued on in a far more positive way. To this day, *even as a successful business-woman – minister – counselor – author*, I still often talk to a Christian Counselor. Life is tough, and no one is *"tough enough"* to handle all that comes our way in one lifetime without needing a little help sometimes. Getting help is not a sign of weakness in a person, but getting help is a sure sign of great strength and deep wisdom.

There is hope for *recovery from depression* beginning with a *real* and *personal relationship* with our Heavenly Father – GOD. Once we choose to commit our lives into the Hands of our personal Savior and bestest friend, *JESUS CHRIST*, we will truly always have *SOMEONE* who will never leave us to handle our pain or to fight our darkest battles all alone. But God often works through people to help and to heal ... *let people help you to handle your pain and to fight your darkest battles, too.*

When *battling depression* we must deal with the *root cause of the depression* rather than isolating ourselves in fear or trying to run away from the problems. *Facing* and *dealing* with *depression* often means *forgiving, letting go, and moving forward with our life.* We will all need to estab-lish *accountability* with God and with ourselves for our actions. This means interacting with someone *trained to recognize depression* – someone who knows how to enable the *depressed person* to seek the *spiritual and professional help* they need in treatment and recovery. It may also mean *medication* to level out the *chemical imbalance in the brain* to make it possible for the *depressed person* to receive the help they need to recover.

A word of caution to those of us who feel that we have a *Calling into the Ministry of Christian Counseling* ... please get some professional training before attempting to diagnose and/or to counsel others who show symptoms of having some serious *emotional, mental,* and/or *physical problems.*

With *wisdom* seek *knowledge* and with *knowledge* get *understanding.* Well-meaning Christians, *without adequate training or knowledge*, can cause more harm than good when attempting to counsel someone suffering from serious problems.

Father God, for all of those who are reading these words and are lost in the tormenting and life-draining darkness of depression, please open their hearts and minds to the "truths" within the words ...they are NOT weak and they are NOT alone. Bring people and books into their lives to enable them to reach out to Your Son, Jesus Christ, in seeking deliverance, healing, and total restoration. And give them the courage and the strength to reach out to other people who have the training and the knowledge to help them recover. "Love On Them – Sweet Jesus" because they need to feel loved and appreciated, and no one does that better than You. Amen.

CHAPTER FIVE

"RECOVERING FROM ABUSE"

Why am I including a chapter on abuse in this book? Because abuse of any type will leave deep scars that have to be *de-scabbed* and *treated* if one is ever to truly heal. I don't want to just talk about *"surviving abuse"*, but I want to talk about *"recovering from abuse"* ... *healing from the abuse in order to move forward into a healthy life in all areas of one's life*. While a *victim of abuse* needs the help of a trained Counselor to overcome long-terms scars of abuse, only the *Love of God* and the *Healing Blood of Jesus Christ* can truly *deliver and heal the abuse victim* from the deeply hidden pain buried within.

My childhood was one of bitter disappointment, confusion, fear, and the bitter pain of abuse. For years *"my heart – my land"* was overrun with the thorns of anger, resentment, bitterness, and unforgiveness. I closed the *"door to my heart"* to all possibility of love, and learned to survive in my *"prison of loneliness"* because no one was ever going to get the chance to hurt me again. But even as I struggled with the abuse of an earthly father who wouldn't, *or couldn't*, love me; I was blessed to have a mother who always made me know that I was special - that I was loved. Living with such a woman, *a true Child-Of-God*, my heart – *while becoming frozen* – never completely lost the ability to hope and trust for a better life.

There are many kinds of abuse: *physical, verbal, emotional, or sexual.* Whether abusive acts have to do with power, things, or people ... *the results lead to destruction.* Abusive behavior can be *aggressive* or *passive, physical* or *psychological, direct* or *indirect.* But regardless of the method ... *all abusive behavior comes from the desire to punish, to manipulate, or to control.*

Abuse breeds an environment of *fear, evil, deceit,* and *pain* <u>versus</u> establishing an environment of *love, truth, wisdom, and patience.* Ongoing abusive patterns destroy the victim's ability to trust in anyone. A desperate need to control becomes a means of struggling to survive that often results in unhealthy addictions to foods, alcohol, drugs, or sex. The effects of abuse are profound: *damage to the victim's relationship to their own bodies; suicidal thoughts and/or self-mutilation; sleep disorders; anger; paralyzing fear; overwhelming grief; etc.* Here are only a few of the many destructive lies taught by abuse: *I am worthless – God is not good – Love doesn't exist – No one is trustworthy.*

Spiritually, the results of abuse are horrendous: there is a distorted *"Image of God"* coupled with a distorted *"Image of Self"* that creates many barriers to experiencing God's Love and Grace. How does a *Victim of Abuse* reconcile a caring God with said abuse? Is God indifferent to pain being subjected upon the victim of abuse? Children who are taught that "Jesus Loves Me" and that God is all-powerful, *yet what is the "Child of Abuse" to believe when they ask Jesus to "Stop Daddy or Mommy from hurting me",* and the abuse doesn't stop?

Children are taught to *obey their parents* because the Bible says so, but how can it be right for Daddy or Mommy to hurt a child and say that it is alright ... *according to God's Rules?* How can *victims of abuse* see God as a *Loving Father* when their own fathers have betrayed, abandoned, or misused them? Where was God, and what does He really think about abuse? *Abuse slanders the "Character of God".*

Abuse has been prevalent upon this earth ever since sin entered the Garden of Eden. There are so many references to *acts of abuse* throughout the Holy Bible that it would take an entire book just to cover them. No human being, *in the free world*, is the *property* of someone else. This *fact* includes *one's spouse and their children*. The Word of God commands us to *love one another* ... abusive behavior is not about love. Our own nation should be shocked and horrified to realize the spreading effects of the abuse of God's Law, and the resulting abuse of persons created in His Image.

- **Genesis 9:6 ...** *"Whoever sheds man's blood, by man his blood shall be shed; for in the image of God he made man."*

Today we live in a violent society ... *just open any newspaper or listen to any news program.* Where does a large percentage of violence start? It starts in the home among family members. Violence reflects the darkness of the human soul – *the sinful nature.* People's violence toward one another grieves God. God instructs those who are in authority to hold people accountable for their violent behavior and to punish them appropriately. It's okay to desire that the people who are abusing you, or someone you know, receive just consequences for their violent behavior. But leave *revenge* to God. In the end ... *He will deal justly with all people.*

- God hates violence. **Psalm 11:5 ...** *"The Lord examines the righteous, but the wicked and those who love violence His soul hates."*

- God judges violence. **Genesis 6:13 ...** *So God said to Noah, "I am going to put an end to all people, for the earth is filled with violence because of them. I am surely going to destroy both them and the earth."*
- God is angry with people's violence. **Ezekiel 8:17 & 45:9 ...** *God is angry with the people's violent behavior, and commands those who are violent to change.*
- God calls us to help bring an end to violence. **Psalm 7:9 ...** *"O righteous God, who searches minds and hearts, bring to an end the violence of the wicked and make the righteous secure."*

Abuse is an inexcusable act. The consequences of abuse, *no matter how someone may try to justify it,* are far-reaching and destructive. Abuse, *in any form,* results in low self-esteem, conflict over sexual identity, inability to trust, isolation, fear, jealousy, guilt, and shame. If the *victims of abuse* do not get the help to end the abuse and to deal with the trauma caused by the abuse ... *it will leave deep scars or long-term physical, psychological, and even spiritual damage.*

As in the case of all sinful actions, the abuser usually fabricates a rationale for his or her conduct. And the *cycle of abuse* has been proven to continue from one generation to another generation until someone is strong enough to get the help they need to *"break the cycle".* Turning to God, *our Heavenly Father,* is one sure way to find the strength and the help to stop the abuse and to begin the healing process. I know what He has done in my life, and He will do the same in yours.

Physical Abuse: whenever a person in a position of authority uses undue force to make another person do whatever they want them to do ... *they are behaving in an abusive manner.* Often beginning with *verbal threats of physical harm*, the *verbal abuse* escalates to *physical violence*. Often abuse is heaped upon wives and children by angry husbands and fathers simply to prove to them *"who is the boss"*. NOTE: while the major percentage of abuse is perpetrated by men – *husbands and/or fathers* – never doubt the real existence of abuse perpetrated also by women – *wives and/ or mothers* – in our society.

- Statistics {*world wide in 2000*} regarding *wife abuse*: 45% of battered women – *are pregnant;* every 15 seconds – *a woman is beaten;* 40% of women murdered – *are murdered by their husbands or boyfriends;* 50% of all wives – *will be physically abused sometime during their marriage.* Worldwide we still have the *universal problem* when it comes to abuse … *women are still seen as man's possession.*

People with deep insecurity or fear themselves often abuse those of lesser strength in order to try and prove their own superiority. Many *victims* suffer *repeated abuse* at the hands of alcoholics or drug addicts. Often the *perpetrators of abuse* were once the *victims of abuse* who are still caught in a vicious *cycle of abuse*.

Verbal Abuse: *the use of words or tone of voice to control or to hurt another person or to destroy self-worth.* Verbal abuse can be as devastating as physical abuse … *a destroyer of respect, trust, and intimacy.* Anytime one attempts to hurt or to control another by: *intimidating with threats, shaming with accusations, belittling with name calling, confusing with mind games, badgering with excessive questioning, deceiving with lies, or insulting with profanity* … they are guilty of being *verbally abusive.* Verbal abuse carries its own deep scars … *feelings of inferiority, rejection, emotional abandonment, low self-worth, difficulty with trust, etc.*

Emotional Abuse: while all forms of mistreatment are *emotionally abusive*, certain behaviors can be overtly labeled as *"emotional abuse"*. An emotionally abusive behavior will fit one of two categories ... *passive* or *aggressive*.

- *Passive Emotional Abuse*: characterized by ... *withholding emotional support; not giving affection or compliments which are due; using the "silent treatment"; refusing to express true feelings; neglecting important family gatherings; failing to return home at a reasonable time; etc.*

- *Aggressive Emotional Abuse*: characterized by ... *not allowing any part in major decisions; withholding money and access to the checkbook; hiding car keys as a means of control; driving recklessly to instill fear; inflicting sleep deprivation; isolating from family and friends; physically abusing a pet; etc.*

Emotional abuse often leaves the *victims* feeling they are incapable of running their own lives; thus, making them become *prime targets* for the manipulation and control tactics of *physical abusers*. Victims of emotional abuse often display erratic behavior patterns, and often display a total lack of self-confidence or a tendency towards unexpected and violent anger.

Sexual Abuse: if there is any form of abuse that is more evil than another ... *sexual abuse is it*. No one wants to think about sexual abuse ... *especially abuse of children or young people or the elderly*. However, statistics show that _one in four females_ and _one in six males_ are *sexually molested* prior to the age of eighteen. Such numbers indicate that many people are looking at life and spiritual matters through the *lens of sexual abuse*. And with such numbers, it is also certain that our church congregations include many people who are aching from having been sexually abused ... *people who are often too scared and ashamed to ask for help.*

Because there are many who believe a *wife is to be submissive* to all her husband's desires, many married women experience *sexual abuse* without realizing it. Sexual abuse and/or violence includes ... *sexually degrading attitudes and treatment; threats or force to get unwanted sex (male rape); unjust accusations of extramarital affairs; brazen flirtation with members of the opposite sex; homosexual activities; committing adultery; coercing spouse to perform sexual acts with others; etc.*

Sexual abuse occurs when an older person sexually exploits a child in order to satisfy the abuser's needs. *Sexual abuse* occurs when any person sexually exploits another person in order to satisfy the abuser's needs. *Sexual abuse* occurs when any person forces another person to engage in sexual activity against their will ... *including a wife or child of the abuser. Sexual abuse* consists of any forced sexual activity ... *verbal, visual, or physical:*

- *Verbal Sexual Abuse*: includes comments about a person's body, lewd remarks, and/or the discussion of sexual activity.
- *Visual Sexual Abuse*: includes pornography and being forced to view sexual activity of any kind.
- *Physical Sexual Abuse*: including fondling or sexual contact.

The sexual abuse of children is most often perpetrated by an adult who has ready access to the child by virtue of *authority* or *kinship*. It can be a one-time occurrence or span many years. The *majority of abusers* of both *male* and *female* victims are *males*. When sexual abuse begins, the average age of the child is between <u>six</u> and <u>twelve</u>. The child is considered unable to consent due to development maturity and an inability to understand sexual behavior. Sexual abuse is illegal in all fifty states.

- **Scripture** says much that relates to the topic of sexual abuse. **Scripture** constantly demonstrates God's love and care for children as an example for all people to emulate. **Scripture** also has direct references to sexual abuse. If anyone thinks that God condones any kind of abusive behavior towards another human being, you had better think again!
- **2 Samuel 13:20 ...** Tamar was raped by her brother, Ammon, and from that point on *"remained desolate in her brother Absalom's house".*
- **Judges Chapter Nineteen ...** this story from the **Old Testament** describes a woman's gang rape by a group of crazed men. That *hideous abuse* and the *protection of the abusers by the Benjamites* caused a terrible war in Israel that cost 40,000 men their lives.

To be abused is to be touched by evil. Evil, like good, has an impact. There are many things that contribute to the impact of abuse in a life – *no two people are alike.* If you are a *victim of abuse*, you need to understand how the abuse has impacted YOU. Where has IT harmed YOU?

Healing is applied *knowledgeably* only when a *wound* is *understood.* And the *wounds of the abused person* go far deeper than can be seen with the naked eye. Another very crucial factor, *for the victim of abuse*, is to *know* that no matter what the extent of the damage done to you no matter how badly one has been wounded ... *there is hope for healing and recovery, and that you are the victim – the abuse was not your fault.*

"Victims of Abuse" are people who need understanding and help to heal. Yet, instead, a large number of the abuse

victims – *especially those who have been sexually molested* – try to bury their pain inside ... *locked deep within their hearts along with their many tears and feelings of guilt and shame.* If we, *as their Brothers and Sisters in Christ*, can't step outside of our own comfort zone to reach out to these victims ... *who will?*

Until I was about five years of age, I was Daddy's little angel. I had no idea that many things going on in my young life were wrong. I just loved Daddy and wanted to always make him love me. I saw the way my mother, brothers, and sisters were treated ... *but Daddy never hurt me – not then.* Shortly after my fifth birthday, things changed all of a sudden. Daddy acted like he couldn't stand to look at me, he didn't want me around him, he started to hit me and call me bad names. No matter how hard I tried to make him happy ... *my Daddy didn't love me anymore!* My heart was broken and my world, *as I had always known it to be,* was shattered. For years I tried to figure out *what I had done that was so bad* that it had made Daddy stop loving me? It took years for me to realize that he was the one with a serious problem ... *not I.*

After awhile I started hiding my true emotions beneath an outer persona of arrogance and haughty pride. There was no way that I was ever going to let anyone know that underneath it all I felt *scared, inferior, ugly, like a failure, and so very much alone.* By the time I was in high school I was as cold and hard as they come. The only thing I clung to was the knowledge that soon I would be old enough to leave home and get away from Daddy. The crazy thing was, *as often is the case with abuse victims,* while I had grown to hate him ... *I still desperately loved Daddy and needed for him to love me.*

I knew my best hope to get away from the abusive home environment was to get an education in order to be able to take care of myself once I moved out. God blessed me with a high degree of intelligence, and I studied hard to graduate at the top of my senior class. There was no financial way possible for me to attend college, even though that was a dream of mine. Instead, I went to work and moved away from home.

I began to build a *false world* where the *pain and the shame of my past* would never be revealed. I was living under the *false impression* that *hidden pain* would one day become *forgotten pain*. But the hidden pain of our past will one day resurface to devastate our present and to rob us of our future *unless and until* we get the help we need to be healed of the wounds of our past. For years, *as an adult*, I kept making personal sacrifices to try and earn or to buy Daddy's love and approval.

Over the following years, I rapidly climbed higher and higher in the business world. I worked hard and spent a lot of my free time in pursuit of knowledge pertaining to whatever position I currently held. I was blessed by employers who noticed my efforts ... *opening doors for advancement that I would otherwise have not known.* I now realize that even back then my Heavenly Father loved me and was watching out for me.

Please believe these two truths ... no matter who is abusing you, no matter what form your abuse has taken, no matter what your age – *you are the victim and you are not to blame.* Also, no matter how helpless you may feel or how hopeless your situation may seem ... *God knows where you are, He knows what is happening to you, and He wants to help you because He loves you.* You have absolutely nothing to feel guilty or ashamed about and you are not alone!

- **Psalm 27:10 ...** *"Though my father and mother forsake me, the Lord will receive me."*

- **Psalm 34:18 ...** *"The Lord is close to the broken-hearted and saves those who are crushed in spirit."*

- **Psalm 107: 19&20 ... *'Then they cried to the Lord in their trouble, and he saved them from their distress. He sent forth his word and healed them; he rescued them from the grave."***

Abuse that is frequent and of long duration has more severe effects. The more closely related the perpetrator and the victim, and the wider the age difference, the more severe the effects. Abuse by males is often considered more harmful, as is abuse involving penetrations of any kind or abuse that is sadistic or violent in nature.

Abuse at any age, of any form, and of any duration will leave scars upon the victim that often last for a lifetime. Chronic childhood abuse does damage to the body, the mind, the emotions, and the ability of the victim to relate to another person in a healthy relationship. The damage is multiplied over and over again during the essential development time when the child is forming a foundation for adulthood. Just as a young sapling can be trained to grow straight and tall – *or misshapen and twisted* – during its formative years ... *so a child can be impacted by life's early experiences.*

People who have been chronically abused learn that bodies are for hurting and believe they have no choice about what happens to them. Healing will mean learning how to care for their bodies to protect them from harm and to maintain their integrity. It is very healing for *survivors* to see that Jesus lived in a body that was also abused. He was hit, spit on, humiliated, and left naked in front of others. *The Healer* – who is scarred for all eternity – *knows the pain of abuse.*

As a *Survivor of Abuse* I will tell you that this world does include evil ... *an evil that many find it virtually impossible to accept or believe.* One of the *first steps* for a *Victim of Abuse* to take in escaping the abuse and beginning to heal is to *tell someone about the abuse.* Please, if you are honored by someone turning to you regarding an abusive situation ...

- Be kind, be compassionate, be understanding. Most importantly – be trustworthy and believe them.
- Ask God to help you to understand the complex issues of the abused and to show you how to truly help the victim of the abuse.
- Please don't run away in fear – unless you have suffered abuse, personally, you have no idea the strength it took for the victim to reach out for help in the first place.
- You must understand that in abuse … human relationships have been smashed beyond recognition in the victim's life.
- Try, with the help of God, to put yourself in the shoes of the abused … ask God to give you empathy for them.

To the *Victim of Abuse* … trust, hope, and love are foreign concepts. They are the *unwilling victims* of an ultimate betrayal and the *consequences of such evil* runs deep and will not heal overnight. In order to help a *Victim of Abuse* you must prove yourself to be caring, loving, and trustworthy … the *"Character of God in flesh"* over time.

The *abused* needs a *'team"* of people who will stand by them and walk with them through the long and painful process of recovery. They will need *professional help* from an expert in the field of abuse; they will need *practical help* to move away from the abusive situation and to start to rebuild a healthy lifestyle; they will need *spiritual help* from people who will love them, accept them, mentor them, educate them, intercede for them, and stay along side of them while they heal.

- There are many private church related services that are available to help *victims of domestic violence*. Talk to your Pastor. If you do not have a church family, talk to some Pastors of churches in your neighborhood.

Often Pastors will be able to guide you in choosing appropriate avenues of help in your community. If you talk to a Pastor, *or any one else,* who tries to make you believe you are to *submit to the abuser* as a Christian … run from them because you are literally running for your own survival!

- If you can not afford professional counseling, the city and county governments have free counseling services available. Counseling Services that usually include individual and/or group counseling for both the abused and the abuser.

- Most communities also have shelters that can provide emergency housing for extreme situations that will provide you some time to make other arrangements for housing and provision.

- You can find out what services are provided by your local city or county government by looking in your phone book listing under domestic violence, social services, legal aid, etc. If you cannot find any local help, you can always call the National Domestic Violence Hotline at 1-800-799-SAFE.

Abuse often results in damage to the emotions. Feelings of fear, shame, grief, anger, and guilt often govern abused people's lives. It will take hard work for the abused to learn to deal with these emotions. But it can be done … *absolutely nothing is outside of God's Power to deliver, and to heal, and to restore.*

My earthly father was also a minister. As a result of the abuse I endured while I was growing up, *and watched my mother and siblings endure,* I grew hardened and confused by God and by the concept of religion. As a result, I not only left home to escape my father's physical and emotional abuse at a very early age, *I ran as far and as fast as I could to escape any concept of God or religion in my life.* I never doubted there was a God ... *a God I wanted no part of at the time.*

Abuse damages people's thinking. Abused people lie to themselves that the abuse was not really that bad, that the abuse was their fault, or that the abuse occurred because they were worthless and unlovable. Abuse also deeply damages the *victim's spirit* and their ability *to relate to God.* Abuse hinders their ability to hope, may make them afraid of God, or make them unable to trust Him. Victims often struggle to understand *"why"* God allowed the abuse to occur.

In my case, I was unable – *at first* – to understand why God didn't make Daddy quit hurting me. *Then* I couldn't understand why God didn't fix whatever it was that was wrong with me that made it impossible for Daddy to love me. But as I grew older, *repeatedly being threatened with hellfire and brimstone*, I grew very afraid of this God. *If I couldn't be good enough to please my own Daddy, how could I ever be good enough to please God?* Finally, *in order to somehow survive emotionally*, I began to hate the Concept of God ... yet knowing that He existed – *in a cold, far away, and uncaring place.*

By the time I was thirty-seven years old, my life was an emotional void. I was cold and unapproachable to most everyone. An *over-achiever*, I tolerated no less than perfection from myself or my associates. *Sexually*, I had gone from being frigid and non-responsive *(to the point of sexual intimacy making me physically ill)* to becoming sexually promiscuous ... using sex to assuage the temporary loneliness of another empty night – *to the power of controlling a man as I had once been controlled by a man.*

But something happened to me in 1987 that changed the entire course of my life. I, *personally*, met this man called Jesus and began to truly know the *"Character of God"* ... *my loving and forgiving Heavenly Father.* I want us to look at so many of the "wrong beliefs" taught in some Christian circles:

- Wrong Beliefs: when Jesus said *"turn the other cheek"* ... He was telling Christian wives, *and/or their children,* that we should willingly submit to abuse?

  Answer: **Jesus was not promoting abuse in Matthew 5: 38&39 ...** *"You have heard that it was said, 'An eye for an eye and a tooth for a tooth.' But I tell you not to resist an evil person. If someone strikes you on the right cheek, turn to him the other also."* **The backdrop of *"turning the other cheek"* in this Scripture was in *refusing revenge* rather than *advocating abuse.***

- Wrong Beliefs: since Jesus submitted Himself to abuse, *if a woman wants to be Christ-like*, she must also submit herself to the abuse of her husband?

  Answer: **Jesus did not randomly submit to abuse. John 7:1 ...** *"After this, Jesus went around into Galilee, purposely staying away from Judea because the Jews were waiting to take His life."* **John 10:39 ...** *"Again they tried to seize Him, but He escaped their grasp."* **Jesus submitted to *abuse* and *death* to fulfill His Purpose. He bore the sins of the world – *our sins* – so that we might have eternal life, and He bore the Stripes for our healing. He *chose to endure the sufferings* to understand and to intercede for mankind in their sufferings.**

- Wrong Beliefs: **First Peter Chapter Two** says we are called to endure *"unjust suffering"*; therefore, wives should take such suffering as *"Commendable Before God"?* **1 Peter 2:19** ... *"For it is commendable if a man bears up under the pain of unjust suffering because he is conscious of God."*

Answer: the context of this Scripture is suffering ridicule, criticism, and rejection for our faith. 1 Peter 3:7 ... *"Husbands, in the same way be considerate as you live with your wives, and treat them with respect as the weaker partner and as heirs with you of the gracious gift of life, so that nothing will hinder your prayers."*

- Wrong Beliefs: an abused wife should view her suffering as the *"cross"* she is called to bear? **Matthew 16:24** ... *Then Jesus said to his disciples, "If anyone would come after me, he must deny himself and take up his cross and follow me."*

  Answer: nowhere does the Bible indicate that the *"cross"* is an instrument of physical and emotional pain to be inflicted upon a wife – or any person. Matthew 16:25 ... *"For whoever wants to save his life will lose it, but whoever loses his life for me will find it."*

- Wrong Beliefs: God made women inferior to men, giving men greater superiority?

  Answer: nowhere does the Bible say that God regards men as superior and women as inferior. Galatians 3:28 ... *"There is neither Jew nor Greek, slave nor free, male nor female, for you are all one in Christ Jesus."*

- Wrong Beliefs: since **Ephesians 5:24 says ...** *"Wives should submit to their husbands in everything"*, a wife must submit unconditionally – even to her husband's abuse?

  Answer: for a wife to *"cooperate"* **with her husband's violent behavior by willfully submitting to it and taking no action to prevent it is for her to actually join with him in sinning against God. Acts 5: 29b ...** *"We must obey God rather than men!"*

- Wrong Beliefs: a wife must not resist the abuse of her husband because the **Bible** says, *"The husband is the head of the wife"?*

  Answer: a wife is to be submissive to the *headship of her husband*, **but the Bible nowhere implies that she is to submit to the** *abuse of her husband*. **Ephesians 5: 23, 28, & 29 ...** *"For the husband is the head of the wife as Christ is the head of the church, his body, of which he is the Savior. In this same way, husbands ought to love their wives as their own bodies. He who loves his wife loves himself. After all, no one ever hated his own body, but he feeds and cares for it, just as Christ does the church – for we are members of his body."*

HEALING AND RECOVERY FROM ABUSE IS POSSIBLE! There is indeed a Redeemer, but He usually works through people and in time. Submitting to His Process and His Time is difficult ... *seemingly impossible at times.* You can't do it all alone. Please don't be afraid or ashamed to seek the help you need to heal and recover from whatever the abuse you may have suffered.

Yes, we do have a Heavenly Father who loves us more than we can even begin to imagine. But He created mankind to operate based on Free Will. He didn't create us to be robots. Furthermore, there is an evil prince – *Satan* – who brings death, who deceives, who leads people to grab power, to use others – *even children* – for their own selfish gratification.

Abuse is the work of the enemy of our souls ... *it is a hideous attempt to destroy a life and to confuse a mind.* Any battle against that force is a fierce battle. Survivors find the battle hard because of the reality behind the scenes ... *a battle about truth and lies, life and death, redemption and destruction, hope and despair.* Yes, it is a battle against memories, fears, coping mechanisms, but ... *ultimately it is a fierce battle against the Powers of Darkness.*

To win the battle will take much hard work. *Lies must be exposed and truths sought.* Unfortunately, there will also be battles to be fought with other people ... *the unaware, the uneducated, the afraid, and those hiding behind their own bitter lies and half-truths.* But it is not a battle we must fight alone. In the middle of the devastation, we have a *"Champion" – Jesus our Redeemer and our Savior.*

- **Isaiah 19:20 ...** *"It will be a sign to the Lord Almighty in the land of Egypt (land of sin). When they cry out to the Lord because of their oppressors, He will send them a Savior and Defender, and He will rescue them."*

It is JESUS who is big enough to fight the Powers of Darkness and Evil. It is HE whose Power is greater than the enemy. It is HE who persevered unto the end. Yes, the war is hard and grueling ... *taking much longer than we want it to.* But JESUS is present in the midst of the devastation and HE is working to bring ... *Beauty Where There Was Devastation – Truth Where Lies Ruled – Life Where Death Reigned.*

112

Through Jesus Christ of Nazareth, *as a Victim of Abuse,* you can choose to cross over the threshold of despair and damage to Hope and Healing.

Here is the prevailing <u>Characteristics of A B U S E</u>:

- <u>A</u>ffects the lives of every one in the family.
- <u>B</u>ridges all racial, religious, geographical, and economical levels.
- <u>U</u>ndermines the value and self-worth of others.
- <u>S</u>eeks to dominate and control.
- <u>E</u>scalates in frequency and intensity.

Victims of Abuse have a *sense of being powerless* ... most often afraid to show any real emotions of anger, disappointment, or tears. If you want to become a *"Survivor of Abuse"* and not continue to be a *"Victim of Abuse"*, you must begin with a new way of thinking about yourself, about God, and about abuse. God did not save you so that you could be abused. *Abuse* is a *sin* against God's creation. You were not created to be abused. You can *overcome your fear of the unknown* by trusting God for the future.

- **Psalm 34:4 ... *"I sought the Lord, and he answered me; he delivered me from all my fears."***

- **Isaiah 41:10 ... *"So do not fear, for I am with you; do not be dismayed, for I am your God. I will strengthen you and help you; I will uphold you with my righteous right hand."***

Understand the Biblical mandate to hold the abuser accountable ... *Confrontation is Biblical.* Confrontation can be used by God's Spirit for conviction, and lack of confrontation enables abusers to continue abusing others.

- *Notify others of your needs*: supportive and trust-worthy friends, relatives, or other people. **Galatians 6:2 ... *"Carry each other's burdens, and in this way you will fulfill the law of Christ."***
- *Develop God's perspective on "submission"*: submission does not give license for abuse. Submission is not demanded, but is a voluntary deference to the desire of others. Submission is a way of life designed by God for everyone. **Ephesians 5:21 ... *"Submit to one another out of reverence for Christ."***
- *Admit your anger and practice forgiveness*: confirm the hurt, confess your anger, and choose to heal.
- *Recognize your own patterns of relating, and change the way you respond*: don't respond fearfully; don't hide the truth; don't think you can change the abuser; and don't take responsibility for the abuser's behavior.
- *Identify healthy boundaries for yourself and commit to maintaining them*: communicate your boundaries; state what you will do if the abuser crosses over the boundaries; and then follow through when the boundaries are crossed.
- *Ensure your personal safety, and that of your children, immediately*: have an action plan; know ahead of time where you will go and who you will call – have numbers easily accessible; involve your church; notify the police of the abuse so it will be a matter of record; and know whom you will contact ahead of time.
- *Redirect your own personal "sense of identity"*: see your identity not in your role as a spouse or as the abuser's child, which can change, but as a precious Child of God, which can't change ... He chose you; He adopted you; He redeemed you; He protects you; He forgave you; He defends you; and He loves you.

- *Focus on the "Character of God":* the person of Christ and the Word of God teach the Truth about "Who" God is.

As you learn more about God's power and ability to heal, you can place your past and your future in His Hands. There is *someone* whom we can trust. He is the *"friend who will never leave or forsake us"*. He is the *"friend who sticketh closer than a brother"*. He is the *Father* who loves us with an *unconditional* and *never-ending love*.

My friends, there will always be the *"what if's"* and the *"if onlies"* compounded by the *"suddenlies"* and the unanswered *"whys"* left upon the *"soil of our souls"* by our journey through the *transitions of life*. We will be forced to walk through *changes* with no earthly guarantee of any given outcome. But there is *one sure guarantee* that we can have ... *we can have a Friend in Jesus who will never leave us or forsake us, a Friend who will stick closer than any brother, and a Heavenly Father who will never let us be tested or tempted beyond what we can bear but will always provide a way of escape.* Faith with Perseverance ... those are the "Keys".

- **James 5:11 ... *"You have heard of Job's perseverance and have seen what the Lord finally brought about. The Lord is full of compassion and mercy."***

- **2 Peter 3: 8&9 ... *"But do not forget this one thing dear friends: With the Lord a day is like a thousand years, and a thousand years are like a day. The Lord is not slow in keeping His promise as some understand slowness. He is patient with you, not wanting anyone to perish, but everyone to come to repentance."***

It was awesome for me to realize that God loved me, *and always had*, just as I was. He constantly sought ways to comfort and help me during all those years that I was running in fear, pain, confusion, anger, resentment, and bitterness. When I finally turned and cried out to God in desperation ... *He heard and answered my cry for help*. He started a process of truths, awareness, healing, and restoration that has freed me from a prison where my past had constructed wall after wall of solid steel around my emotions and had robbed me of all trust.

Not only has God healed my deepest wounds, but He began to teach me new and healthier ways to think, to feel, and to act. By His understanding and forgiveness, He has taught me understanding and forgiveness for others and for myself. He restored to me my lost confidence and gave me new self-respect. He taught me how to trust ... *in Him, in others, and in myself as His Beloved Child*. He taught me the beauty of loving and of being loved as a mutually shared healthy emotion ... *an emotion not to be feared – but a gift to embrace*. This FRIEND would love to do the same for you as He has done for me. His name is JESUS, and ... *He wants to become your Very Bestest Friend!*

God truly is *"healing my land"*. I no longer live in the fear and confusion of the *"what if's"* and the *"if onlies"* or the possible *"suddenlies"* of my life. In spite of all my personal losses and deep pain, Jesus Christ – *My Bestest Friend* – has walked through the *"Valley Of The Shadow Of Death"* with me ... delivering me with new hope, a stronger faith, new direction, and complete trust in His Plan for my life.

I pray daily that God use my experiences to help someone who is struggling and/or hurting. I ask that God give me the opportunity to *share the blessing of loving and of being loved* ... free from the fear of the *"what if's"*. By the Grace and Mercy of God and the Love of my Heavenly Father ... *I am free to live again – free to love again!* I have learned to believe in the Love of God and to trust in His Plans for my life.

Dear friends, your healing is possible. Your future does not have to be a condition of your past. You may not have had the ability to choose while under the control of another person in your past, but you do have a choice to make now. I pray that you will ... *"Choose To Heal"*.

CHAPTER SIX

"MANAGING THE STRESS"

W hat is stress? Webster's New World Dictionary: <u>Stress</u> *... a mental or physical tension or strain; urgency; pressure; etc. causing this.* <u>Stressed Out</u> *... tired, nervous, or depressed as a result of overwork, mental pressure, etc.*

Let's look at some Scriptures that warn us of becoming *stressed out* that will help us to identify the signs when our lives are moving in an unhealthy and stressful direction.

- <u>Stress = cares of this life</u>: **Luke 21:34** *... "Be careful, or your hearts will be weighed down with dissipation, drunkenness and the anxieties of life, and that day will close on you unexpectedly like a trap."*
- <u>Stress = cares of this world</u>: **Matthew 13:22** *... The one who received the seed that fell among the thorns is the man who hears the word, but the worries of this life and the deceitfulness of wealth choke it, making it unfruitful."*
- <u>Stress = worldly plans</u>: **Matthew 6: 25–34** *... "Therefore I tell you, do not worry about your life, what you will eat or drink; or about your body, what you will wear. Is not life more important than food, and the body more important than clothes? Look at*

the birds of the air; they do not sow or reap or store away in barns, and yet your heavenly Father feeds them. Are you not much more valuable than they? Who of you by worrying can add a single hour to his life? And why do you worry about clothes? See how the lilies of the field grow. They do not labor or spin. Yet I tell you that not even Solomon in all of his splendor was dressed like one of these. If that is how God clothes the grass of the field, which is here today and tomorrow is thrown into the fire, will he not much more clothe you, O you of little faith? So do not worry, saying, 'What shall we eat' or 'What shall we wear?' For the pagans run after all these things, and your heavenly Father knows that you need them. But seek first his kingdom and his righteousness, and all these things will be given to you as well. Therefore, do not worry about tomorrow, for tomorrow will worry about itself. Each day has enough trouble of its own."

- <u>Stress = vanity of seeking more</u>: **Ecclesiastes 4:8 ...** *There was a man all alone; he had neither son nor brother. There was no end to his toil, yet his eyes were not content with his wealth. "For whom am I toiling," he asked, "and why am I depriving myself of enjoyment?" This too is meaningless – a miserable business.*

- <u>Stress = vanity of worry</u>: **Psalms 127:2 ...** *"In vain you rise early and stay up late, toiling for food to eat – for he grants sleep to those he loves."*

At times we all experience physical, emotional, and spiritual exhaustion. Many of us try to get more done in less time with better results. We try to juggle the demands of home, church, work, and family life. Living on the ragged edge, we become worn out, stressed out, and eventually we burn out.

Several years ago in my own life a close friend and business associate tried unsuccessfully to make me face the fact of this *"truth"* within my own life. That is I wouldn't face the truth UNTIL the day came when I experienced first-hand ... *emotional, mental, and physical burnout!* Trust me, *dear friends;* you do not want to push yourself that far ... *it is a long hard road back – if you really ever make it back at all.*

How often do we fret and worry – *stress out* – about things that we have absolutely no control over? How many of us get so worked up over circumstances or people that we have absolutely no control over? WHY? Worry and stress is very detrimental to our frame of mind and has a very negative effect upon our physical well-being. So why do we, *as humans*, push ourselves to the point of emotional, physical, or spiritual *burn-out* over circumstances or people whom we have absolutely no control over?

As intelligent human beings whom God has blessed with common sense, let's learn to do all that we can to take care of ourselves and the people in our lives, and then simply trust God to take care of the rest. Many times our stress is a direct result of our over-inflated egos ... *we want to be in control!*

Stress not only dampens our spirits and frazzles our nerves, but the constant rush of adrenaline over stimulates the heart and can weaken the immune system which leaves us prone to more illnesses and stress-related problems. Stress is an inevitable part of life, so we have to learn how to effectively manage it.

In *managing stress*, let's first look at using our common sense to protect our minds and bodies from undue *stress-related* consequences. *There is no magic bullet to manage stress!* Stress researchers from Yale to the University of California have shown over and over that the best way of managing stress, *from both a physical and psychological perspective*, is to adhere to these basic concepts ... *eat right, get sufficient sleep, and get some physical exercise daily.*

I must admit that I have not always *"practiced what I am preaching"* in these areas of my own life. However, I made a *personal decision* several months ago to change some *unhealthy habits*, and now Jesus is helping me to replace *unhealthy habits* with far more *healthy habits*. As a result of my *choice to change*, I am enjoying improvement in a couple of important areas of my health. Overall, *my choice to change* is making a *positive impact* upon my entire life.

- *Avoid stress* whenever you can. Obviously, the goal of avoiding all stressful situations is unrealistic. However, *with planning*, it may be possible to avoid some of them – or at least to plan effective strategies for dealing with situations that cause you the most stress.

  It is important to understand that each person will have a different strategy for avoiding their own *personal stressors*, but the *"key"* is to make *positive lifestyle changes* that will have the greatest benefit in *your* life.

- Obviously, if you can't avoid stress, then you need to *manage stress* as effectively as possible.

  Try to maintain a healthy diet as much as possible: *greasy burgers and fries, lots of refined sugars, and heaping cups of caffeine do not a healthy diet make.*

  Get some physical exercise every day: *take a twenty minute walk at lunch to relax the stress of the morning, go biking, join a gym, take up ballroom dancing, whatever works for you – just spend some time out in the fresh air and away from stress-filled environments on a daily basis.*

  Get some sleep: *establish a regular bedtime and a regular wake-up time and stick to it for one week – even on the weekend. Sleep researchers tell us that within a week our body clocks will reset themselves to the new and healthier schedule. Do something calming in the hour or so before bedtime. Avoid exercise within three hours of bedtime as this allows time for the body to calm down and return to resting levels.*

Supplementation: after doing what you can in terms of stress avoidance/management, getting adequate amounts of sleep and exercise, and eating a balanced diet ... *you will find it very beneficial to use dietary supplements.* Take a comprehensive multi-vitamin and multi-mineral supplement that will provide adequate amounts of the most anti-stress nutrients that are needed at increased levels during periods of high stress: *Vitamin C, Magnesium, Calcium, and the B-Complex Vitamins.*

Consider what God is doing: **James 1: 2–4 ...** *"My brethren, count it all joy when you fall into various trials, knowing that the testing of your faith produces patience. But let patience have its perfect work, that you may be perfect and complete, lacking nothing."*

CHAPTER SEVEN

"FEAR – WORRY – ANXIETY"

Anxiety disorders *(fear, worry, anxiety)* are the most common emotional struggles of today ... affecting some twenty to thirty million people. An estimated one in five adults suffers from some kind of *phobia*, and that includes one in five persons sitting in our churches. While we often contribute to these *disorders* by our unwise choices – *living disconnected lives, carrying too much debt, living at too fast a pace* – other factors can also contribute to our lives being literally *paralyzed* by *fear, worry,* and *anxiety.*

If we are carrying deeply imbedded, *often deeply hidden,* scars from our past ... this, too, can leave us *paralyzed by fear* and unable to move forward in a healthy and fulfilled life. This is the type of *fear – worry – anxiety* that we are going to focus on in this book ... *emotional disorders that are a result of the scars of the heart.* Often we, *as adults,* end up paying for the *abuse* that others have perpetrated upon our lives ... *paying with fear, worry, and anxiety.* We may not have had any choice or any control over what others have done to us in the past, but we do have the choice to take control of what others try to do to us – *emotionally* – now and in our future.

That control begins by our facing our fears and getting the help we need in order to understand them, overcome them, and to stop allowing the same things to happen to us over and over again in future relationships. God did not create us to be punching bags for others ... *physically or emotionally.* Please don't continue to allow your past to control your future.

<u>What is Fear</u>? Fear is a natural and necessary alarm system that is triggered whenever we feel threatened. This God given emotion ignites a response to a *real* or *perceived* danger. The experience of fear is very real and, *provided the fear is justified,* it is perfectly normal and can lead to protective behavior.

Other types of fear, *fear over imagined outcomes,* can literally paralyze us and control our future in very unhealthy ways. This type of *paralyzing fear* can cost us valuable relationships, great jobs, good times ... the list of potential losses is endless. Some of the fears we want to talk about here include ... *death, betrayal, rejection, abuse, grief, and relationships.*

Unresolved fear will gnaw at your innards and twist your guts with *timidity, dread, terror, apprehension,* and *unrealistic concern.* This kind of fear will make it impossible for you to move forward with your life until you get the help you need to understand the fear and to overcome the fear. *Unhealthy fear* will wreck personal relationships, family relationships, jobs, and cheat you out of so much that life has to offer. But there is hope, there is deliverance, there is healing, and there is SOMEONE who can lead you out of *your prison of paralyzing fear.* That FRIEND is JESUS, and HIS HELP is as close to you as taking your next breath.

<u>What is Worry</u>? Worry is not an emotion but a mental activity that produces anxiety. Worry is a by product of *stinking thinking* that is an unhealthy and unreasonable exercise that attempts to solve situations beyond our control. And

worry never solves anything … *it simply creates stress and increases our level of anxiety* – resulting in an unwelcome visit from our old enemy *"fear"*.

Instead of praying or simply letting go of things that cannot be controlled, worriers obsess about controlling the problem … *talking to themselves about how terrible it is and imagining all sorts of horrible things that are going to happen if the problem is not solved immediately.* Over enough time, worriers even begin to believe that if they worry hard enough or long enough, their worry will somehow solve the problem. But that is never the case. Worrying never solves a problem. Worry only increases our anxiety and adds to our fear.

What is Anxiety? Anxiety keeps a person from relaxing – from resting. Anxiety lies at the root of so many physical and emotional illnesses. Anxiety is at the core of so much professional and relationship failure. Anxiety is one major by product of religious confusion. Anxiety breeds disease. Disease destroys and kills!

Anxiety is a pervasive and long-term inner feeling of nervousness, unrest, and uneasiness. The *symptoms of anxiety* can include … *tense feelings, rapid heart beat, dry mouth, increased blood pressure, jumpiness or feeling faint, excessive perspiring, feeling clammy, and anticipation of trouble.*

Everyone experiences some anxiety from time to time. But *frequent* and *intense anxiety* may indicate a clinically diagnosable and treatable disease. An *anxiety disorder* can be a sudden and unexplained uneasiness that lasts a few hours, or it can be a constant state of mind. Simply wishing the symptoms away will not work. Some forms of *troubling anxiety* include …

- *Generalized Anxiety*: a pervasive form of *chronic tension* that manifests itself in many different situations. When it exists longer than six months, it is diagnosable as an *anxiety disorder* and may require treatment to bring the level of continued anxiety back under control.

- *Phobia:* one of the many irrational fears that haunt and torment otherwise normal, healthy people ... *Christians included.* An estimated one in five adults suffers from some kind of *phobia. Phobia* is a fear that is strongly associated with a single object, place, or event. Many face *phobic fears* of elevators, heights, tight places, open spaces, the dark, medical professionals, animals, and even public speaking.

    Exposure to the *phobic trigger* causes rapid breathing, pounding heartbeat, and sweaty palms. Many are barely able to travel by air, cross an ocean in a ship, use an elevator, go shopping, hold down a job, take a trip on a freeway to visit family, and the list goes on. Worst of all those who suffer with any *form of phobia* think that they are the only ones who must live with this misery. In addition to being paralyzed by their *phobia*, they suffer acute embarrassment, feelings of rejection, feelings of being misunderstood, and often excruciating loneliness as a result of isolating themselves in a misguided attempt to protect themselves from the fear. *There are three defined types of phobias:*

    {1} *Specific or Simple Phobias:* fear of an object or situation, such as spiders, heights, or flying.
    {2} *Social Phobias:* fear of embarrassment or humiliation in social settings.
    {3} *Agoraphobia:* fear of being away from a safe place, such as your home, and exposed to deadly risk ... *this often accompanies Panic Anxiety.* Severe *agoraphobia* can imprison a person in their homes for a lifetime.

While no one knows how *phobias* develop, it clearly seems like it is learned, as a parent with a *phobia* can easily instill the same *phobia* in a child at an early age. A part of the brain called the "Amygdala" has been programmed to create this fear, bypassing any reason. Often there is no explanation for the origin of the fear though sometimes a person can identify an event or trauma, *such as being chased by a dog,* which triggered the *phobia.*

What puzzles experts is why some people who experience such an event develop a *phobia* and others do not. Many psychologists believe the cause lies in a combination of genetic predisposition mixed with environmental and social causes.

Christians can also struggle with phobias. Christian believers, in particular, find that even a *'small phobia'* can be very devastating because they see it is as a failure to achieve God's healing or ... *lack of faith.* They hide their pain for fear of rejection. Often they feel a profound sense of having failed God in some ways. Satan can have a field day with *phobia* sufferers.

If you are suffering from a *phobic fear* to the extent that it is affecting the quality of your life, you need help in order to understand the root cause of the fear and to learn how to overcome it. *That includes Christians!* There is effective treatment for *phobia sufferers,* and Christian leaders need to become more aware of such *phobias* and to encourage *believers* to seek professional help. God does not want to see His Children suffer unnecessarily. Since there is effective help for undoing even the *most entrenched of phobias* ... God's people need to be willing to seek such help.

SEASONS OF THE HEART

- *Obsessive-Compulsive Behavior:* known as OCD, this is a fear hidden behind a variety of obsessions and compulsions, such as highly ritualized/repetitive behavior like constant hand washing. These maladaptive patterns are attempts to manage anxious thoughts and feelings.
- *Post-Traumatic Stress Disorder:* as a result of being victimized or even from having witnessed a traumatic event ... *recurring visions, dreams, and memories of the trauma induce fear and are relived in debilitating ways.*

  First recognized in prisoners of war, *Post-Traumatic Stress Disorder* (PTSD) is now seen as a common experience across a wide range of traumatic life experiences ... *physical and sexual abuse, natural disasters, injurious accidents, etc.* Often referred to as *"flash-backs"*, episodes of *Post-Traumatic Stress Disorder* can result in a person becoming so paralyzed with fear that they are unable to function normally. This illness can cost a person their career, their marriage, family, and even their life if they refuse to seek the help they need to understand what is happening to them and accept the help they need to heal.
- *Panic Attack:* the sudden onset of panic is an overwhelming state of anxiety ... *being flooded and paralyzed by the fight-or-flight response.* Symptoms include a racing heart, sweating, dizziness, ringing ears, choking, and vertigo. The physiological reaction to *panic* is so strong that the *panic sufferer* often imagines that he or she is having a heart attack or going crazy. *Agoraphobia* can set in ... *the fear of returning to the people and places where panic occurred.*

  At its worst, a *sufferer of panic attacks* ends up housebound ... *fearful of panic away from home and excessively vigilant.* More than *three panic attacks* in a month, or the onset of *agoraphobia,* indicate a disorder that needs professional treatment.

Many Christians think that God condemns all anxiety and that He condemns those who suffer with different forms of it. God doesn't condemn the *person* with the *illness* ... just like God doesn't hate the sinner – He hates the sin. What He doesn't condone is our refusal to seek help in understanding these types of fears and how to overcome them. We can seek God for His Supernatural Help and we can seek help from a trained professional.

- **John14:1 ... *"Do not let your hearts be troubled. Trust in God; trust also in me."***

- **Matthew 6: 25–34 ... *"Therefore I tell you, do not worry about your life, what you will eat or drink; or about your body, what you will wear. Is not life more important than food, and the body more important than clothes? Look at the birds of the air; they do not sow or reap or store away in barns, and yet your Heavenly Father feeds them. Are you not much more valuable than they? Who of you by worrying can add a single hour to his life? And why do you worry about clothes? See how the lilies of the field grow. They do not labor or spin. Yet I tell you that not even Solomon in all his splendor was dressed like one of these. If that is how God clothes the grass of the field which is here today and tomorrow is thrown into the fire, will He not much more clothe you, O you of little faith? So do not worry, saying, 'What shall we eat?' or 'What shall we drink?' or 'What shall we wear?' For the pagans run after all these things,*** *and your Heavenly Father knows that you need them. But seek first His kingdom and His righteousness, and all these things will be given to you as well. Therefore do not worry about tomorrow, for tomorrow will worry about itself. Each day has enough trouble of its own."*

In these Scriptures Jesus is not condemning us for our anxiety ... *He is telling us how pointless and harmful it is to worry about things that we have no control over.* Jesus' familiar expression, *"Take no thought for your life"*, refers to *anxious worry.* He calls attention to the destructiveness of anxiety about the future. His teaching is startlingly clear ... *such worry is futile, pointless, and unable to solve the problem.*

No worrisome thought about tomorrow can help people live better or keep evil away. Worry is not an emotion ... *it becomes a pattern of thinking that takes hold when people try to live independent of God.*

Do you want a healthy relationship? Are you willing to think about the person in the relationship – *to relax and enjoy the relationship* – rather than focusing on the *"what-ifs"* of the relationship? Do you want a better job – a more challenging career? Do you want to live out that desire deep within your heart to write a book, sing, become an actor, learn to ski, go to college, change careers, start a new business, move to another part of the country, have a great marriage, be a father or mother ... *the list is endless with possibilities?* You will never be successful in any of these things as long as you are consumed by the *"what-ifs"* that result from *fear, worry,* and *anxiety.*

Unless *fear, worry,* and *anxiety* are honestly faced and worked through, people can end up in a pattern of avoidance ... *organizing their lives around people and situations that they must avoid.* It is much healthier to practice another pattern for living your life.

- <u>Turn to God first</u>: **1 Peter 5:7 ...** *"Cast all anxiety on Him because He cares for you."* And again we find answers for overcoming destructive emotional behaviors by reading from **Philippians 4: 6–7 ...** *"Do not be anxious about anything, but in every-thing, by prayer and petition, with thanksgiving, present your requests to God. And the peace of God, which transcends all understanding, will guard your hearts and your minds in Christ Jesus."*

- <u>Focus on the solution – Not the problem</u>: **Matthew 14: 22–32 ...** this is the story of Jesus coming to the disciples in the midst of a great storm. He came to them *walking on the water.* And when Jesus spoke to the disciples, He kept it very short and simple, *"Take courage! It is I, Don't be afraid."*

  Jesus is still telling us the very same thing today, *"Take courage! It is I. Don't be afraid."* There is absolutely no storm in your life that with the help of Jesus you can't weather. There is no problem so big that it can't be solved. But *solutions* take *courage* and *creative thinking* ... we will never solve anything as long as we suffer from *stinking thinking*.

- <u>Stop wasting energy on worrying</u>: **Matthew 6: 25–34** tells us in great detail that our *Heavenly Father* loves us, and instructs as to *why* we are not to waste our energy with *worry. Worry* causes *stress* which drains our immune systems making us more susceptible to illness and disease. *Worry* creates *anxiety* which leads us into a *pattern of paralyzing fear* causing us to miss out on so many good things that our Heavenly Father has in His Plans for our lives. *Worry never has and never will solve anything!*

- Keep your thoughts on God in order to have peace: **Isaiah 26:3** ... *"You will keep in perfect peace him whose mind is steadfast, because he trusts in you."* I don't know about you but there is nothing that I desire more than to live in perfect peace ... *free of fear, worry, and anxiety.* I much prefer living in an environment of peace *versus* residing in an atmosphere of confusion and anxiety. I enjoy waking up each and every morning knowing that no matter what the day brings ... *everything is going to work out okay because God is in control of my life and nothing can touch me without His permission.* Even when life gets tough, *and it will*, I have peace in knowing that Jesus will walk right beside me and bring me through – no matter what happens.

    This is the *peace* that my *personal relationship with Christ Jesus* has given me. You, *too*, can have this peace just by asking and by trusting in God. I promise that if you are willing to do your part to get your life back on the right track ... *God will never fail to do His part in helping you.*

- Pray: as we read from **Philippians Chapter Four**, we are *not to be anxious about anything, but in everything, by prayer and petition, with thanksgiving,* **we are to** *present our requests to God.*

    Let's look at **Verse 7** ... *"the peace of God".* This is not merely a psychological state of mind, but an inner tranquility based on peace with God – *the peaceful state of those whose sins are forgiven.* The opposite of *anxiety,* this *peace* is the *tranquility* that comes when the believer commits all his or her cares to God in prayer and worries about them no more.

- Direct your attention toward your true source of hope: **Psalm 91:2** ... *I will say of the Lord, "He is my refuge and my fortress, my God, in whom I* *trust."* You are not alone. Pray to God for help, and if you need professional help in order to understand and to overcome your worries and fears, there are many excellent Christian Professionals available. Just don't let your fear and insecurity keep you from seeking the help you need to be an over-comer and not a victim of these devastating and destructive emotions.

Before you try to tell yourself that it is easy for someone like me to sit here and tell you that living with *unhealthy* and *paralyzing fear* will destroy you and hurt others around you so you need to *face your fears* and to *deal with your fears* ... let me remind you that I have faced many of my own monsters – too many for one lifetime. With faith in the love of God and hard work teamed up with perseverance on my part ... I AM FREE AND HEALTHIER TODAY!

With the help of God, I have overcome obstacles and losses that would have overwhelmed many. I have survived abuse; bitter divorce; an annulment; miscarriages; a complete hysterectomy at age twenty-eight; the sudden brutal death of a husband and a daughter; and professional and personal betrayal with professional, personal, and financial losses too grave to even attempt to discuss here. But God has delivered me, healed me, and restored me in ways far above anything I could have ever imagined, and ... *He ain't though with me yet!!!*

GOD IS A GOOD GOD ... what He has done for me, He will also do for you if you will ask Him into your heart and into your life. However, God will never force Himself on you. He loves us, but He also created us with free will. *To heal or not to heal ... the choice is up to each one of us.*

- **Deuteronomy 31: 6&8 ...** *"Be strong and of good courage, do not fear nor be afraid of them; for the*

Lord your God, He is the One who goes with you, He will not leave you nor forsake you."

God will never leave us alone. God encouraged Joshua through these words of Moses. I pray that you will let God encourage you by the words I have written here, and that you will seek encouragement from other Brothers and Sisters in Christ.

God promised to be with Joshua in the coming task of conquering the land, so Joshua should be *"strong and of good courage"*. God also promises to be with us in the pressures and challenges of life. The tasks ahead may be difficult, the work immense, and the enemy powerful, but God calls His people to trust Him ... *He is the One who goes before you to prepare the way. He will be with you. He will not leave you. He will not forsake you. He will not reject you. He will not betray you.*

- **2 Timothy 1:7 ... *"For God has not given us a spirit of fear, but of power and of love and of a sound mind."***

   When we worry we are not truly trusting God. Worry can be a natural first reaction to an uncertain situation, but to persist in worry reveals a lack of trust that God is in charge. Besides, God has not given believers *"a spirit of fear, but of power and of love and of a sound mind"*.

   Power helps us have strength of character and confidence in any situation. *Love* helps us graciously deal with difficult people. A *sound mind* helps us remain self-controlled and self-disciplined no matter what happens. We can set aside our worry and replace it with these gifts from God.

In closing, I would like to ask you to take your Bible and read what Paul had to say about *fear – worry – anxiety.* Paul certainly had plenty of reason to feel anxious. Sitting in a Roman prison, he didn't know if he would be released or put to death. Writing to the believers in Philippi, however, he urged them ...

- **Philippians 4: 6–13 ...** *"Do not be anxious about anything, but in everything, by prayer and petition, with thanksgiving, present your requests to God. And the peace of God which transcends all understanding, will guard your hearts and your minds in Christ Jesus. Finally, brothers, whatever is true, whatever is noble, whatever is right, whatever is pure, whatever is lovely, whatever is admirable – if anything is excellent or praiseworthy – think about such things. Whatever you have learned or received or heard from me, or seen in me – put it into practice. And the God of peace will be with you."*

Anxiety and its companion *worry* do their best to immobilize believers. People are *anxious* about the future ... their days filled with *worry.* They are *anxious* about events that haven't happened but could happen. *Anxiety causes physical problems. Anxiety makes people fearful and distressed. Anxiety makes people ill.*

So what can believers do about their *anxiety?* Paul gives us the answer ... *"In everything by prayer and supplication with thanksgiving, let your requests be made known to God."* When we give our *anxiety* to God, He replaces it with *His peace* that *"surpasses all understanding".* God's peace is beyond comprehension because it makes no sense. *The circumstances seem to require anxiety, but instead we feel God's peace.* When we feel *anxiety* rising, we should turn to God in prayer. He will give us the *peace* He promised.

I have no idea of who originally wrote this, *it came to me in an email*, but I feel I would be remiss if I didn't share this with you now.

- *Ten Guidelines From God:* effective immediately … please be aware that there are changes you need to make in your life. These changes need to be completed in order that I may fulfill My promises to you to grant you peace, joy, and happiness in this life. I apologize for any inconvenience, but after all that I am doing, this seems little to ask.

1. *Quit Worrying:* life has dealt you a blow and all you do is sit and worry. Have you forgotten that I am here to take all your burdens and carry them for you? Or do you just enjoy fretting over every little thing that comes your way?

2. *Put It On The List:* something needs done or taken care of … *put it on the list.* No, not your list. Put it on My to-do-list. Let Me be the one to take care of the problem. I can't help you until you turn it over to Me. And although My to-do-list is long, I am after all God. I can take care of anything you put into My hands. In fact, if the truth were ever really known, I take care of a lot of things for you that you never even realize.

3. *Trust Me:* once you've given your burdens to Me, quit trying to take them back. Trust in Me. Have the faith that I will take care of all your needs, your problems, and your trials. Problems with the kids? Put them on My List. Problems with finances? Put them on My List. Problems with your emotional roller coaster? Put it on My List. Problems with your physical health? For My sake, put it on My List. I want to help you. All you have to do is ask.

4. *Leave It Alone:* don't wake up one morning and say, *"Well, I'm feeling much stronger now, I think I can handle it from here."* Why do you think you are feeling stronger now? It's simple. You gave Me your burdens and I'm taking care of them. I also renew your strength and cover you in My Peace. Don't you know that if I give you these problems back, you will be right back where you started? Leave them with me and forget about them. Just let Me do My job.

5. *Talk To Me:* I want you to forget a lot of things. Forget what was making you crazy. Forget the worry and the fretting because you know that I am in control. But there's one thing I pray you never forget. Please, don't forget to talk to Me – OFTEN! I love you. I want to hear your voice. I want you to include Me in on the things going on in your life. I want to hear you talk about your friends and family. Prayer is simply you having a conversation with Me. I want to be your dearest friend ... YOUR BESTEST FRIEND *(my words).*

6. *Share:* you were taught to share when you were only two years old. When did you forget? That rule still applies. Share with those who are less fortunate than you. Share your joy with those who need encouragement. Share your laughter with those who haven't heard any in such a long time. Share your tears with those who have forgotten how to cry. Share your faith with those who have none.

7. *Be Patient:* I managed to fix it so in just one lifetime you could have so many diverse experiences. You grow from a child to an adult, have children, change jobs many times, learn many trades, travel to so many places, meet thousands of people, and experience so much. How can you be so impatient when it takes Me a little longer than you expect to handle

something on My to-do-list? Trust in My Timing, for My Timing is perfect. Just because I created the entire universe in only six days, everyone thinks I should always rush – rush – rush.

8. *Be Kind:* be kind to others for I love them just as much as I love you. They may not dress like you, or talk like you, or live the same way you do, but I still love you all. Please try to get along, for My sake. I created each of you different in some way. It would be too boring if you were all identical. Please know I love each of your differences.

9. *Love Yourself:* as much as I love you, how can you not love yourself? You were created by Me for one reason only ... *to be loved and to love in return.* I am a God of Love. Love Me. Love your neighbors. But also love yourself. It makes My heart ache when I see you so angry with yourself when things go wrong. You are very precious to Me.

10. *Don't ever forget to touch someone with your love:* rather than focus upon the thorns of life ... *smell the roses and count your blessings.*

CHAPTER EIGHT

"UNDERSTANDING THE EMOTION OF ANGER"

A NGER ... is one of those *emotions* that we, <u>as Christians</u>, often try to hide or to run away from. ANGER ... is often the *emotion* we see expressed that is really a cover-up for more intense emotions of the heart. We use ANGER to hide behind rather than deal with the *real emotions* we are feeling ... *fear, insecurity, jealousy, betrayal, guilt, hurt, etc.* Uncontrolled ANGER often explodes into verbal and/or physical violence.

ANGER, *like all other emotions,* is a God-Given emotion that can be used in a healthy productive manner or in an unhealthy destructive manner. But the same is true of all our God-Given emotions ... *fear, passion, sexual desire, anxiety, insecurity, drive, ambition, love, and so forth.*

We can not, *for a lifetime,* hide or run away from any of our God-Given emotions ... *including anger.* So what do we do with our human weaknesses and negative emotions to stop their destructive force within our lives and the lives of others around us?

- We need to learn how to *understand the emotion* in order to take this *knowledge* into our innermost being. By *getting the knowledge* to *understand our emotions*, with the *wisdom* and *strength* we have available to us through Christ Jesus, we can not only learn to control our negative outbursts but also to *channel our emotions* in a positive and productive way.

- Be willing to do whatever it takes to get the *knowledge* to *understand your emotions*. With this *knowledge – pray for wisdom*, and as you begin to grow in *knowledge* and *wisdom - seek understanding*. Then make the *personal choice* to *start applying* what you have learned in your relationships.

- Anger is an emotion, but anger is not an action. Anger is a form of energy. Anger is not violence. People fear anger because anger is associated with violence. *Anger* is an *emotion*. *Violence* is an *action*.

We need to understand the *distinction* between *anger* and *violence* in order to develop a healthier attitude about the *emotion of anger*. Once we begin to *understand the emotion of anger*, and we become able to *accept the existence of the emotion of anger* within ourselves and in others, then we can begin to develop a much healthier attitude about anger.

One reason that we are afraid of anger is that anger is so often associated with someone getting hurt ... *an expression of anger in a very negative and unhealthy way.* Another reason that we have difficulty with the emotion of anger ... *we have not been given the skills to manage our anger in a positive and healthy way.* All around us in our daily lives we see anger expressed in negative, unhealthy, and hurtful ways. Unfortunately, we have far less examples of seeing anger being expressed in positive, healthy, and productive ways.

As mentioned earlier, what people often experience as anger is actually other emotions. It is amazing how often the *true emotion* motivating a person's anger is *fear, pain,* or *helplessness.* Usually the angry person is not even aware of anything but their anger. If we do not know that the emotion we are really feeling is helplessness, fear, or pain and we are experiencing anger ... *anger is the emotion that we will show.*

Here are a few examples of underlying emotions that can trigger anger. We immediately get angry if someone cuts us off in traffic ... *usually the underlying emotion is fear of being involved in an accident.* We are stuck in traffic, *or some other uncontrollable circumstance,* that prevents us from getting home or causes us to miss an important meeting and we get angry ... *seldom do we realize that we are feeling helpless to get what we want or need.* We get angry because someone we loved and trusted betrayed us, we may be aware that we are hurt, but ... *seldom do we recognize that the anger stems from the pain related to the betrayal.*

ANGER (Webster's New World Dictionary): *a feeling of displeasure resulting from injury, mistreatment, opposition, etc., and usually showing ITSELF in a desire to fight back at the supposed cause of this feeling. Anger is broadly applicable to feelings of resentful or revengeful displeasure; indignation implies righteous anger aroused by what seems unjust, mean, or insulting; rage suggests a violent outburst of anger in which self-control is lost; fury implies a frenzied rage that borders on madness; ire, chiefly a literary word, suggests a show of great anger in acts, words, looks, etc; wrath implies deep indignation expressing itself in a desire to punish or get revenge.*

ANGER (The New Unger's Bible Dictionary): *the emotion of instant displeasure and indignation arising from the feeling of injury done or intended, or from the discovery of offense against the law.*

The anger attributed to God in the New Testament is that part of God that stands opposed to man's disobedience, obstinacy (*especially in resisting the gospel*), and sin, and manifests itself in punishing the same.

Anger is not evil, per se, being, as love, an original susceptibility of our nature. If anger were in itself sinful, how could God Himself be angry? The Apostle Paul commands the Ephesians, *and all believers*, that when angry they are not to sin.

- **Ephesians 4: 26&27 ...** *"Be angry, and do not sin; do not let the sun go down on your wrath, nor give place to the devil."*

Paul does not forbid the *being angry* in itself, and could not forbid it, because there is *holy anger*; but the *being angry* is to *be without sin*. Anger is sinful when it rises too soon, without reflection; when the injury that awakens it is only apparent; when it is disproportionate to the offense; when it is transferred from the guilty to the innocent; when it is too long protracted and becomes revengeful.

- **Matthew 5:22a ...** *"But I say to you that whoever is angry with his brother without cause shall be in danger of the judgment."*

- **Colossians 3:8 ...** *"But now you yourselves are to put off all these: anger, wrath, malice, blasphemy, filthy language out of your mouth."*

The Bible doesn't say, *"Never get angry"*. It does say, however, *"Be angry, and do not sin"*. Anger is a God-given, powerful emotion. Handled well, anger can cause positive change. When handled poorly, anger can cause great harm. So what should believers do with their angry feelings?

1. They should NOT indulge the anger because that could cause them to speak or to act in ways that they will later regret.
2. They should NOT stuff the anger down deep inside with people pretending they never feel angry. Doing so can cause a host of personal and relational problems. *Stuffed anger* will eventually cause a *"system overload"* whereby years of resentment erupt when a small spark sets it ablaze.

Recently, a friend and I were driving to San Antonio, Texas for a few days of relaxation and sightseeing. This friend was a Christian who had struggled with anger and even violence before giving his life over to Christ. However, *as his friend and a trained counselor*, there had been a couple of times over the past three years when I had witnessed inappropriate angry outbursts towards someone over things that were actually a result of his own actions or lack of taking necessary action at the time.

Over a period of time spent with him in talking and praying, he seemed to have made peace with many issues that lay at the root of his anger. However, on our trip, I soon realized that he was still *"stuffing"* his anger rather than dealing with it. I also realize that what erupts from him as *anger* is so often based in *insecurity, fear, and a feeling of helplessness*. My prayer is for him to also come to understand this and to finally be free of the hidden issues in his life that disrupt in anger and will continue to do so until he deals with the real emotions at the root of his angry reactions.

- The HEALTHY WAY to handle anger is to deal with it as quickly as possible so that we do not nurse the anger and thus *"give place to the devil"*. Satan loves to use angry feelings to divide believers. We should seek to resolve our differences with others quickly. Then we can get on with the Lord's work.

But what about the times we get angry with God? And, *yes*, even believers will go through things sometimes that will bring such pain and/or confusion that they can not handle it on their own ... *so they turn their anger towards God for "letting it happen" in the first place.* This can be a *healthy anger* that God will use in *His Pathway Of Healing,* or it can become an *unhealthy and deadly anger* that Satan will eventually use to deceive us about the Love and Goodness of God in order to ultimately destroy us.

HEALTHY *versus* UNHEALTHY ANGER: anger is a fact of life, but is all anger bad? Is it always a sin to be angry? While rage, fury, wrath, resentment, and hostility are often used to describe the emotion ... *anger is simply a strong feeling of irritation or displeasure.*

Actually people experience anger much more frequently than we care to admit. When we begrudge or disdain others, when we are annoyed, repulsed, irritated, frustrated, offended, or cross ... *we are probably experiencing some form of anger.* Studies have shown that most people experience the *emotion of anger* at least eight to ten times each day. Since we all have to realize that we do possess within ourselves the God-given emotion of anger, we need to strive to understand this emotion in order to deal with it in a positive way.

Having grown up in an environment of anger and abuse, I know that my natural tendency was *to react in an angry and hostile way* when I felt threatened or scared. But, *more importantly,* I learned from living in such a negative and destructive environment that I did not want to continue *this cycle of negative destructive emotions* in my own life. With counseling and the help of God, I have come to *understand the emotion of anger,* and I have learned how to channel my frustrations in a more positive and productive manner.

Please understand that I am very human and I do slip up on occasion and respond with a negative form of anger. However, now I have the *knowledge* to recognize what I have done, the *understanding* to know why I reacted in a negative manner, and the *wisdom* to quickly do whatever I need to do to undue the damage and to turn the situation into a positive one.

Depression, anxiety, fear, and grief drain our human body of emotional and physical strength. Anger, on the other hand, releases energy into the nervous system and makes us ready for action. It is a *personal choice* whether we use that burst of energy in a constructive way or in an abusive destructive way.

- *When people allow anger to control them, it becomes unhealthy anger.* Unhealthy anger expresses itself in a desire for revenge and can easily distort one's perspective, block their ability to love, and even limit their capacity to think clearly. At that point, people are more likely to spend their anger energy in destructive actions such as emotional, verbal, or physical abuse and violence.

- *The opposite of unhealthy anger is healthy anger, which could also be called "quality anger".* As we read in **Ephesians 4:26 ...** ***"Be angry and do not sin".*** This type of healthy *"quality"* anger depends on the help and guidance of the Holy Spirit.

  Healthy anger enables people to invest their emotional energy into confronting evil, righting wrongs, and changing things for the good in a positive way. The energy of anger, *when invested wisely,* can provide greater focus and intensity and can lead to greater productivity.

147

Often in grief we feel great anger ... *towards the loved one for leaving us, towards ourselves for things we either wish we had done or had not done while our loved one was still alive, and even towards God for taking away someone so precious to us.*
IT IS OKAY TO FEEL ANGER IN A "HEALTHY" SEASON OF GRIEVING ... *even towards God Himself?* God made you and He knows your heart and He feels your pain. Just understand that this *anger* is in reality coming from a place of deep life-changing grief ... *helplessness, fear, guilt, loneliness, and so forth.* You can talk to God about your anger, *even your anger towards Him,* knowing that He loves you, He understands your pain, and – *if you choose to let Him do so* – He will bring you through the loss to the other side.

In order to confront and control unhealthy anger, a person needs to decide upon a plan to counter-attack the emotion in advance. When *unhealthy* anger is not under control, it will block the ability to think clearly and to respond in a productive way. We all have to deal with anger, so how do we do so in a *healthy* manner?

Think and pray about your anger and how you can apply the following steps to respond in a healthy way to your anger *versus* reacting in an unhealthy and often lethal way.

1. *Be aware of the anger*: a person with an anger problem may not always show it through his or her appearance or actions ... *a battle may rage inside a person with a seemingly calm demeanor.* Try to understand why you are angry. Identify what makes you vulnerable to anger, become aware of how your body responds when you are getting angry, and what physical manifestations of anger do you adopt when

enraged? Remember that there is a big difference between normal irritations in life and a persistent state of anger.

2. *Accept the responsibility for anger*: stop blaming others for your problems, and make the decision to invest the time and energy into changing your overall negative reactions to people or to situations. Blaming a personal reaction on someone else is not accurate. People don't *"lose"* their temper. People *"choose"* their own temper.

3. *Count the cost of anger*: negative unhealthy anger has ruined more friendships, caused more divorces, destroyed more careers, been at the root of more financial losses, and destroyed more lives than any other emotion. One psychologist has said that <u>one</u> angry confrontation can erase <u>twenty</u> acts of kindness! My point is ... *unhealthy anger can cost us dearly if we do not learn to keep it in check.*

4. *Identify the source of the anger*: anger is a *secondary emotion* that is experienced in response to a *primary emotion* such as hurt, frustration, or fear ... *people who are hurt feel vulnerable to more hurt.* For many people, anger is a *defense mechanism* against being hurt.

   Frustration occurs when expectations are not met or people cannot meet their personal goals. Oddly enough, the things that frustrate us the most usually have one characteristic in common ... *they really aren't very important in the long run.*

   Identifying frustrating personalities or situations will prepare a person for handling similar encounters in the future in a far more healthy way.

5. *Let the anger out*: release your anger to God. Tell Him how you feel. He can handle it. Then go and talk with a friend whom you can trust to be totally honest

149

with you, or talk with a counselor trained in anger management. Whenever you are up to doing so, *and make it soon*, go and talk to the person with whom you are angry in a constructive way.

As Christians, we do not have the right to remain angry towards someone. In Christ, we have given up that right, and holding onto our unhealthy anger is a very destructive thing to do. We are to surrender our anger to Him and to forgive others as He has forgiven us. When we forgive, we are free ... *free from resentment, bitterness, and unhealthy anger.*

6. *Set limits on your anger*: learn to control your words and your behavior. God tells us to get a grip on our tongues. Don't cross the line of verbal or physical abuse no matter how frustrated you become. Don't justify or excuse such abusive behaviors by blaming it on someone or something else. We alone are responsible for our words and our actions.

Proverbs 10:19 ... *"When words are many, sin is not absent. But he who keeps a tight rein on his tongue is wise."*

7. *Choose how to invest anger energy*: this is a critical step in controlling our anger. While we cannot always control when we will experience anger, we can choose how we will express our anger. With God's help, we can find creative and constructive ways to deal with anger. We can allow anger to dominate us and ultimately destroy so many good things in our lives, or we can harness anger's energy into healthy and quality responses.

Quality anger involves open, honest, and direct communication. *It* involves speaking the truth in love. *It* involves declaring truth and righting wrongs.

It involves being open to an apology or explanation. *It* apologies and forgives and seeks to work towards a mutual healthy agreement.

Understanding Anger: anger is an emotion, a feeling. In itself, anger is not a bad thing. It will help to remember that anger is the second emotion – not the first. How we respond to the feeling of anger is where we can make it work productively for us – or not. We have *choices* when angry ...

- An *Aggressive Response* is when anger is expressed overtly for the purpose of hurting someone else either with verbal put-downs, threats or physical actions. The message from this response is that my anger is not okay so I will blame someone else for this feeling and will take out my anger on him or her.
- A *Passive Aggressive Response* is when anger is repressed, internalized, or denied such as in snide comments, the cold shoulder, and keeping feelings bottled up inside until they explode. The message from this response is that my anger is not okay so I will deny it and I do not value my feelings nor do I respect myself.
- An *Assertive Response* is when anger is expressed directly in non-threatening ways that do not hurt oneself or another person. The message from this response is that my anger is okay and I can use the feeling to help me understand what appropriate action I want to take next. "I" statements are used to share feelings and state what is needed from the other person at an appropriate time and place for the discussion.

For many Christians, both the *experience of anger* and the *expression of anger* have become a habit. Habits can take some time to change. The good news is that with God's help we can all change and grow. As we allow the Holy Spirit to fill us and we apply the promises from God's Word ... *we will begin to replace old, unhealthy ways of responding into new, healthy and God-honoring emotional responses.*

As we learn creative ways to invest the God-given emotion of anger energy, and as we approach anger from a Biblical perspective, we will find that our anger can be used as one of the most powerful sources of personal motivation available!

CHAPTER NINE

"THE TRIAL OF REJECTION"

Living in a sin-broken world is painful. Not one person will get through life without facing trials of various types in various degrees. Some people face trials in their physical lives, others face financial difficulties, and others face trials in their family relationships or friendships. But none of us will make it through life without at one time or another suffering the *"Trial Of Rejection"*. How we decide to handle rejection will truly affect the quality of our life, and subsequent relationships, from that moment on.

Whether it is *rejection* that is a result of childhood abuse, divorce, loss of a job or promotion, betrayal by a friend or family member ... *the pain of rejection is very real.* One of the *most painful trials* that we as humans can experience is feeling *rejected, forsaken,* or *abandoned.* The pain associated with the *feeling of rejection* affects many areas of our lives.

Rejection rips at not only our heart's emotions, but attacks the core of our self-confidence and feelings of self-worth. Being *rejected* by someone you love and trust will leave scars that often get in the way of other relationships unless we choose to allow ourselves to heal from the pain of the rejection. There will be times in our life that we will be *rejected* by someone no matter how hard we try or how much we are willing to sacrifice in order to keep a relationship intact. How we deal with *rejection* is critical for our emotional and spiritual health.

In March of 2003, I met someone whom I grew to respect, trust, and love over a period of several months. Because I had already suffered a great deal from broken trust, betrayal, and loss by death, abuse, and *rejection* ... it took me a long time to open up my heart entirely to this man. He was very patient and understanding during those initial months of our relationship. He promised he would never intentionally hurt me, never leave me voluntarily, never be untruthful to me, and always strive to love and cherish me. He made me believe that *together* we could work through anything.

Day by day and step by step ... I was able to allow my defenses to come down and to begin to truly trust in him and in his love for me. I became confident and excited about our future together. On the day that I finally told him that I also had grown to love him, he asked me to make him one promise ... *that if we began a committed man/woman relationship that I would never leave him.* When we had problems, we would stay together and work them out with the help of God. I was happy to make this promise as I wanted the same from him ... *which he once again gave to me.*

In July of 2005, he asked me to marry him. I said "YES", without hesitation, because I trusted in him completely. Together that day, we made a commitment to each other and to God for our lives together. A few weeks later we bought our rings and set a date for our wedding. Shortly after this, I began to sense a withdrawal within him whenever we were together but I couldn't get him to talk to me about what was bothering him. Time went by. Very early one Sunday morning I got a short phone call from him telling me that it was over. The reasons he gave to me made no sense whatsoever. I was devastated, *emotionally and spiritually*, by this unexpected *rejection* ... filled with confusion and a deep feeling of betrayal.

With God's help, over the next several weeks, I was able to accept that it was over ... *able to accept, but not to understand, what had happened.* Then in May of 2006, he came to my home with roses for my birthday. Still telling me how much he loved me ... *we agreed to be friends.* A couple of weeks later, he came up again. This time he told me he felt that we could have the Blessings of God in a committed relationship, so we decided to take it one day at a time and see if we could once again become more than friends. Three days later, *once again over the phone,* he ended "us" again ... *for the third time.*

This last time the *confusion and pain of his rejection* cut so deep I was having a very hard time handling it. I told God that I never wanted to go through this kind of pain again with anyone, and I made a decision to not allow myself to ever get caught up in another possible relationship with any man ever again. I would just focus on my job and my ministry work, and build my personal life only on friendships – nothing more. However, the *confusion* of this man's actions would not go away, and he would not answer any of my questions. I got only silence from him. I got angry! In trying to get him to at least talk to me about what had happened, I sent him some pretty heated emails. Still I got nothing in return.

After a time of healing, *anger helping to get through the pain,* I knew that no matter what he had done to me ... *I needed to make peace within myself, as a Child-of-God, about all of this.* I needed to ask forgiveness for some of the things I had said in my anger, *justified though they were,* and I had to forgive him from my heart.

The Holy Spirit began to deal with me that the way we had left things between us was not Christ-like ... *we needed to deal with each other, and our pain, as Children of God.* After some time spent in praying about the matter, I emailed this man and left it in God's Hands to provide the opportunity for us to sit down and truly talk to each other.

As a result of hours of our spending time together and our really talking to each other, we began to have a deeper understanding of what the other was feeling. By owning my feelings of rejection and insecurity and letting go of the unhealthy anger, I once again was able to move forward without the *fear of rejection* holding me prisoner in a lonely world of self-imposed isolation. I am now able to pray God's Very Best for this man's life in all areas, and truly mean it from my heart.

Jesus suffered brutal *betrayal* and *rejection* at the hands of those people whom He came to save. Jesus knows firsthand the *pain of rejection* ... even His closest friends and disciples forsook Him – Judas even sold Him into the hands of His enemies for thirty pieces of silver. We can learn so much about living through the *trial of rejection* from Jesus. He is always ready to walk with us through the pain and to bring us out on the other side as a stronger and healthier person. I know from personal experience that Jesus truly is ... *the one friend who will never leave us or forsake us – the one friend who will never reject us.*

The Bible offers God's great promises for us as we face any trial: **James 1: 2&3 ...** James wrote to all believers, ***"Count it all joy when you fall into various trials, knowing that the testing of your faith produces patience."* 1 Peter 1: 3–9 ...** Peter wrote that all believers who are ***"grieved by various trials"*** can trust that God is working through those difficulties to perfect their faith.

Recognizing *rejection* and *choosing to deal with the wound left by rejection* is critical to our mental, emotional, physical, and spiritual well-being. Some people attempt to protect themselves from *rejection* by adopting an <u>under-dependent</u> *approach* to relationships ... *they refuse to trust anyone or to invest themselves emotionally in a misguided attempt to avoid getting hurt again.* Others become <u>over-dependent</u> ... *they cling tenaciously to relationships to avoid feeling rejected – yet they simultaneously live in fear of it.* Most people use some combination of these extremes to *cope with rejection.*

Whether you are personally living through a *trial of rejection*, or are trying to help someone else to heal, here are some *traits* identified in people who have been *wounded by rejection:*

- *They will have difficulty trusting people:* many try to hide their fear of rejection by appearing cold and even abusive in their relationships with others.
- *They often mask their fear of rejection by living a very self-destructive motto:* "Do unto others BEFORE they do unto me."
- *They will be hypersensitive to rejection*: often mistaking constructive criticism or well-meant advice as rejection of either themselves or of their ideas.
- *They approach every relationship with fear of criticism and anger:* they are unable to accept a person as being what they seem to be. Instead they are always analyzing everything in an attempt to protect themselves from the inevitable rejection.
- *They go from one relationship to another, one job to another, or one church to another in search of the impossible*: an environment free of the possibility of rejection.
- *They will habitually try to rescue needy people because they doubt, sometimes subconsciously, that healthy people would want to be with them or even choose to relate to them*: getting into unhealthy relationships over and over again.

- *They continually tolerate disrespect and even abuse from others*: desperately needing relationship – even unhealthy relationship – often feeling they deserve no better.
- *They have a very real difficulty in trusting God and His Word:* how can they believe that God really loves them ... look at how He allows other people to treat them?

People who are *suffering from rejection* desperately need to understand that they can be delivered from their paralyzing fear, they can be healed emotionally, and they can be restored into healthy and productive relationships. I want to talk briefly about *three principles* that are important in *healing from the hurt of rejection.*

- *Cultivate Increasing Intimacy With God:* when we intentionally cultivate a spiritual environment that fosters intimacy with God, we learn to really KNOW GOD instead of just knowing about God. Please believe me ... *a Personal Relationship With God is NOT about religion – it is about relationship.*

    In a personal relationship, God is not only a loving and merciful Heavenly Father, He is our friend. His loyal love and eternal Presence become more than just theological certainties ... *they become experienced realities in a way that anchors us when trials assail us.*

    As a little girl who was rejected by her Daddy, *no matter how hard I tried to be good or to make him love me,* I learned at a very early age to swallow my tears and to bury my pain deep inside. But that *early rejection* shadowed every relationship in my life long after Daddy was gone. And because Daddy was also a preacher, *raising us in a very strict "reli-*

gious" environment, I also felt *betrayed* and *rejected* by God. For more than thirty years I felt that I could never be *good enough* for God to love me, and I finally turned my back on Him completely.

But the love of our Heavenly Father is so awesome ... *He never turned His back on me.* In 1987, *when I had no where else to turn and no one else to turn to*, I desperately cried out a *challenge* to God. I told Him that I knew there was a God but I had no idea what He wanted from me. *(You see, in my religious confusion, I thought that I had to earn God's forgiveness and God's love. I didn't understand that He already loved me – right where I was.)*

I *challenged* God to take my life that was in such a mess and to change it and to change me ... *if He truly loved me*. WOW! God took me at my word, *knowing that I was crying out to Him from a broken and frozen heart*, and that day I took the first step out of the pain and darkness and onto the *road to healing and restoration*. That day I met Jesus Christ of Nazareth for myself. Jesus became my Lord and Savior, my Healer and Deliverer ... *My Bestest Friend!*

I have made many mistakes on my journey since 1987, and I have walked through some *fiery trials*, but the difference is that I have never had to walk through them all alone. Each *trial* has become a *stepping-stone* to a healthier and fuller life for me. And God ain't through working on me yet! That is why I can understand what James and Peter wrote in the Scriptures above, and that is why I can say with David who was called "a man after God's own heart" ... ***"When my father and my mother forsake me, then the Lord will take care of me"*** (Psalm 27:10).

- *Cultivate Increasingly Balanced Relationships With Others:* God's Word contains many relational principles that promote balanced and mutually respectful relationships. Don't confuse trying to help someone with the need to cling to an unhealthy person just to have someone with you.

Jesus exemplified guidelines for respectful interactions with people. Read the Four Gospels – **Matthew, Mark, Luke, John** – and you will see that Jesus didn't let people tell Him what to do. He modeled the *truth* that we don't have to hide our views or values to be congenial and kind. The thought of *not hiding* or *compromising* their views or values to a person *suffering from rejection* most likely sounds terrifying, especially if stating a different opinion exposes us to the *risk of rejection* by people whose opinion we value.

But here is the truth of the matter: compromising our views and values just to avoid the *possibility of rejection* is not only emotionally unhealthy, but it will leave devastating and destructive relationships in its wake. There can be no real communication or understanding between two people when one person holds all thought inside *to avoid rejection* by the other person in the relationship. Furthermore, our *fear* will prevent us from pursuing healthy relationships in all areas of our life. Living one's life motivated and controlled by *unhealthy fear* is to live one's life in an isolated and very lonely prison.

- *Cultivate Increasingly Realistic Expectations of Ourselves, Others, and of God:* Jesus clarifies this principle in **John 16:32** ... *"Indeed the hour is coming, yes, has now come, that you will be scattered, each to his own, and will leave me alone. And yet I am not alone, because the Father is with me."* Jesus' words summarize two truths that guided His relationships and that hold the key to overcoming the *hurt of rejection.*

The *first truth* is that we can't trust people completely. Jesus never put *unrealistic trust* in people because He knew what was in their sinful hearts. All people deserve respect because they bear the image of God, but not one of us is perfect. In our respect of others we need to be realistic enough to know that all people make mistakes. *People will always disappoint us. We will always disappoint other people.* How we choose to deal with the disappointments will determine the quality of our life and our relationships both with people and with God. Jesus knew that the disciples, who had just declared that they believed He came from God, would soon abandon Him.

The *second truth* is that *dependence* on God helps us to handle the *hurt of rejection.* Jesus' confidence in His Father's love created a sense of being *"alone but not alone"*. Yes, it is true that Jesus knew God's faithfulness within a uniquely intimate relationship. But as we grow in our own *Personal Intimate Relationship With God,* and follow Jesus' God-Dependent way of relating, we too will be able to better handle *experiences of rejection.*

If you've been deeply hurt by *rejection*, you may face a long process of *relearning* how to relate to people. But don't give up on yourself, don't give up on others, and don't give up on the love and healing power of a Personal Relationship With God. He loves you and wants you to be healthy and prosperous in *all areas* of your life. That includes having deep and meaningful relationships with others ... *including a happy marriage and a rewarding home life.*

We will know that our relationships are becoming healthier and more God-Dependent as we increasingly ...

- Reach out to others from a deepening sense of fullness in Christ.
- Accept the truth that others can never meet all of our needs.
- Recognize that we can never meet all of the needs of another person.
- Choose to forgive others for their inevitable failings.
- Acknowledge our inevitable failings and ask for forgiveness.
- Forgive ourselves for our failures.
- Learn to turn our failures into stepping-stones of recovery.

When subjected to intense heat ... gold is refined. Impurities are burned away and pure gold remains. Like gold, faith that is tested by the fire of trials and difficulties is strengthened and purified. Believers learn that their faith depends on God alone, and that such faith is precious to God.

When we face trials, *including the trial of rejection*, we can *"greatly rejoice"* for we know that God will strengthen our faith if we continue to hold on to Him. As we are strengthened in our faith, we grow to know that we have *one friend* who will *never leave us, forsake us, betray us, or reject us.* That Friend is Jesus!

- **1 Peter 1: 6–9 ...** *"In this you greatly rejoice, though now for a little while, if need be, you have been grieved by various trials, that the genuineness of your faith, being much more precious than gold that perishes, though it is tested by fire, may be found to praise, honor, and glory at the revelation of Jesus Christ, whom having not seen you love. Though now you do not see Him, yet believing, you rejoice with joy inexpressible and full of glory,*

*receiving the end of your faith – the salvation of
your souls."*

There is but *one source* of *deep healing* from *rejection*.
Only when we find *ultimate acceptance* and *security* in God
can we experience *personal peace*, *relational peace*, and
healing from the *pain of rejection*. Trials are inevitable ...
rejection is inevitable. Everyone experiences problems and
pain. **The Bible figuratively describes it as rain falling
"on the just and on the unjust" in Matthew 5:45.**
Believers can look at their *trials* in a different light. They
can know, as it tells us in **Psalm 34:18 ... *"The Lord is near
to those who have a broken heart, and saves such as have
a contrite spirit"*.** Even more, however, believers can rejoice
in their trials because through trials God can work in our
lives to make us more like Christ.

If you are struggling with self-doubts and self-incrimina-
tions over your own failures, and if as a Christian, you are
dealing with guilt over mistakes that have hurt yourself and
others, you are not alone! Remember King David – *the man
after God's own heart?* Talk about someone who made some
whoppers when it came to mistakes and bad choices ... *adultery, deceit, betrayal, murder, etc.* But God forgave David,
and still loved him.

Let's take a look at how our mistakes and bad choices
can not only have a negative effect upon our lives, but can
also devastate and destroy the lives of those whom we love.
Again let us look at King David and his daughter, Tamar, in
2 Samuel Chapter 13.

- *Tamar – A Legacy Of Trials*: the painful legacy
  of turmoil that David provoked by his sin with
  Bathsheba soon spread to other family members.
  David's children, *Amnon and Tamar*, were snared by
  the curse of David's sin. Amnon acted out a sexual

obsession with Tamar, *his half sister*, by conspiring with a friend to trick her into being alone with him.

The trap worked. Tamar begged for mercy and desperately suggested an honorable solution of marriage to Amnon. Since they were half siblings, *in their culture*, the arrangement was possible and acceptable. But in spite of Tamar's pleading, Amnon raped her. Once he had raped her, Amnon shamefully rejected Tamar.

By her own flesh and blood, *her half brother Amnon*, Tamar was tricked, betrayed, abused, and then rejected. But Tamar's betrayal didn't stop with Amnon. David, *her own father*, betrayed her trust when he learned of what Amnon had done. For although David was aware of the tragedy unfolding in his family and got angry, he actually did nothing to help Tamar heal.

Tamar lived in disgrace as a desolate woman in her brother Absalom's house. The painful loneliness of her life was a *trial of betrayal and rejection* that she faced for the rest of her life as part of the legacy of her family. Tamar's brother, *Absalom*, festered in hatred and planned vengeance on Amnon. There was more than Tamar's honor at stake. Amnon's position as the firstborn son and likely heir to the throne certainly increased Absalom's desire to see him eliminated. Years later, Absalom lured Amnon away from the palace and killed him.

These *trials for David's children* could have been avoided. Even though David's heart was broken by the behavior of his children, he never tried to correct the injustices. *Perhaps David was immobilized by guilt and shame over his own past mistakes.* However, his denial and delay only let matters fester and worsen, and the consequences were devastating.

If we think that living our lives with *unresolved pain and fear* as the result of the *betrayal* or the *rejection* we have suffered in a past relationship isn't going to leave *devastating consequences* within our lives and the lives of those we love ... think again! If we think that *unresolved guilt* and *shame* over past mistakes won't leave *devastating consequences* upon our lives and the lives of those we love ... think again! Hidden pain and anger will resurface again and again until we do the work necessary to deal with the root cause, forgive, and learn to move forward.

No matter what trials we face, God cares deeply for His Children. He promises us in **Psalm 145:18 ...** *"The Lord is near to all who call upon Him, to all who will call upon Him in truth"*. Whatever difficulties come into our lives, God is always near to us. He is stronger than *rejection* ... stronger than any trial we can ever experience. He is able to meet our every need. He already knows us – every little thing about us. Yet, He still loves us and yearns to have a deep personal relationship with us.

You have to begin to trust someone if you ever want a healthy and fulfilled life. Why not begin by making the choice to trust in God and in His Unconditional Love for you?

TRUST JESUS ...

HE IS THE ONE FRIEND WHO WILL NEVER LEAVE YOU OR REJECT YOU!

CHAPTER TEN

"PERSONAL GROWTH THROUGH LONELINESS"

*B*eing alone and *being lonely* are two different things ... *being alone is a physical state while being lonely is an emotional state*. People can be alone and be very content, while other people can be in a crowd and still feel very lonely. If you feel lonely, you are not alone!

- Over 23.6 million people in the United States live alone according to the US Census Bureau figures: 38% are elderly. In 1950, only 10% of households in the United States consisted of just one person. By 1994, this number had increased to 24%.

The causes of loneliness and rejection may vary: physical disease or long-term illness; circumstantial difficulties, such as, geographical relocation, the death of a loved one, childlessness, divorce or family breakdown; and sometimes God will set us aside for Himself for a Purpose in which we may be misunderstood and even rejected by friends and loved ones because we have chosen to obey God.

We are living in the Year of 2008 here in the United States, and yet even in a world of email, videoconferencing, voicemail, and other inventions that keep people instantaneously connected ... *many people still succumb to the age-old problem of loneliness.* From the Garden of Eden to the present day, people have struggled with a sense of *loneliness* and *separateness.*

These are the facts: loneliness has existed since the beginning, still exists in our modern and highly technological world, and will continue to exist until the end of time as we now know it. So how do we, *as lonely people*, learn to deal with our loneliness in a healthy way so that it can become a Period of Personal Growth *versus* a Time of Self-Destructive Actions?

That is the purpose of this Chapter entitled "Personal Growth Through Loneliness". I want to invite you to take a journey with me – *Biblically and Personally* – down some roads of loneliness that could have destroyed, but instead became times of great personal and spiritual growth.

From the moment of birth, humans seek attachment and connection. Without attachment or relationship, infants will fail to thrive. Children who are raised in an abusive or neglectful environment will not learn how to form healthy attachments. Without the warmth of feeling loved and wanted, these children will develop a deep sense of insecurity and often paralyzing fear. They have very low self-esteem, and they most often feel no self-worth. Without help, they will carry these negative emotions, *and the negative ways they learn to use them to simply survive,* into their adult relationships.

Wasted Childhoods: there is nothing lonelier than being raised by an uncaring and/or abusive parent or some other adult. I know because I have been there. A wasted childhood can never be regained, although many of us have tried, but it can be overcome and – as adults – we do not have to pass on the mistakes our parents made with us to our children.

Without a feeling of being connected, adults may yield to depression which often leads to very serious actions that have severe repercussions upon their lives and the lives of others. Because God created people in His Image – He made them relational. When God saw Adam *alone* in the Garden of Eden, He said *being alone was not good.*

Despite His own presence and relationship with Adam, God knew people also need human relationships. Human beings need both *vertical intimacy with God* and *horizontal intimacy with people* in order to be fulfilled. Without these relationships, people become vulnerable to a complex set of emotions described as "*loneliness*".

- *Loneliness* is a normal response to the *perception of being alone* when one desires intimacy. It is different than solitude. Loneliness comes when people don't desire to be alone or disconnected, and yet perceives themselves to be either emotionally or physically isolated.
- *Solitude* is *a state of being alone.* Solitude may be desirable at certain times. Everyone needs moments of personal quietness and reflection when they are alone and free of distraction. We can choose to take advantage of our *time of solitude* and embrace it as a Godly Purpose, as His Provision for us. If we use our *time of solitude* to spend time with Him, it can become a productive experience with positive results.

Loneliness, on the other hand, is painful and distressing to the core human need for intimacy. The *pain of loneliness* can in actuality overwhelm a person with such an "*ache of the heart*" that it becomes almost impossible to breathe. Have you ever known such *overwhelming loneliness* that you could feel your heart aching so bad that you wanted to reach inside of yourself and hold your heart within your hands to somehow ease the pain? I have known that kind of pain in loneliness, and that pain caused me to make some decisions in my life that were not always healthy ones.

Loneliness is an emotional response that is linked to a perceived cause. For example: *situational loneliness* is a frequent response to physical or emotional separation. *Situational loneliness* is that feeling of isolation or loss that people experience as sadness, anxiety, or a sense of deprivation in connection with a loss of some kind. *Situational loneliness* may be brief and contained, or it can be deep and overwhelming.

Physical separation is often a cause of *situational loneliness*. People may find themselves swept away by a *sense of loneliness* in response to being separated from family and friends. They know there are people who care, but their situation demands separation. The intense longing that accompanies the separation is compelling and sometimes overwhelming. When the period of separation is brief, the loneliness increases the joy of the reunion. If the period of separation is extensive, *such as death or some other unavoidable circumstance*, the loneliness is harder to handle. Death, divorce, life transitions, and personal mobility are the most common causes of *situational loneliness*. Intimate relationships are severed, changed, and forever disrupted in some way.

Emotional separation can also lead to loneliness. The loneliest people are often found in a crowd ... *people can feel very lonely when they are surrounded by those with whom they perceive little or no intimate connection.* This sense of being disconnected seems to *accentuate the loneliness* and often leads to even deeper despair.

This *kind of loneliness* is often felt as a *form of anxiety* that drives some people to frantic efforts at superficial connection. Single bars, clubs, internet dating, chat rooms, and other gathering places thrive on those who are struggling to hold this deep loneliness at bay. When *physical separation* is coupled with *emotional separation,* the loneliness can seem to become unbearable.

Chronic loneliness can result from underlying feelings of not belonging or of not being understood. Many people desperately desire intimacy, but are unable to connect due to deeply held personal beliefs or social deficits. This person feels *chronically alone* and *isolated* and unable to have any hope of *"connecting again"* in the future. Such chronic feelings of loneliness can lead to deep personal isolation and despair that often ends in suicide or angry, violent alienation.

Personal Periods Of Great Loneliness: I, *too*, have known the depths of *life-sucking loneliness.* Being raised in a home where my dad forced strict and legalistic religious doctrines upon us – *both as a father and as a preacher* – I learned very early to swallow my tears and to hide my emotions.

Before I was even a teenager, I struggled with finding ways to stop Daddy from hurting Mama and I feared every day that he would start hurting my little sister. I tasted the bitter dregs of humiliation when the other kids in school would laugh at my out-of-style and hand-me-down clothes. I made up excuses to explain to my teachers why I couldn't participate in after school activities, and why I often had bruises. Quickly I learned how to cover-up my pain by becoming the best student in the class, and by building a façade of arrogant pride to hide my real emotions.

To this day, I can still remember the humiliation, the feelings of such confusion, and a deep lack of self-worth ... *what was I doing that was so awful that my own daddy could not love me and only wanted to hurt me?* And how could God possibly love me if my own daddy didn't even want me around? And how was I supposed to trust in a God who did nothing to make my daddy stop hurting us? Many years went by before I come *to know God* and *to know His Unconditional Love for me.*

For years I tried so hard to make my daddy love me, but nothing I tried made any difference. It was a very long time before I truly understood that he was the one with a serious problem. With the love of Jesus and His healing power of restoration, I was able to forgive Daddy and to grieve his inability to show love or compassion to us. Yet, *the loneliness of my childhood*, stayed with me in a negative way for a very long time as an adult. I spent years in deep loneliness trying to do everything right so others would like me and/or approve of me when I didn't even like or approve of myself.

As a child, I had one consuming goal. I was going to do whatever it took to get an education so I could leave home, get a job, and to have money so no one would ever have a reason to ridicule me again. I also vowed very early in my young life to never let down my emotional guard ... *no one was ever going to get close enough to hurt me the way Daddy hurt Mama.* I thought that once I left home, my life would be so much different ... *there would be times of laughter instead of tears.* I thought that getting away from Daddy would end the confusion and the deep loneliness, but it didn't.

The scars of my childhood went very deep. I had never learned, as a child, how to receive love or to give love ... *only to pretend whatever emotions I needed to show others in order to survive.* Getting away from home didn't end the loneliness. Being on my own, *and alone*, only added a deep feeling of hopelessness over time. As a result of all this, I went from one unhealthy relationship to another in search of belonging to someone in order to stop the excruciating pain of deep loneliness.

I longed for a husband to love me, a child to need me, and a real home for all of us. Yet, *feeling unattractive and unworthy*, I continued to pursue the wrong relationships for all of the wrong reasons. By the time I was thirty years of age;

I had been married and divorced twice. After surviving two life-threatening miscarriages, *against the doctor's advice*, I became pregnant again and God blessed me with a beautiful and healthy baby girl on January 21st, 1970. Susan gave me a reason to find the inner strength and courage to keep going many times over the next fourteen years. But I didn't always "keep going" in a healthy way. I was still very lonely at the very core of my being as a person - as a woman.

After I lost my husband and my only child, there was no reason left to go on. Each day just sort of phased into the next as time passed on by. The "walls of steel" I had built around my emotions were so thick and so solid that even a hurricane could not have broken them down. My "heart" was locked away ... *buried beneath layers of hard frozen emotional ice.* Yet to the outside world, I appeared to be a person who had it all together ... *successful, independent, and in control of her own world.*

I stayed excessively busy to avoid *"aloneness"*, but I was too proud to admit that what I was really afraid to face back then was the devastating *"loneliness"*. So by day – it was work, and by night – it was nightclubs, or anywhere else that I could mix in with a crowd. For years, I kept on running, running, running ... *but never fast enough or far enough to outrun the bottomless pit of loneliness.*

When I was told what had truly happened to my husband and child, when I learned that I had a contract out on my life, and when my only way out was to become a Civilian Operative for the FBI for three years of my life ... *I soon found out that I had only thought that I had known loneliness.* All of my ties, *personal and professional,* were severed - even to the point that my mother received a copy of my death certificate.

For three long excruciatingly hard years, I lived on the run. I lived wherever I was told, and had no control over the conditions under which I lived or worked. Each day was another twenty-four hours of uncertainty and buried fear for my very life. I was allowed to have no real friends – *only contacts* – and my name changed so many times that I have long since forgotten most of them. I pray that you, *the readers*, never experience that type of aloneness or such unbelievable depths of loneliness.

But this is the part I truly need for you to take deep within yourself ... there was ONE FRIEND that no one could take away from me, and that FRIEND walked with me every step of the way through my time of hell on earth. You see, right before I met with the Feds for the first time, I gave my life over to Jesus Christ. He became not only my Lord and Savior; He also became my Deliverer and Restorer and my "Bestest Friend"!

I was told repeatedly that if I managed to stay alive during the course of those three years, I would have to undergo a complete identification change once it was over. But the last words my mother spoke to me the morning that I left her standing on the sidewalk outside of her apartment before daybreak, *her prayers and her deep never-faltering faith*, stayed with me always until God brought me back home. Mama told me to go and finish what had to be done, and then to come home. She told me that she would still be there, *praying and believing every day while I was gone*, that God would bring me back to her ... still alive and still "me". Thank God for a praying mother of faith and perseverance.

I am here as living proof that we serve a "God Of The Impossible". I not only lived through those three years, my God has delivered me and restored me in ways too numerous to tell here. Yes, my name was and still is Vel Hobbs, and I have known great "Personal Growth Through Loneliness".

Admitting loneliness is not a negative confession but an honest, sometimes humbling, expression of human need. Thinking that we are independent of others and have no need for anyone is not a commendable trait, but it is a sure sign of a deeper emotional – often spiritual – problem. The desire for companionship is a legitimate need within each of us. God Himself recognized fellowship and companionship as a valid need.

- **Genesis 2:18 ...** *The Lord God said, "It is not good for the man to be alone. I will make a helper suitable for him."*

Without female companionship and a partner in reproduction, the man could not fully realize his humanity. God's provision of a "helper" for Adam was not a condescending comment on singleness but an approval on marriage. God was concerned for Adam's loneliness, for God created people to have relationships with Him and with others.

By refusing to admit – *often even to ourselves* – our innate need for companionship and real fellowship with others, *by refusing to own our loneliness,* we are setting ourselves up to ultimately seek unhealthy solutions to temporarily assuage the loneliness that constantly gnaws away at our inner peace and feeling of self-worth. Unhealthy and temporary solutions often include promiscuous sexual relationships, pornography, alcoholism, drugs, isolation, etc.

Though issues may differ as to the <u>why</u> of being alone - single adults that may include the never-married as well as separated, widowed, and divorced persons; death of a loved one, relocation, separation from family members, long hours at work, abusive relationships, and the list goes on – each face the potential problems of aloneness, such as ... isolation, insecurity, and feelings of rejection.

Being "unattached" can foster destructive responses, or it can encourage the development of a deeper relationship with God. There is nothing wrong with being single – just don't try to go it alone! We were created as social beings with a need for others. Let us look at the "Trinity of the

Godhead" ... *at Him in Whose Image we were created.* Man and woman were created with the capacity for fellowship ... *even as the Holy Spirit fellowships with the Son and the Son with the Father.*

King David, *whom God called a man after His own heart,* admitted to feelings of loneliness and expressed them through the writing of songs. Millions of people throughout time have looked to the writings of the Psalms for comfort in their own times of loneliness and personal need.

- **Psalm 25: 16&17 ...** *"Turn to me and be gracious to me, for I am lonely and afflicted. The troubles of my heart have multiplied; free me from my anguish."*

- **Psalm 102:7 ...** *"I lie awake; I have become like a bird alone on a roof."*

- **Psalm 142:4 ...** *"Look on my right hand and see, For there is no one who acknowledges me; Refuge has failed me; No one cares for my soul."*

Jeremiah Chapter Twenty – Jeremiah the Lone Prophet ... Jeremiah didn't get a ticket to an easy life when God called him to be a prophet. In fact, Jeremiah complained that his life was too difficult. The more he was faithful to speak God's Word to the people of Israel, the more rejection he suffered. Jeremiah bemoaned the fact that he was mocked and derided daily because he had taken a stand for God. He felt that he was a *solitary voice* speaking the truth to a nation that did not want to hear the truth. He acknowledged, however, ***that God's Word was like a fire burning within him and it could not be held back*** ... **Jeremiah 20:9.**

As we read of Jeremiah's life and of his "mission" from God, we see into the life of an intensely lonely man. His feelings spilled over each other as the prophet prayed. He spoke of very intense feelings ... *anger, resentment, and self-loathing jostle with Jeremiah's praise and confidence.* The very fact that he continued to communicate with God shows us that Jeremiah knew he was never completely alone. As overwhelming as his gripes and challenges were, Jeremiah still found comfort in having *SOMEONE* to whom he could gripe.

One of Jeremiah's most memorable messages from God provides an encouraging perspective about life that still pertains to our lives today. When we think we are all alone and facing the greatest challenges of our lives, the Spirit of God within us will continue to shape us and to draw us out to live for God.

- **Jeremiah 29: 11–13 ...** *"For I know the thoughts that I think toward you, says the Lord, thoughts of peace and not of evil, to give you a future and a hope. Then you will call upon Me and go and pray to Me, and I will listen to you. And you will seek Me and find Me, when you search for Me with all of your heart."*

People need to understand the source of their loneliness. Perhaps someone's loneliness is based on perception, and not an unchangeable circumstance. Perceptions can be changed once a person sees the cause of their loneliness. Are you feeling lonely due to a mistaken perception, or can the situation be changed?

If the loneliness is based on a real circumstance, *not just a perception*, you need to accept the situation and learn to handle it in the best way possible. This was the case in my situation:

- I had no control over my childhood environment.
- I had no control over the cruel and untimely deaths of my husband and child.

177

- I had no choice in the three years of my life that were spent in personal isolation from friends and family as a Civilian Operative for the FBI.
- *I did have a choice as to how I would handle these uncontrollable situations in my life* ... was I just going to lie down and grieve myself to death <u>OR</u> was I going to use this time to grow personally, professionally, and spiritually?

The *best remedy for loneliness* is to use the *alone time* to grow in all the areas of your life, and to focus on reaching out to someone else who is in need. Get Up and Get Busy ... *or choose to sit there in your misery and eventually dry up and die.* I am not trying to sound harsh here. I do understand deep loneliness, *but I have also learned that in our times of deepest loneliness,* we have choices to make that will affect the rest of our natural lives. Furthermore, the choices we make will touch the lives of others around us in either a positive or negative way.

It is hard to keep going, *to not just give up and quit,* when it seems we are all alone in an often very cold world. With the help of Jesus, it is possible to keep going through the pain until we reach the other side. Most of us will find it necessary to "*walk through a valley of deep loneliness*" at some point in life. Loneliness is not a new condition of lifestyle prevalent to our modern age. Read your Bible ... *loneliness has existed ever since sin entered the Garden of Eden!*

When sin entered the Garden of Eden, genuine intimacy disappeared. Adam and Eve blamed each other, lied, and excused themselves. From that moment on genuine intimacy with God and with other human beings was lost. Without genuine intimacy, we will all know loneliness.

Jesus Christ was the Only Begotten Son of God, and yet He knew a deeper loneliness than it is even possible for us to begin to comprehend. Jesus was left alone during His most difficult time, *there in the Garden of Gethsemane*, and He had to make a decision not to quit although He knew what lay before Him ... *the horrendous suffering on His way to the Cross, and the unbearable pain of God – His Father, turning away from Him as Jesus took our sins upon Himself.*

The **Apostle Paul** was left alone at his first trial. No one acted in his defense. All of his friends forsook him, but God never left him alone.

- **2 Timothy 4: 16&17 ...** *"At my first defense no one stood with me, but all forsook me. May it not be charged against them. But the Lord stood with me and strengthened me, so that the message might be preached fully through me, and that all the Gentiles might hear. Also I was delivered out of the mouth of the lion".*

In 1992, *when God showed me the vision of the three books I was to write as a personal testimony to Him and to encourage others*, I had no idea the personal cost I would pay by being obedient to God. When the first book, "A House Divided", was released in 2000 ... *it cost me the personal loss of several of my family members – and I was already very much alone.* But I have never regretted writing the books that God showed me to write. I never wrote one word to hurt anyone nor to speak badly of my earthly father. I was led by God to share my testimony to encourage others going through the same things that He had delivered me from.

- **2 Corinthians 1: 3&4 ...** *"Blessed be the God and Father of our Lord Jesus Christ, the Father of mercies and God of all comfort, who comforts us in all our tribulation, that we may be able to comfort those who are in any trouble, with the comfort with which we ourselves are comforted by God".*

In 1995, when I returned to Missouri to care for my ill mother – *at her repeated request* – I had no idea that I would experience such resentment from some family members, that I would use every penny I had to do so, and that I would drive myself to physical illness by fulfilling my call to take care of Mama and keep her out of a nursing home. I had left my job and sold all I had in Houston to go back home to help my mother and my family. I was not prepared for the resentment or the rejection heaped upon me by some family members. Only by the Grace of God was I able to forgive them and to not grow disillusioned and bitter.

While I may not have found the inner strength to *obey God* if I had known beforehand the *forthcoming consequences*, I will never regret my decision to do as God asked and I have been deeply rewarded by Him for doing so. During those long months of trials, I held on very tightly to *two truths*:

1. *I knew that I had obeyed God in going back to Missouri to take care of Mother.* Was my family treating me fairly? NO! So, why did I stay?

   Because I knew I was operating in God's Will. I knew that He had more reasons than I might ever realize for my being there. I knew, *from personal experience*, that God will never let me down – no matter what anyone else might say or do. He will always make a way where there is no way.

2. I believed strongly enough in God's love and God's provision that *I hung in with the right attitude* until He brought me through to the other side. When we choose to follow God's Purpose for our lives – God's Purpose will be completed.

   Only later did I get to see the incredible blessing of having my brother, Carl, give his life to Jesus. Carl and his wife, Jackie, and I shared several years of closeness as family and friends as a result of my initial obedience to God. Carl has gone on to be with his Sweet Jesus now, but Jackie is still my closest friend and dear sister.

I am pretty sure you, too, have had lonely times … *times when you felt no one cared about you, no one understood you, and no one believed in you.* In these times of aloneness, *we may not realize it,* but these times are actually very good for us. God often uses our times of being all alone to teach us to rely on Him, and not upon ourselves or someone else.

A person's loneliness may be a healthy part of the *grieving process* as we deal with a deep loss. This is a natural and healthy thing unless we allow the loneliness to cause us to isolate ourselves from others. There is much more information on "grieving" in the section entitled, "A Season Of Grief". If you haven't read it, I recommend you do so because grieving someone's death is not the only kind of loss that we need to grieve in a healthy way in order to move on with our lives.

The *experience of loneliness* can be a healthy experience if we use the experience to draw closer to God and to others. If you are dealing with loneliness, you need to reach out to God and to others. Don't allow yourself to become emotionally involved in a personal relationship in a misguided attempt to find a way out of your loneliness. Take the time, *in your temporary aloneness,* to get to know and to appreciate YOU … *the remarkable person whom God created you to be.* Then, *and only then,* will you become a healthy person that is ready to truly share yourself and your life with another person.

If you know someone who is lonely, you can help them by spending time with them and by not allowing them to become isolated and alone. Become a friend to someone who is experiencing loneliness, and remind them that *in Christ* they are never alone!

Before you say you don't know anyone whom you can reach out to help, let me remind you that the world is full of lonely people ... *in the hospitals, in the nursing homes, in the jails, in your neighborhood, and most likely in your church or place of work.*

- **2 Corinthians 9:6 ...** *"Remember this: Whoever sows sparingly will also reap sparingly, and whoever sows generously will also reap generously".*

If we will reach out to help someone else – God will always send someone to reach out to help us in our times of need. God is a God of Seed-Time and Harvest, and ... our *seeds sown* are not just about money, but are also about how willing we are to *sow seeds of ourselves* into the lives of others by giving of our time and energy.

- **Isaiah 41:10 ...** *"Fear not, for I am with you; Be not dismayed, for I am your God. I will strengthen you, Yes, I will help you. I will uphold you with My righteous right hand".*

God reminds us – HIS PEOPLE – that in our loneliness and inadequacy we need not fear or be dismayed. WHY? Because HE is OUR GOD and because HE is with us always ... *we can find strength and comfort in knowing that He is holding us in His "righteous right hand".*

Everyone feels lonely at times. Sometimes, however, loneliness can become so desperate that it causes fearfulness and an overwhelming feeling of hopelessness. Prolonged periods of aloneness can cause us to become depressed by a deep state of loneliness and a paralyzing fear of hopelessness that this "time" will never end.

If you are going through a time such as this, please turn your attention away from your current situation and back towards God. God promises each of us that He will always hold His people close to Him.

Crawl up into the lap of your Heavenly Father and ask Him to wrap His loving arms tightly around you. Tell Him how desperately you need to feel and to know His love. Don't be embarrassed or afraid to approach your Heavenly Father in this way ... *"unless you come to Him as a little child"*, you will never be truly free to feel His comfort and to know His love. Remember that Jesus has called us His friends, and with Jesus we are never alone.

- **Hebrew 13:5b ...** *because God has said, "Never will I leave you; never will I forsake you".*

Are you experiencing loneliness? What are you going to choose to do about it? You have *one* of *two* choices:

1. You can choose to give into those *feelings of loneliness* by sitting around and doing nothing but feel sorry for yourself, by blaming others for your loneliness, by refusing to accept responsibility for your own decisions and actions, or by waiting for someone else to come along and *"fix your loneliness"*, well ... *it ain't gonna happen.*

    If this is the choice you make, you are moving from loneliness into depression, isolation, and often times something far worse. Loneliness, *left unattended*, can lead to alcoholism, drug use, unhealthy relationships and/or sexual behavior, and even suicide.

2. You can choose to assuage those *feelings of loneliness* by deciding to become involved with other people: start attending church and become part of the activities offered through that church, be a friend to someone else instead of dwelling on your own prob-

lems all of the time, listen to uplifting and positive music, read some good books, go back to school or take a course over the internet that involves something of interest to you, join a gym or just get out there and take a long walk, talk to a counselor, or do whatever – *just get up, get out there, and get involved.*

You can begin by asking God to work with you in what you are doing to take away the lonely feelings. When we are willing to do our part ... God will always do His part.

If you are currently experiencing a season of loneliness, what is it going to become for you ... a *Period of Personal Growth* or a *Time of Self-Destructive Actions*? The choice belongs to you.

CHAPTER ELEVEN

"FACING THE REALITY OF DEATH"

Ecclesiastes 3:2 ... *"A time to be born, and a time to die."* There are so many emotions, *so many words,* that can be applied to death ... *tears, sorrow, anguish, fear, dread, pain, suffering, etc.* Facing the reality of death can be especially difficult for Christians when they have been praying and holding on in faith for the healing and restoration of their own body or for the healing and restoration of a loved one.

How do we hold on to our belief in a loving and merciful God as we watch the pain and the devastation within the physical *(and sometimes mental)* being of a body tortured by the onslaught of death? If God is all powerful, if He is all loving, if He is a compassionate and merciful Father ... how can He just stand by and *seemingly* do nothing in the midst of so much pain?

We could have asked the same question regarding the suffering and death of God's Only Begotten Son - Jesus Christ. Why should His Own Father, *who held the power of the universe within His hands,* stand by and allow the persecution and the death of an innocent man ... His Own

Son? But let us remember the words of Jesus, Himself, as He prayed in the Garden of Gethsemane.

- **Matthew 26: 39&42 ...** *He went a little farther and fell on His face, and prayed, saying, "O My Father, if it is possible, let this cup pass from Me; nevertheless, not as I will, but as You will." Again, a second time, He went away and prayed, saying, "O My Father, if this cup cannot pass away from Me unless I drink it, Your will be done."*

The Paradox of Healing: no one will experience complete healing and recovery until they go to glory in heaven ... *we live with imperfect earthly bodies in an imperfect world.* Jesus Christ chose to die so that we, *as believers*, can live for eternity. Never allow Satan to cause you to doubt how very much God loves you.

- **John 3:16 ...** *"For God so loved the world that He gave His Only Begotten Son, that whoever believes in Him should not perish but have everlasting life".*

- **John 11: 25&26 ...** *Jesus said to her, "I am the resurrection and the life. He who believes in Me, though he may die, he shall live. And whoever lives and believes in Me shall never die".*

Christ died for people's sins and those who accept His sacrifice are made righteous before God. However, people – *as human beings* – must still struggle with the sin nature, and we need to come before God daily for healing and recovery from sin. Moreover, *as believers*, we have another enemy who is running to and fro upon this earth seeking to deceive and to destroy God's ultimate creation ... mankind.

That enemy is Satan, *and as much as our Heavenly Father loves us and longs to save us,* Satan strives to deceive us and to turn us against the love of God in order to ultimately destroy us.

Please don't allow the pain and the fear of death to cause you to turn away from the *love* and the *ultimate healing* of God. As you walk through the SEASON OF LOSS AND GRIEF, you can hold onto the unchanging love and strength of your Heavenly Father. Don't allow Satan to turn your natural healthy need for a SEASON OF GRIEVING into a lifetime of bitterness, regrets, loss of faith, and final destruction.

People's bodies, souls, and relationships will continue to groan for the healing that will only be experienced in the Presence of God. So, *in a very real sense,* God's people are already healed – *but not yet healed.* God's *paradox of healing* is far beyond our human comprehension.

Another *paradox for healing* exists in the *need for healing.* James encourages *believers* to pray over sick people, anointing them with oil in **James 5:14 ...** *"Is anyone among you sick? Let him call for the elders of the church, and let them pray over him, anointing him with oil in the name of the Lord."* Surely God should be petitioned when people are ill. However, this is not a formula for certain recovery while still upon this earth; *it is submission to God regarding His will for that person.*

God may choose not to heal on this earth in this lifetime. *Why?* Because the very illness, *the very suffering and weakness,* that so disturbs can be used by God to help people. God took the Apostle Paul's physical weakness, *for example,* and used it to glorify Himself. Paul wrote:

- **2 Corinthians 12: 7–9 ...** *"A thorn in the flesh was given to me, a messenger of Satan to buffet me ... I pleaded with the Lord three times that it might depart from me. And He said, 'My grace is* *sufficient for you, My strength is made perfect in weakness.'"*

Though Paul repeatedly asked that the *"thorn"* be removed, God told Paul that He would make His power perfect through Paul's weakness. God did not leave Paul helpless, however. God promised His grace to help Paul endure the struggles ... *that same promise is extended from God to all of us as well.* Paul would gladly boast about his weakness so that Christ's power would rest on him. **2 Corinthians 12:10 ...** *"For when I am weak, then I am strong."*

In other words, when we can't do it alone, then we have to depend on God to do it in us. Therefore, we can boast ... *not about being healed, but about being weak enough for God to use.* God's work of healing and recovery is not always to take away our wounds; rather, His work may simply be to enable us to join with Christ in His suffering and to glorify Himself through it.

We may ask God to heal and we rejoice whenever He does so. We may also rejoice, however, when He chooses instead to use our weaknesses as a platform to display His grace and power in our lives. Through suffering, we may bring help and hope to others who are suffering in the same way. We can point them to our Savior. Through our wounds ... *others may be invited to make an appointment with the Great Physician.*

If healing is to occur, the Lord will do it. Sometimes He performs a miracle that cannot be explained naturally; sometimes He works through doctors and medicines; sometimes it's just the body's natural God-Given healing processes at work. *And then there are the cases where God performs the ultimate healing by taking the person to be with Him.*

The true "Prayer of Faith" acknowledges God's sovereignty over each person's life. The "Prayer Offered In Faith" reveals complete trust in God to do His Will. Healing prayer should be held by all of those who hurt. And we should *rest in the peace of knowing* that God does answer prayer ... *in His Perfect Timing and according to His Perfect Will for each person's life.*

God does not heal every person who prays for healing – while on this earth. He does, however, heal many who ask. **In the story of Hezekiah, from 2 Kings 20: 1-11**, we are taught the importance of throwing ourselves on God's mercy. Take the time to pick up your Bible and read this interesting and inspiring story for yourself.

God can and does still heal. He has the power to do so. At times, healing a person while that person is still on this earth is within His Plan, while at other times – *it is not.* We must always remember, however, that *total and permanent healing* will come when we see Him face to face. God will work in our brokenness to show His deep love and give His abiding peace.

FINALLY HOME ... *joy, freedom, healing, newness, and eternity!* For believers, these words as well apply to death. Loss hurts. Even Jesus wept at the death of a loved one as shown in **John 11:35 ...** *Jesus wept. Then the Jews said, "See how much He loved him!"*

While we sorrow, however, we sorrow not as those who have no hope. Along with the tears and the sorrow, through our belief in Christ Jesus we know that death is only the end of life on earth and the beginning of life with HIM. **Psalm 116:15 ...** *"Precious in the sight of the Lord is the death of His saints."*

Death is real. Everyone who lives will one day die. For some, death is a great tragedy. It is sad when loved ones die, and it is natural to grieve. But God tells us that the death of a *born-again believer* is *"precious in the sight of the Lord".* For believers ... *death is merely a gateway into their heavenly home where they ultimately belong.* Our time on this earth is merely a pilgrimage through a strange land. Or, *as my big brother Carl liked to put it,* this life is only *boot camp* where we are being prepared for our eternal home.

Carl had endured unbelievable suffering since a logging accident in 1998 left him paralyzed from the waist down with his spine severed in several places and severe damage was done to his brain. Over a period of eight years, Carl suffered multiple strokes, consecutive amputation of both legs, and the tragic death of his teenage son before he went home to be with his *Sweet Jesus* on January 14th, 2005. My big brother had always been my champion, but never more so than how he chose to live his life through those long years of horrendous physical and emotional loss and constant suffering.

My last phone conversation with Carl, *just hours before his mind began to succumb to the confusion of his illness*, once again confirmed his deep and unwavering trust in God – his unfaltering love for his Sweet Jesus. And, *once again*, my desperately ill brother strengthened and inspired my own personal walk as a Child-of-God. In his dying hours ... *Carl was still being used to bring Glory to God and to encourage others around him.*

In that phone conversation, Carl told me that he would soon be <u>running</u> down the streets of gold on both of his legs with all his pain gone forever. He also told me ... *"Sis, don't you worry about me. My Sweet Jesus is coming to take me home soon. But you'll be okay. And someday, when your work on earth is done and God is ready for you to come home, I will be there waiting for you. You can't come with me now because you still have a job to do, but my work here is finished and I am going home!"*

When I was talking with Carl that day, I didn't know that I would never have another conversation with my brother on this earth. What I knew then and know now, beyond a shadow of a doubt, is that – *in spite of what we saw him suffering in the human aspect of his life* – Carl is at peace in the love of his Sweet Jesus, and he is resting nestled close in the Hands of His Heavenly Father. I know where he will be spending eternity ... *THE BEST IS YET TO COME*!

- **2 Peter 3:13 ...** *"But in keeping with His promise we are looking forward to a new heaven and a new earth, the home of righteousness."*

- **Revelation 21: 1–5 ...** *Then I saw a new heaven and a new earth, for the first heaven and the first earth had passed away. Also there was no more sea. Then I, John, saw the Holy City, New Jerusalem, coming down out of heaven from God, prepared as a bride adorned for her husband. And I heard a loud voice from heaven saying, "Behold the tabernacle of God is with men, and He will dwell with them, and they shall be His people. God Himself will be with them and be their God. And God will wipe every tear from their eyes; there shall be no more death, nor sorrow, nor crying. There shall be no more pain, for the former things have passed away." Then He who sat on the throne said, "Behold, I make all things new." And He said to me, "Write, for these words are true and faithful".*

Often when I am struggling with a difficult situation, I think about how differently Carl handled betrayal, fear, loneliness, and pain BEFORE he turned his life over to God *versus* how he handled the most excruciating of pain AFTER he invited Jesus Christ to become his Lord and Savior and to carry his pain with him.

- Carl was never in a hurry to *"give his heart"* to someone, and I understand *why* doing so is so difficult for those of us raised in an environment of rejection and abuse. But then he met a young, and very beautiful, woman who stole his heart. They were married, and were blessed with a baby girl. Over the next few years, Carl was betrayed by his young wife while serving the second of three tours of duty in Viet Nam and he also lost his relationship with his daughter.

Carl served one year in the Korean Conflict and three tours in the Viet Nam War as a soldier in the United States Army. He was severely injured at one point by enemy fire while on duty. How did Carl survive his loneliness, deep emotional and physical pain, and the constant fear of intimate torture or death at the hands of his enemies while at war? He shut down his heart by freezing out his emotions, and he begin to drink more and more as the days turned into weeks and the weeks turned into months and the months turned into years of deeper and deeper isolation.

Yes, my brother turned his Army Career into success, promotions, and achievement until he finally retired with honor ... *a man who never allowed the disappointments of his life to lessen his deep respect and love for his country!* But, he also came home frozen inside and an alcoholic-in-denial.

For several years, he isolated himself and lived hours of every day deep inside of a whiskey bottle. He controlled his drinking, for the most part, during the days as he continued to run the logging company he started after retiring from the Army, but at night ... *he locked the doors and strived to drown his pain and loneliness in booze.*

Carl told me more than one time that the booze only dulled his physical pain and made his memories a little more tolerable, but that it never quite freed him inside. He so desperately longed for some real peace.

- Carl finally gave his life over to Christ Jesus, and began his own *"Journey of Recovery"*. Not a quick or easy *journey* by any means. But if my brother were still alive today, he would tell you himself ... *it became a journey he would never have missed taking with a final destination so incredible that it is above all human imagination! Death* was but the *doorway* that our Heavenly Father used to take my dear brother home ... *a "home" filled with such peace and love that he would never choose to leave!*

After his logging accident, and the subsequent years of pain and suffering, Carl never feared *death* although he often stared *death* square in the face. In fact, during the years following the accident, several different doctors sent him home to die on three separate occasions. When faced with dying, my brother didn't fear leaving this earth ... *he just longed to go home.*

One day I know I will be reunited with Carl again, and I will also be reunited with my precious Mother who went home to be with the Lord in 1999. There, *once again*, I will see my daughter, *Susan*, who was taken home in 2004 at the tender age of fourteen. And most of all, I will see my God face-to-face and worship my Lord who chose to die that I might live for eternity in that glorious new place being created by God for His Children.   Such a place is impossible to imagine because this world is filled with so much loss and sorrow. The **Book of Revelation** describes a better time and a better place:

- **Revelation 21:4 ...** ***"And God will wipe away every tear from their eye; there shall be no more death,*** *nor sorrow, nor crying. There shall be no more pain, for the former things have passed away."*

God has promised to *"wipe away every tear"* and *"there shall be no more pain".* No matter what we experience here on this earth, God promises a perfect future with Him. Through the hard times of today ... *we can trust this hope, this truth, for our future.*

- **Revelation 21:5 ...** *Then He who sat on the throne said, "Behold, I make all things new." And He said to me, "Write, for these words are true and faithful".*

Everything that has been perverted by sin, death, and decay will be created over again at the end of this history. All pain, sorrow, and death will pass away. Once again, everything will be perfect ... *straight from the Hand of God.*

God promises that He will *"make all things new".* Broken lives will be healed. Tears will cease. Souls will be renewed. Believers will be given heavenly bodies for living with God forever. This recreated and renewed world is God's spectacular gift to those who have trusted in Him. We must stand strong for God ... *His promises will surely come to pass.*

Death was not God's original desire for humanity. God created human beings for life and not for death. Adam had received the *"breath of life".*

- **Genesis 2:7 ...** *"And the Lord God formed man of the dust of the ground, and breathed into his nostrils the breath of life; and man became a living being."*

It was not until Adam and Eve sinned that death arrived. God said that Adam's punishment for his sin would be as follows:

- **Genesis 3:19** ... *"In the sweat of your face you shall eat bread till you return to the ground, for out of it you were taken; for dust you are, and to dust you shall return."*

- **Genesis 5:5** ... *"So all the days that Adam lived were nine hundred and thirty years; and he died."*

So began the *cycle of birth and death* that will continue until Christ returns. As the Apostle Paul explained in **Romans 5:12** ... *"Therefore, just as through one man sin entered the world, and death through sin, and thus death spread to all men, because all sinned."*

Death is difficult because it is loss ... real and painful because loved ones are gone – symbolic because it reminds us of lost innocence, sin, and punishment. Death is a painful reality faced by every person. We lose people whom we love, and we will one day die ourselves. How should believers view this dreaded event called death?

Death is distasteful and it is dreaded. Few of us would say that we look forward to dying. *Death is viewed very differently from God's perspective, however.* And our perspective on death will dramatically affect our ability to handle it.

- Humans see death as something to be avoided for as long as possible ... *God sees death as something to be anticipated.*
- Humans see death as a gloomy, dark night ... *God describes death as a glorious new day.*
- Humans see death as the end of the journey ... *God sees death as the beginning of the best journey of all.*

Carl, *sitting in Mom's hospital room in his wheelchair,* watched her lifeless body wasting away. In the last few seconds of her life, *as Carl described it,* Mom opened her eyes, slightly raised her head, looked straight at him sitting in his wheelchair, smiled and said, *"O my Sweet Jesus",* laid her head back upon the pillow, slightly turned her head to the side, closed her eyes as though falling into a peaceful sleep, and drew her last breath.

I have no doubt that witnessing this passing of our Mother, *one of God's children,* often gave Carl the strength to lean into his own faith in God during more than eight years of suffering in his own life. I also have no doubt that it influenced his perspective on life, on death, and on eternity.

For Christians, the approach of death can be a time of positive anticipation because we enjoy God and long to be with Him forever. **Like Abraham, we are looking for a city,** *"whose builder and maker is God"* ... **Hebrews 11:10.**

Death is not a time to be shunned or feared. **It is a time to anticipate hearing our Lord and Savior say,** *"Well done, good and faithful servant; you were faithful over a few things, I will make you ruler over many things"* ... **Matthew 25:21.** Who would not welcome such a reception?

Death entered the world because of sin. When Adam sinned, death came to all human beings. **As Paul wrote in Romans 6:23 ...** *"The wages of sin is death".* One man, Adam, caused sin to enter the human race, and so death from sin. One man, JESUS, came with the promise of resurrection from the dead. Jesus accomplished this by becoming human, dying, and then rising again.

Someday, *in God's new creation,* death itself will be destroyed. Until then, all human beings will die. But for believers ... *death is not to be feared – for it is a gateway to eternal life with God.* **1 Corinthians 15:26 ...** *"The last enemy that will be destroyed is death".*

First-century believers were persecuted for their faith and faced death continually. Like them ... we must always be ready to die, ready to stand before God, and ready to thank Him for all He has done in giving us salvation.

Most people know the wonderful feeling of having a place where they are wanted and cared for, a place they can call their own ... *a home*. **In Revelation 21: 10–27, John described the** *heavenly home* **that is waiting for those of us who** *choose to follow Jesus.* In the New Jerusalem the streets are made of gold and the foundations are adorned with jewels. And most importantly ... *God lives there – His Glory gives light to the city.* Although we may have a home we enjoy on this earth, one day we will reach our ultimate destination. Our true home is with God forever, *if we are a born-again believer.*

This is one very real certainty ... *we will each spend eternity in one place or another depending on which Master we have chosen to believe in and to follow on this earth.* Choose JESUS and spend your eternity with HIM. Choose Satan and you will spend your eternity in hell. Please don't think that by not choosing Jesus Christ you are also not choosing an eternity in hell with Satan and his demons because, my dear friend, there is no such thing as "NO CHOICE".

Please don't listen to the lies of Satan telling you that you have plenty of time to repent and to accept Jesus Christ as your Lord and Savior. The only breath that we have any guarantee of taking is the breath we are taking this very second, and ... *it could very well be our last breath before death and – ETERNITY.*

Mama was eighty-six years old when she died, and she had suffered with a serious heart condition for more than four years before her final breath. Carl survived three tours of duty in the Vietnam War, one tour in the Korean Conflict, years of alcoholism, and more than eight years as an invalid before going home to be with his Sweet Jesus. A few more days, and he would have celebrated his sixty-seventh birthday.

Do you hear Satan whisper in your ear, *"See, there is no need to hurry to serve Jesus. Have a little more fun first. You're young and healthy – you have a long time to live before you will die"*. Do these words sound like a replay of what goes through your mind whenever something or someone forces you to take a serious look at your own death? They sure sound a lot like what used to go through my mind before I finally invited Jesus Christ into my own life in 1987 at thirty-seven years old, and ... *He became my Lord and Savior, my Healer and Deliverer, and my Very Bestest Friend!*

What about AGE – HEALTH – DEATH? My husband, *Leonard Hobbs*, was strong and healthy one minute and dead from an unforeseeable and unstoppable accident the next minute at thirty-six years of age. My strong and healthy four-teen-year old daughter, *Susan*, was laughing one moment and shortly thereafter she lay dead on the bathroom floor. Both were young, strong, and healthy. Neither had any known reason not to live to a ripe old age, but ... *they didn't.*

As I stated earlier ... *the only breath we have any guarantee of taking is the one breath we are taking right now.* But there are _two definites_ that we can all be certain of ... *we each will die and we each will spend our eternity either with God in heavenly bliss or with Satan and his demons in hell.* Each and every one of us must make the choice for ourselves as to where we will spend eternity because no one else can make it for us.

I have been asked this question ... *"If God is such a good God who loves us so much, why would He send anyone to hell?"* God does NOT send one single person to hell. In fact, He yearns for each of us to choose to accept His Plan of Redemption by accepting Jesus Christ as our Lord and Savior in order to not only spend our eternity in bliss with Him, but also that we can have a far more abundant life while we are still on this earth.

God does not send a person to hell. God made it possible for each and every human being to exercise their free will to make a personal choice to either serve God, or to deny Jesus Christ as their Lord and Savior and to choose to follow Satan. Jesus chose to die for our sins in order for us to choose eternal life with Him, but ... *the choice of where we spend our eternity, and with whom, is entirely our own choice to make.*

- **John 3: 16&17 ...***"For God so loved the world that He gave His only begotten Son, that whoever believes in Him should not perish but have everlasting life. For God did not send His Son into the world to condemn the world, but that the world through Him might be saved."*

AM I PREPARED TO DIE? Death is a reality. No one has found a cure for it. On this earth, no one ever will.

- **Hebrews 9: 27&28 ...** *"And as it is appointed for men to die once, but after this the judgment. So Christ was offered once to bear the sins of many. To those who eagerly wait for Him He will appear a second time, apart from sin, for salvation."*

Sooner or later, therefore, all people have to face death. Each person must eventually ask themselves the question ... *"Am I Prepared To Die?"* The Bible is very clear about how to prepare for our eternal future. In fact, it is as simple as **A B C**. All people need to ...

- **A**dmit that they are not ready to go to heaven when they die because they are sinners. **The Bible tells us in Romans 3:23 ...** *"For all have sinned and fall short of the glory of God."* All people have sinned; therefore, no one deserves to be with God

SEASONS OF THE HEART

for all eternity. **Romans 6:23 ...** *"The wages of sin is death."* Fortunately, God made a provision so that people can choose to spend their eternity with Him. In order to do so, they must ...

- Believe that although they are sinners, Jesus Christ died to pay the penalty for sin and to save them from its punishment. Salvation is not a matter of turning over a new leaf or trying to live so that good works outweigh bad works. Salvation is the loving act of God whereby He sent His Son, Jesus, to die on Calvary's Cross to pay the penalty for sin once and for all time for those who will receive Him. Those who believe in Him must ...

- Confess to God that they believe what God's Word says – *that they are sinners, and that they believe Jesus died to save them from sin and its penalty of eternal damnation.* They must confess their sins, repent of their sins, and ask Jesus Christ to become Lord and Savior of their lives. **The Apostle Paul wrote in Romans 10:9 ...** *"If you confess with your mouth the Lord Jesus and believe in your heart that God raised Him from the dead, you will be saved."*

How does it all end? For Christians, pain and suffering may not be alleviated on earth, but our time on this earth is only temporary. What God has for us *as believers* is a glorious future because we have chosen to trust in Jesus Christ as our Savior, our Healer, and our soon coming King. For the Christian ... *death is not the end – it is a glorious new beginning!*

- **1 Corinthians 15: 55–57 ...** *"O Death, where is your sting? O Hades, where is your victory?" The sting of* *death is sin, and the strength of sin is the law. But thanks be to God, who gives us the victory through our Lord Jesus Christ. Therefore, my beloved brethren, always abounding in the work of the Lord, knowing that your labor is not in vain in the Lord.*

Death is the doorway to our final destination ... ETERNAL LIFE. If you are a Christian, that eternal life will be with God. Then, *as believers*, we will finally be truly ... *HOME!*

Do you have the *peace of knowing that you know that you know* that if you die within the next instant you will spend your eternity with God? **Can you truly say with David in Psalm Chapter Twenty Three ...?**

> *"The Lord is my shepherd;*
> *I shall not want.*
> *He makes me to lie down in green pastures;*
> *He leads me beside the still waters.*
> *He restores my soul;*
> *He leads me in the paths of righteousness*
> *For His name's sake.*
> *Yea, though I walk through the valley of the shadow of death,*
> *I will fear no evil;*
> *For you are with me;*
> *Your rod and Your staff, they comfort me.*
> *You prepare a table before me in the presence of my enemies;*
> *You anoint my head with oil;*
> *My cup runs over.*
> *Surely goodness and mercy shall follow me*
> *All the days of my life;*
> *And I will dwell in the house of the Lord forever."*

I ran from God until I was thirty-seven years old. I had no doubt that God existed. I knew that one day everyone dies, and I knew that – *without salvation* – after death comes an eternity that will be spent either in heaven or in hell. I was running as a result of *religious confusion* and *deep anger.*

The God most presented to me as I grew up was a God of anger, condemnation, and eternal judgment. *Out of fear,* I went to the altar a few times during my childhood years of attending church … *the fear of burning in hell.* But because I never really came to <u>know</u> God, my *religion* didn't last too long. Finally, *in anger and desperation,* I made the decision to put God out of my mind once and for all. After all, *since I couldn't be good enough or live good enough to go to heaven,* I might as well do whatever I wanted and have all the fun I could because I was going to hell anyway.

In October of 1982, *on the day of my husband's funeral,* I screamed at my mother for the first and last time in my entire life. After the funeral Mom walked up to me, put her arm around me, and said to me, *"Honey, God wants to help you through this if you will only let Him".* I screamed at Mother to never say the name GOD to me, or in my presence again, if she ever wanted to see me again. I will never forget the pain that my words put into the heart and the eyes of my mother. But she simply hugged me, told me that she loved me, and walked away. Thank God, *literally,* that she never stopped interceding in prayer for me.

Mama's prayers were finally answered at a little Indian church on the outskirts of Oklahoma City in 1987. I finally cried out to God in desperation and invited Jesus Christ into my heart as my personal Lord and Savior. From that day until this day, I awake each morning with a peace deep within my heart because …

- I <u>know</u> that God is my Heavenly Father who truly loves me.

- I <u>know</u> that I have been forgiven and set free of sin through the Blood of Jesus Christ.
- I <u>know</u> that no matter what happens it will be okay because my life is in God's Hands and He is in control.
- I <u>know</u> that through Jesus I have an abundant life here on this earth – no matter what happens.
- When my journey here is finished – *when my times comes to die* – I <u>know</u> that I will spend my eternity in the glorious home prepared for me by my Lord and Savior and my very Bestest Friend ... JESUS CHRIST!

I have heard people say, *"Living for Jesus is so hard"*. Then they have never met my Jesus. Because my years spent living in sin, *with the underlying fear of dying*, were the years of living that were so hard. A life of denying the love of God and Salvation through Christ Jesus almost destroyed me.

My whole life, *my entire world*, changed when I finally met Jesus for myself! Knowing Jesus Christ, *and walking in a Daily Personal Relationship with Him*, is the simplest and easiest thing I have ever done. For **"the joy of the Lord is my strength"**, and I know that **"I can do all things through Christ who strengthens me"**. I no longer fear *death* because I know my Savior is waiting for me just on the other side of that *doorway!*

Yes, I have made mistakes – *and have been forgiven for them* – since I began my walk with the Lord. Yes, I have suffered loss – *personal, professional, financial* – as a Christian. Yes, I have suffered physical and mental devastation from a debilitating illness – from which I was ultimately delivered and restored. Yes, I have tasted the bitterness of betrayal and rejection as a result of my choice to follow God's Purpose for my life ... *knowing firsthand the agony of loneliness*. Yes, *I have come before God in anger on occasion*, but never doubted His love for me. So why would I say that *"living for Jesus is the easiest thing that I have ever done?"*

- Because <u>HE</u> is the <u>ONE FRIEND</u> *who will always stick closer than any brother.* <u>HE</u> is the <u>ONE FRIEND</u> *who will never leave me, forsake me, reject me, use me, or betray me.* I know that I know that I know … I can always trust in God and in His love for me, and that is why I say *"living for Jesus is the easiest and the smartest thing I have ever chosen to do in my entire life".*

Do you want to know this Jesus? Do you want this kind of Personal Relationship with the Creator of the Universe? Do you want a Friend who will stick by your side no matter what? Do you want to <u>know</u> where you will spend eternity after you die? Do you want to be free to *enjoy your life* without *fearing death?* Jesus is as close as your next breath … *just a whisper away.* He is standing there right now *"knocking at your heart's door".* Do you want to invite Him in? Pray with me …

Heavenly Father, I know that you sent your Son, Jesus, to die for my sins. I know that He rose again and that He gave His life as the ultimate sacrifice for me. I now confess my sins, repent of my sins, and ask you, Lord Jesus, to come into my heart and to be my Lord and Savior and my Bestest Friend. I know that I am saved. I accept the Gift of Salvation by Faith through the Blood of Jesus. I choose to live my life on this earth for you, and I know that I no longer need to fear death because my eternal life is secured in Christ Jesus. Help me to grow in my daily relationship with Jesus. Father God, I ask in Jesus' Name. Thank You, Lord Jesus, from the bottom of my heart for my new life in you. Amen

Where Will You Choose To Spend Eternity?

Jesus Loves You

Please Choose Jesus!

CHAPTER TWELVE

"A SEASON OF GRIEF"

Ecclesiastes 3:4 ... *"A time to weep, and a time to laugh; a time to mourn, and a time to dance."* A deep hurt due to the loss of a loved one can cause feelings of depression, pain, emptiness, loneliness, and anger that often take longer than you would like to overcome. For Christians, these feelings – *especially the feelings of anger at the deceased and/or God* - often bring shame and fear as they struggle to overcome their grief through faith.

YES, Jesus will walk with you every step of the way and bring people into your life to help you walk through the *"Season of Grieving"*, but we all at one time or another will have to take this personal journey. Furthermore, each loss will bring a different level of grief. From my own deep personal losses, I can tell you that knowing a loved one has accepted Jesus Christ as their Lord and Savior will make a big difference in your level of grief ... if you, *too*, are a Child of God. But even as a Christian, you will still have to deal with the *"Stages of Grief"* in order to truly heal.

I hope that if you are dealing with personal grief, you will come to realize that it is okay to struggle with your emotions. It is okay to be angry ... *to be confused and angry with God or even with the person who died*. It is how you decide to deal with your emotions that will ultimately determine how you will eventually heal - or don't truly heal.

What is Grief? Webster's New World Dictionary: *intense emotional suffering caused by loss, disaster, misfortune, etc.; deep sadness.* Grief is a normal, healthy response to loss. One of the greatest losses that can occur is the death of someone you love. Other losses can include the loss of your health or the health of a loved one, the end of an important relationship, such as a divorce, loss of a job or financial security, etc.

Healing from such a loss involves coming to terms with the loss and the meaning of the loss in your life. Whether it is a job, friends, home, status, a loved one or a pet ... *all people experience loss in one way or another – to one degree or another.* And please don't minimize someone else's loss ... *different things have different meanings to all.* Loss can make us *bitter* or *better.* It all depends on how we choose to deal with the loss and the grief.

Unfortunately, no one likes to talk about loss and grief very much. We all have a tendency to struggle with how to comfort someone who is grieving. We all have a tendency to become uncomfortable around a grieving person. So many times we don't reach out to help the person struggling with grief ... *we seem to have an unspoken agreement not to talk about the loss.* Or, instead of talking with the grieved person, we talk at them ... *trying to placate them with our own ideas of what they should be doing and feeling or by trying to stuff well-meaning Scriptures down their throat as a "quick fix".*

Some losses are very minor and the effect they have on the person is short-term and minimal. Other losses, however, are felt very deeply and can affect us for a lifetime. How people respond to their losses and how they allow those losses to affect them can make a lasting difference in their lives.

Whenever loss occurs, it is important for us to see it in the correct perspective so that we can understand the full impact of what has happened. We must identify how the loss will impact our current life, as well as the effect the loss will have on our thoughts and actions in the future. Let me give you a couple of examples here:

- *October 1982* ... my thirty-six year old healthy and strong husband was killed without a moment's notice. At that time in my life, *after years of deep religious confusion,* I had no desire to turn to God for help. I was so angry, so alone, so empty, and yet so determined that no one would ever see the depth of my pain. *How I was handling my loss began to cause me to grow even more cold and bitter – not better.*
- *May 1984* ... my only child, a fourteen-year old daughter, was killed without a moment's notice. After two miscarriages, and months of not knowing whether my child would be born alive or dead, I finally had a beautiful little "miracle" to call my very own. Susan was so healthy, so beautiful, so strong, and so loved. Then in one moment of time she was lost to me forever.

  The pain of this loss was so deep and so over-whelming that I couldn't breath, I couldn't sleep, and yet I buried it very deep inside and sought no help from anyone ... *certainly not from God.* Not even contemplating suicide, *just desperately needing to end the pain in order to finally get some sleep,* I came within a breath of taking my own life.

  The *loss of my daughter* made the *walls of steel* that I had erected around my heart's emotions become even thicker and the *deep anger and coldness* even stronger. I need to add here that while I wanted no part of God at this point in my life ... *only His Love and Supernatural Intervention is responsible for my still being here today.*

- *September 1999 ...* my little mother, Jewell Mahurin, left her pain and suffering behind to go home to be with Jesus. By this time, I did have a deep and personal relationship with Jesus Christ, and so I was able to handle this loss far differently than my losses of the past.

  My Bestest Friend and Ultimate Healer walked every step of the way with me through this *"Season of Grief"*, and what a difference *His Presence* made in my life. While I do still miss Mama, *whenever I think of her*, it is with feelings of peace, joy, and the happiness of knowing that I will be with her again one day for Eternity.

- *January 2005 ...* Carl, *my big brother and last close family tie*, drew his final painful breath and went home to be with his Sweet Jesus. My heart was heavy with his passing as I knew that I would miss him very much, but my heart was also very light with the *knowing* that he would suffer no more and that we would be together again when my journey *(or as Carl put it in our last conversation – when my job on earth)* is finished.

Loss is not the enemy, but avoiding or ignoring the loss is. Trying to avoid a loss by hiding the feelings will only cause problems in other areas ... *emotionally, spiritually, or physically.* Dealing with the loss in a healthy manner can be a major avenue to growth and life-transforming change. With each loss comes the potential for growth, insight, and understanding. Since these results are not immediate, people often fail to see these future blessings.

We live in a society where everything is geared towards *"instant gratification"*. When people suffer a deep loss, they often want to rush through it and move forward. Moving on with our life is important and a critical part of the healing process. However, when we try to *move forward* by *running away* from the pain in an attempt to *escape the pain* of the loss, we are not truly *moving forward*. In order to *move on* with our life in a healthy manner ... *we will have to work our way through the stages of grief.*

We will all *experience grief* at some time in our life. The word *"grief"* is derived from a Latin verb meaning *"to burden"*. To *"mourn"* is defined as *"to feel and express sorrow"*. Mourning is the expression of grief.

Grieving is like entering the valley of shadows. Grief is not fun. It is very painful ... *life-changing painful.* Grieving is hard work. It is a lingering process ... *often taking one to three years for significant losses.* I strongly urge someone who is caught up in grief *(any traumatic loss)* to please take the time necessary to work through the *grieving process* before making any decisions that will dramatically change the fundamental foundation of their life.

When *grieving,* our natural instinct is to *run* from anything and everything that is a constant reminder of *our loss.* You can't run away from the pain or the memories ... *they will follow you wherever you go.* Once you reach where you are going, *emotionally or physically,* you will find that all you have done by *running away* is to create a whole new set of problems.

In order to *heal from the loss in a healthy way*, we must *face the loss* and *work through the loss* in order to truly *be free of the loss* in order to *move forward* with our life. In order to heal we must deal with all kinds of loss in a healthy manner. A multitude of emotions are involved in the *grieving process.* Many of these emotions seem to conflict with one another.

- *Here are some of the emotions of grief:* anger, blaming yourself, blaming another person, blaming God, blaming the deceased, crying spells, dizziness, diarrhea, headaches, insomnia, fast heartbeat, a lump in your throat, a feeling that everything around you is unreal, hyperventilating, sighing and yawning, nausea, disorganization, lack of focus, loss of appetite or overwhelming desires to constantly eat, restlessness, irritability, sadness, deep discouragement, depression, shortness of breath, seeing images of the dead person, exhaustion, trouble concentrating, fear, love, hate, self-pity, emptiness, overwhelming helplessness, etc.

Don't beat yourself up for having many of these emotions. When people grieve, they experience their loss ... *psychologically* through feelings, thoughts, and attitudes; *socially* as they interact with others; *physically* as it affects their health.

- Grief encompasses a number of changes. It appears differently at various times, and it comes and goes in people's lives.
- Grieving is a normal, predictable, expected, and healthy reaction to a loss.
- Grief is each individual's *personal experience* and *manner of dealing* with any kind of loss no matter how minor or how severe the loss may appear to others.

Grief is not just an event – Grief is a process. Grief has *several stages*, although they are not necessarily experienced in exact order, nor does *one stage* have to be completed before a person moves on to the *next stage*. Let's walk through some of the *"stages of grief"*:

- The *first stage* is *denial* or *shock*. Intellectually, the bereaved may comprehend what has happened, but their emotions may not experience the pain yet. They may feel numb.

- The *second stage* is when the bereaved can *release their emotions*. They often release these emotions in the form of anger towards others, towards the deceased, towards themselves, or towards God. Grieving people become preoccupied with memories of what has been lost and they may withdraw for awhile.

- The *third stage* involves *wrestling with feelings of guilt and anger*. People who are grieving will beat themselves up emotionally as they blame themselves for not somehow preventing the loss. They feel disorganized and don't know how to move on with their life. Very often some *level of depression* may set in as the grieving person becomes more apathetic toward life as a result of their loss.

- The *fourth stage* is *acceptance of the loss*. Reorganizing their lives, filling new roles, and reconnecting with those around them are all healthy and important facets of the healing process.

- The *fifth stage* is *reconciliation of grief*. The balance of life returns little by little ... *much the same as when healing from a physical wound*. There are no set timeframes for healing from grief as each individual is different and unique.

- The *sixth stage* is *hope*. The sharp, ever present pain of grief will lessen and hope for a continued – *albeit different* – life will begin to emerge. Plans are made for the future and the individual is able to move forward in life with good feelings knowing that they will always remember and have memories of the loved one.

A *key part of the grieving process* is to have true friends who will stay with you and support you emotionally. But well-meaning friends and loved ones should never make the *grieving process* even more difficult by trying to impose their own ideas and concepts of recovery onto the *grief-stricken* person.

It is very important for friends and loved ones to allow the *grieving person* to experience all of the different intense emotions of the *grieving process.* By allowing the person to work through the emotions of the *grieving process*, friends can help the person who has experienced the loss to reorganize and to reconnect with the world.

Grieving is difficult work. Here are some suggestions to help you, *or someone you love,* to navigate – in a healthy manner – the journey through grief:

- *Take time* ... don't allow others to rush you into *"getting over"* your feelings.
- *Don't make major decisions* ... the time of grief is a time of instability, and a grieving person is not in any frame of mind to make major or long-term decisions.
- *Medications or Alcohol* ... while the grieving person may need for their doctor to prescribe a short-term medication to enable the person to sleep or to even function, please avoid the temptation to use alcohol or drugs to numb the painful feelings on an ongoing basis. In order to walk through the *stages of grief* to enable you to recover from the loss in order to move on with a healthy life ... *you will have to feel the emotions of grieving to truly recover.*
- *Cry* ... tears are the healthiest expression of grief. Don't try to hold back crying for the sake of others.
- *Acceptance* ... know that there will be good days and there will be bad days. Pangs of intense grief can

resurface or intensify during holidays or other significant events such as birthdays and anniversaries.

For instance, my daughter was buried on my thirty-fourth birthday. Since we had always made birthdays a big deal for celebration, my birthday now carries with it the memory of the very last time on earth that I will ever see my child's face. So the Month of May is a hard one for me because of my birthday and Mother's Day.

I still miss my child and I still miss being able to pick up the phone and talking with Mother. Knowing this, I make sure to stay busy during this time each year and to be around people whom I love and enjoy. There are moments that the presence of my daughter becomes very real to me. *For just a moment in time I am taken back into another moment in time.* However, because I have healed from my loss, I don't revert back into the dark depths of the grief.

- *Remember the loved one often and as much as you need to* ... look at photographs, read old letters, and retell your memories to friends and loved ones as often as you feel the need to talk about your loved one. Don't try to swallow back the pain or the tears for the sake of anyone else. Do whatever you need to do to take care of YOU.

- *Spend time with people who will understand your need to talk about what happened* ... people who have gone through the *grieving process* themselves will allow you to just be yourself. They will really listen to your remembrances. They will just *be there* as they *allow* you to take all of the time you need to *work through* the *stages of grief.*

  It helps for *grieving people* to have true friends who will stay with them and support them emotionally. It is important for these friends to allow the *grieving person* to experience all of the different intense emotions of the *grieving process.* Such friendships will ultimately help the person who has experienced the loss to reorganize and to reconnect with the world.

I want to share a little piece of my life here as I walked through the *season of grief* following the sudden deaths of my young husband and daughter. You can read much more about this time in my life in my book entitled, "A House Divided".

You see, I wasn't in a personal relationship with Jesus Christ at the time. I wanted no part of God. In fact, I was terrified of Him. I presented a persona to the world around me of being a strong and independent woman who was capable of handling anything that life threw my way. Inside, I was a lost and scared little girl ... *running, running, running,* in a misguided attempt to escape my pain.

Yet, *even in my running*, it was only the mercy and the unconditional love of a Heavenly Father who sustained me during this time ... the same mercy and love that was using the circumstances of my life to lead me to a place where I was willing to ask Him to change my heart and my life.

During the time immediately following the death of my daughter, an older lady who worked with me suddenly lost her husband to cancer. She was absolutely devastated. As far as I know, she and her husband weren't in a personal relationship with God. At that time, neither was I. One day this woman came to me to ask this question, *"You have been through this kind of loss twice in just a few months of time. You have to tell me what to do to make it through this pain."*

216

I wish I had known back then how to lead her into the healing love and restoration of Jesus Christ, but at that time all I could do was to talk to her about my own loss. Doing so helped her because ONLY after we have *"walked a mile in the shoes of the kind of pain the other person is feeling"* can we truly know how they feel and be able to empathize with them.

I say to the friends of a grieving person ... *stand with them, love them, and allow them all the time they need to work their way through the many stages of grief.* Please do not lay well-meaning, *and even religious*, platitudes on them. They are truly suffering and they are truly scared ... *don't add to their pain by making them feel guilty because they can't live up to your expectations of them.*

- *Allow yourself time to heal* ... this is very critical in the *healing process* for many reasons. You must pay special attention to your overall health. Make sure you are getting enough sleep. Eat a healthy well-balanced diet. Get outside in the sunshine for exercise or a mild walk. Without proper rest, nutrition, and exercise ... *your grieving process will lead you into a very dark valley of depression over time.* You must take care of your health in order to work through the *stages of grief* in a positive way.

    Most likely all you will feel like doing is to crawl into bed, pull the covers up over your head, and wish the outside world would just go away. Don't give in to those destructive urges. You have to allow yourself to move through the pain in order to recover from your loss. Recovery takes time and work.

- *Ask for what you need from others* ... don't try to be so strong and independent now. You need to allow yourself to lean upon others. Accept whatever help your friends or loved ones offer. And don't hesitate to ask for any kind of help you need ... *even if it is just to have someone stay in your home with you for awhile.* I don't care how strong you may think you are, now is not the time to try and do everything for yourself or by yourself.

- *Seek out Grief Counseling if you feel that you can not cope alone* ... facing the need for counseling is not a sign of weakness but rather a sign of great strength. Grief Counseling is available through community resources, churches, and therapists. Join a Grief Support Group ... *local community papers often has these types of listings.* Use the internet and join an electronic bulletin board dedicated to supporting individuals who have lost loved ones. However, I must urge anyone doing so ... *don't allow the internet to become the only source of help that you seek* – you need the personal interaction with people whom you can see and touch as well as hear in order to truly heal and to be able to move forward with your life.

- *Remember that your grief is individual to you* ... not everyone's grief is identical to yours. You will share some similarities with others, but *grieving* is a very *personal* and a very *individual* process.

- *Don't allow your "season of grief" to turn into a "lifetime of self-pity"* ... sometimes as badly as it hurts, we grow to "need" the pain. Instead of leaning on others for a period of letting go and recovery, we turn others into a crutch for our weakness. Life is all about seasons ... *we all have to find the inner strength to move through the grieving process so we can pick up our life once more.*

HOW DOES THE BIBLE DEAL WITH GRIEF?

The Bible has much to say about both loss and grief. People who experience loss, *as well as those who come alongside them*, can gain wisdom with knowledge to help them move through the *grieving process*.

- **Psalm 23:4 ...** *"Yea, though I walk through the valley of the shadow of death, I will fear no evil; for You are with me; Your rod and Your staff, they comfort me."*

We have a loving and merciful Heavenly Father who comforts those who must walk through the *"valley of the shadow of death"*, and each of us will make this walk in our lifetime. But rest in this truth ... *during the darkest hours of mourning, God will never abandon His Children.*

Isaiah Chapter 53 describes the suffering of our Savior. He experienced *loss* and *grief* so that He could understand our humanity and die in our place. Isaiah's words communicate the suffering of the ONE who loved us and died for us. JESUS received God's punishment for our sin so that we could have peace with God. **Jesus was despised and rejected.** *"A Man of sorrows and acquainted with grief ... He was wounded for our transgressions, He was bruised for our iniquities; the chastisement for our peace was upon Him, and by His stripes we are healed."*

During 1992 and 1993, while living in Houston, I came into a desperate place with my life ... *physically, professionally, financially, emotionally, and even spiritually.* As a result of a serious throat condition, I grew very weak and very ill. I lost my job which was my only practical source of income. One day in silent desperation, I cried out to God that *if only* there was *someone* who had gone through all of the things I had gone through that I could talk to. I just needed someone who could truly understand my pain because they, *too*, had been where I was.

I needed to talk with someone who had also suffered the betrayal of abuse, someone who had lived in an environment of deep religious confusion, someone who had lived through the betrayal and devastation of a bad marriage and bitter divorce, someone who had finally learned to allow themselves to love and to trust in marriage again – only to have a spouse ripped from their life in death, someone who had lived through miscarriages and a difficult pregnancy to give birth to a beautiful and healthy child – only to have that child taken from her by a sudden and merciless death, someone who had *"pulled themselves up by the bootstraps"* time and time again to regain professional and financial security – only to lose it all once again through no fault of their own. *If only I had someone who could understand my loss, my fear, and my grief.* God was about to answer my cry.

That very evening God gave me a *Vision* with a *Message* that I will never forget, and a *Hope* that has sustained me so many times since. As I was sitting in illness and desperation in my apartment later that same day, the *Presence of God* paid me a visit. I heard a *loud swooshing sound* like a mighty rushing wind, and into the center of my living-room stood a *very large tree trunk*. Swirling all about this *tree trunk* was a *heavy vibrating mist*.

Out of *this mist* I heard a voice, and that *voice* was telling me that there was SOMEONE who had suffered all that I had suffered, and much more. That *HE* had lost all that I had ever lost, and more. This was my *HEAVENLY FATHER* who loved me more than I could ever begin to realize or understand. That I could always talk to a *FRIEND* who would understand … *I could always talk to HIM about anything and everything*. He told me to put my hand in His Hand and He would lead me through all things on this earth to Eternal Peace in His Kingdom one day. Then with another *loud swoosh* the *Vision* was gone, but … the *Truth* and the *Peace of God* still sustains me to this very day.

There are many other times that God used *Supernatural Intervention* in my life and in the lives of others, and you can be strengthened by His Message Of Love in my book entitled, "Angels, Visions & Dreams, Prophecies".

Although loss and grief are common, no amount of technology or experience can make the *grieving process* any easier. The *hard news* is that the *only road* to *true healing* is *through* the *grief.* The *good news* is that we don't have to take *this journey* alone ... *God travels the road with us.* It is natural to feel sad and to mourn the death of a loved one. We deeply miss the close relationship we had with that person. But in our times of sorrow, we can let Jesus hold us close in His compassionate arms ... *knowing that He truly understands our pain.*

The Bible is filled with people who suffered grief. People like you and me ... *people touched by tragedy.* How they chose to respond to the grief is instructive for us because God wants us to know that it is all right to grieve. King David was losing a child and he grieved. He wept bitter tears. He poured his heart out before God on the sacred soil of sorrow. Yes, the Bible affirms the *need to grieve* and *to express sorrow.*

- **Isaiah 61:1 ... *"He has sent me to bind up the broken hearted."* The God of the Bible is the God of the broken-hearted! One of the meanings for the Hebrew word *"bind"* from this Passage of Scripture is *"to wrap around".***

If you are in a *season of heart-breaking grief,* ask Jesus Christ to wrap His pierced hands around your broken heart and allow Him to share in your sufferings. Climb up into the lap of your Heavenly Father and let Him wrap His loving arms around you while you cry your broken heart and broken dreams out onto the bosom of God. You are His Child ... *He loves you and understands you better than anyone else ever will.*

David was called *"a man after God's own heart",* and yet David greatly sinned. David confessed his sin, cried out in repentance, and received forgiveness through the Mercy of God. Don't allow guilt and your own feelings of inadequacy to stop you from seeking the mercy, the forgiveness, the love, and the restoration of your Heavenly Father. David grieved deeply and he turned to God and God's Word for his source of comfort. Friends and loved ones can help, but only the Love of Christ can truly deliver us and restore us in the end.

Grief comes to all of us. How many times have we said, or heard someone say, *"I just can't believe that this could happen to me?"* Grief comes uninvited and is never in a hurry to leave. To some measure, it will occupy a room in our heart for a very long time. We are never the same after tragedy strikes ... *we move through it, but we don't completely get over it.* As individuals, our respective *seasons of grief* will change us for a lifetime. How we *choose to deal with the loss and the grief* will determine the quality of our life and our relationships for the rest of our lives.

The Bible doesn't shy away from the *reality of grief.* It recognizes what people go through when they lose a spouse, a child, a sibling, a parent, or a close friend who dies before we have a chance to say goodbye. At this point, I want to spend a moment with discussing how we choose to handle our grief and the consequences of our choice. First, I would like to look at the *choices* of *two women* in the Bible who suffered great loss and *chose* very different paths in dealing with their grief ... Ruth *versus* the wife of Job.

Everyone grieves. The question is, *"Will we choose to allow the grief to paralyze our lives?"* The **Book of Ruth** is a primer on *handling grief.* It shows that God's compassion and our faithful friends can give us the courage to meet grief head-on. Ruth's life is a great encouragement to those whose souls are bent low by the grief of the past and the seeming hopelessness of the future. **Just hold on to these words from Psalms 30:5 ...** *"Weeping may endure for the night, but joy comes in the morning."*

But how did the wife of Job respond to loss and grief? **Job 2:9 ...** *Then his wife said to him, "Do you still hold fast to your integrity? Curse God and die!"* Shattered by the loss of her children and her wealth, Job's wife was overwhelmed with grief and anger. As her husband agonized with the additional pain of boils all over his body, his wife lashed out at Job and at his God.

Such is the common reaction to suffering of those with no faith or awareness of God's higher purposes. While intense suffering can blind even the strongest believer to God's love and faithfulness ... *this blindness should only be temporary.* Anger that is directed at God in our loss, *over the long-term,* displays an unwillingness to trust in His higher purposes. Anger towards God for our loss over a prolonged period of time ... *denies both the sovereignty and the mercy of God.*

Satan – *the author of pain, suffering, loss, and grief* – hopes to use these weapons to turn people away from the love of God. With Ruth and Job, Satan's plan didn't work. With Job's wife, however, it did.

Once I accepted Jesus Christ as my Lord and Savior, my thinking began to change. I began to realize that my life was in God's Hands, *as were the lives of those whom I had loved and lost,* and while the suffering was no less intense – the outcome began to be different. I began to let go of the pain and the grief and to allow myself to be filled with the goodness and mercy of the Lord ... *I began to truly heal.*

Instead of my old anger that caused me to lash out at my mother for trying to help me to understand that God loved me and that He wanted to help me through my deep loss, I started to accept God's Plans for my life and His Plans for my loved ones. In short ... *I pressed into the healing power of my Heavenly Father instead of falling deeper and deeper into a world of darkness and lost hope.* I have learned that in the midst of our brokenness, *God who is always with us,* joins in our pain and sorrow … *showing that His Heart is for each and every one of us.*

Still we wonder what the point of it all is for. GOD KNOWS GRIEF. **It is said of Jesus that He was** *"a man of sorrow and familiar with suffering".* When we are walking through our own *"Season Of Grief"*, we need someone who is familiar with our suffering. We need someone who has passed through this door and come out on the other side.

Still the question gnaws at us … *"If God is so familiar with the horror of human suffering, why doesn't He spare us from having to go through so much of it in our lives?"* I have often had people, *even friends and family,* ask me, *"Why would a loving God give you Susan in spite of medical impossibilities that should have stopped you from ever giving birth to a healthy child, only to allow her to be taken from you for no apparent reason?"*

Believe me, I asked myself and God that question many times both *before* and *after* becoming a Christian! But now I also know that only God could have known that my love to care for and to protect my daughter would be the only thing from which I drew the strength to survive many obstacles in our lives back then.

Furthermore, only a Loving God could have known that years after Susan's death, *it would be a Supernatural Intervention by way of a Vision of Susan,* which had the power to cut through the *walls of steel* around my emotions to allow me to finally come to know the healing restorative love of my Heavenly Father. Do I miss my daughter and sometimes wonder what might have been? *You bet I do!* Have I ever wished that God had spared me the pain of her loss by denying me the joy of her miracle birth in the first place? *NEVER!*

Many questions will never be completely answered in our journey through this life on earth. Sometimes we just have to *choose* to totally trust in God and in His Plan for our lives without all of our questions being answered. To lean into our relationship with Christ Jesus much as a little child leans into their relationship with a father or mother. In child-like simplistic faith that God, *Our Heavenly Father*, loves us and will always take care of us.

And yet, *according to Scripture*, grief is not entirely negative. It gives us a heart of wisdom. It deposits a spiritual and emotional understanding that is not found on the outskirts of human existence, but at the very center of what it really means to be alive.

Suffering is unavoidable and inescapable. Everyone will know suffering as it is part of being human – of being alive. The **Story of Job** reveals a source of suffering, people's powerlessness in suffering, and ultimately God's Power through the suffering. Job knew great loss and Job knew deep grief. *Job knew unbelievable suffering, but Job later also knew incredible healing and restoration.*

- **Job 3: 23–26 ...** *"Why is life given to a man whose way is hidden, whom God has hedged in? For sighing comes to me instead of food; my groans pour out like water. What I feared has come upon me; what I dreaded has happened to me. I have no peace, no quietness; I have no rest, but only turmoil."*

Job was a Godly man. Through it all, *although he did not understand the "whys" of his loss and suffering,* Job never turned against God.

- **Job 2:10 ...** *But he said to her, "You speak as one of the foolish women speaks. Shall we indeed accept good from God, and shall we not accept adversity?" In all this, Job did not sin with his lips.*

225

God doesn't always explain things to us. Why would a Child-of-God be cut off with no explanation? What good could possibly come of this? What kind of testimony to the *goodness and mercy of God* will this be? One lesson I have learned through my personal losses and deep suffering is to have *unconditional faith* in the Plans that God has for my life. My prayer is that I will know God's Presence ... *even when I do not understand His Ways.*

Suffering is not necessarily a punishment for a believer. Don't get caught up in trying to figure out the *"why"* of your loss – don't choose to look at the plenty of very bad people who live a long life and seem to never suffer at all. *In His Perfect Timing, God will set all things right.* Don't drag out your *season of grieving* by trying to figure out all of the *"whys"*, by staying angry at what Satan tries to convince you is the injustice of God ... *instead we need to lay hold of the WHO.* No matter what happens to us, *no matter what the depth of our loss*, God's hand is still stretched out to us in healing and restoration.

Job didn't know that God had agreed to allow Satan to test him because Satan was convinced that Job loved God because God had so richly blessed him. Job's wife urged him to curse God and die. Job's friends kept telling him that it was his own sins that had caused God to turn away from him. And while Job could not understand why God was allowing everything in his life, *including his health and family,* to be ripped away ... *Job still chose to trust in God.*

The Bible does not promise the absence of grief – only the Presence of God. After Job had suffered loss and grief to a seemingly unbearable point ... *God entered the discussion.* God does not explain to Job his sufferings nor does He help him to make sense of his loss. Instead, God underlined the reality of His Sovereignty, and the fact that He acts on His own without human advice or explanation. God expects

His people to trust Him and His goodness regardless of what happens.

- **Romans 8: 38&39 ...** *"For I am persuaded that neither death nor life, nor angels nor principalities nor powers, nor things present nor things to come, nor height or depth, nor any other created thing, shall be able to separate us from the love of God which is in Christ Jesus our Lord."*

The **Book of Job** shows us that our love for God must not be conditioned upon how we think He is treating us. Great suffering *well-borne* is an indication of unshakable trust in God. Faith in God must be maintained through times of trial as well as times of blessing. Such faith reflects God's nature in us, His redeeming Power in Christ, and His unconditional love toward us for all seasons. No matter what we face in life, *including death and grief*, we can trust that God is in control. We must rely on Him and His goodness.

GOD GROANS ... suffering is not merely earthly and human – it is also divine. **Paul described it this way in Romans 8:26 ...** *"Likewise the Spirit also helps us in our weakness. For we do not know what we should pray for as we ought, but the Spirit Himself makes intercession for us with groanings which cannot be uttered".*

Other religions can not fathom the concept of an all-powerful God suffering on behalf of His people ... *suffering when they suffer – feeling their pain.* God came to earth in the person of Jesus Christ in order to understand humanity and, *ultimately*, to die an agonizing death for us. God's suffering reveals the Path to Glory. Jesus bore the full and complete penalty of sin and suffered judgment so that God's children would never be separated from His love. Jesus' suffering became the Blood Offering for sin that cleanses and heals. It is the redemptive Power of Suffering that allows us to glimpse an incredibly small taste of what Jesus suffered on the Cross while bearing our sins. It also strips us of the illusion of autonomy and the deceit of self-righteousness.

Despite its painfulness, suffering can be very valuable. Suffering clarifies what the heart truly worships, especially when the pain is unexplained and unabated. Do we worship the idea of deliverance ... *or the Deliverer?*

When my brother, Carl, lay suffering month after month and year after year in his hospital bed or his wheelchair ... *what was his attitude?* As the years went by and his walk with his Sweet Jesus deepened, his initial anger and fear changed into Praise and Worship to the Unconditional Love of God that was *using his suffering* to prepare him for a Glorious Eternity with Christ Jesus. He moved from *worshipping the idea of deliverance* to truly *worshipping the Deliverer.* And what a true testimony to his love and faith in the unconditional Love of God he left behind when he left this world to *"go home to be with his Sweet Jesus".*

You see, *in his suffering,* Carl learned that God was *using his suffering* to *purify his heart* by *deepening his desire* for the day when all of his tears would be wiped away. Carl taught me how to quit struggling so much with the *"whys"* and to truly come to rest in the knowledge of the fact that only God knows the Plans that He has for my life ... *"Plans to prosper me and not to harm me. Plans to give me hope and a future".*

When I attended Carl's funeral, I was there to celebrate his life, his faith, and his testimony. Quite a major difference in how I viewed his death than how, *lost and without Christ,* I had faced the deaths of my young husband and daughter years before. And, yes my dear brother, when my job on this earth is done ... *I know that I know that I know that I will walk on those streets of gold with you, and with my daughter, and with my mother, but most of all – with our Sweet Jesus!*

Our growing discontent with the sin and evil in this world increases our hopefulness for heaven. Suffering not only clarifies and purifies, but it also motivates the heart to action.

- If we see a child cry ... *we offer tenderness.*
- If we see the wounds of a victim ... *we offer solace.*
- If we see the grief of another ... *we offer comfort.*

God never wastes a wound. In times of trouble and difficulty, people long for comfort. Through Christ, we learn the ability to empathize with others who are suffering, and we learn firsthand the comforting Power of God. Only then can we come alongside the sufferer ... *knowing exactly what they need.* We can also assure them of God's comfort for we have experienced it for ourselves.

- **2 Corinthians 1: 3–5 ... God comforts us so that** *"we may be able to comfort those who are in any trouble, with the comfort with which we ourselves are comforted by God".*

Human sufferings arouse anger, invigorate action, and as a result ... allows us to be used to push back *some of the darkness.* Suffering humanizes the heart and increases our hunger for God. In his suffering, Job found that his deepest desire was not for relief, restitution of his losses, or a return of his reputation. Job found what he wanted more than anything in the midst of his suffering was the Presence of God. Suffering awakened him to a deeper desire for God. This is the same thing that my brother, Carl, learned in his long period of suffering. It is also what I have been learning through my *personal seasons* of struggle and grief.

What a glorious picture of the Body of Believers ... *comforting one another as difficult times arise.* When facing difficulty, we should trust God and rest in His compassionate arms. Only then will we be ready to offer compassion to those in need.

If you are suffering due to a great loss, give yourself time to grieve. If you are trying to comfort someone who has just experienced a great loss, allow them the time they need to grieve. Grieving takes time, and each person's timetable for healing is different. I found, *through great personal loss*, that each loss is unique and different. Each loss will take a different timetable to grieve and to heal. All loss is not the same loss. All grief is not the same grief.

How long will it take for the words, *"Go on with your life"*, to drift through your consciousness? Lots of time ... *years maybe*. Society, and well-meaning friends and loved ones, want you to get over it and to get on with your life. Just *lean on God* because He understands the *grieving process* and the *timetable* needed for *you* to heal. Consider how different our reaction to multiple deep personal losses can be:

- Consider King David and how his grief for his deceased infant child was different than the grief for his grown son, Absalom. He seemingly resolved the grief of one loss rather quickly, while the death of Absalom all but took the life of David.
- My loss of a young husband left me feeling betrayed, angry, embittered, and even guilty for years.
- The loss of my only child left me empty, hopeless, and cold for a very long time.
- The loss of my earthly father left me confused and sad for years.
- The loss of my mother, *my lifetime rock*, left me missing her but at peace with her passing to be with Jesus.
- The loss of my big brother, *my last close family tie*, left me a little lonely but so happy that his body was now

at rest from pain and I know I will be with him once again when my work on this earth is completed.

God understands that even though we may have buried a loved one, we cannot bury our feelings, nor should we attempt to do so. We need time to vent, and to find ways of coping with the loss in our lives. God records in His Word that people in Biblical days were in no hurry to rush through the *process of grief* and neither should we.

Abba Father, I have walked several times through a season of grief. I have learned to place my hand in Your Hand and to lean into Christ Jesus to bring me through to the other side as a wiser and more compassionate person. Lord, use my words here to encourage and to strengthen others who are struggling with loss and grief. Wrap them in Your Loving Arms and protect them as they work through their pain and suffering. Send people into their lives who will truly under-stand their suffering and will simply stand with them as they walk through the grieving process. We know that You love us with an unconditional love that is far beyond human under-standing. Enable us to trust in You, God, and to trust in Your Plans for our lives and the lives of our loved ones. I ask in the Name of Your Son, Jesus Christ, who loved us so much that He willingly gave His very life so that we could not only have Eternal Life with You but also a more abundant life here on this earth. Amen

From my personal *"Seasons of Grief"*, as both a non-believer and as a Christian, I can tell you that one of the most consuming aspects of grieving the loss of a loved one is in the area of regrets ... *the "if onlies"*. *"Give me the flowers while I live"* is so much more than just an old cliché. It is a *truth of living* that will have profound effects upon the *truth* of *dying* and of *grieving*.

231

- One of the devastating memories I have of my husband's funeral was when they started to lower his casket into the grave. I was not a person given to emotional displays. My life had taught me to *"hide my pain"* and to *"swallow my tears"*. However, that day it took six grown men to stop me from throwing myself into the grave after my husband. I knew that once the dirt covered the casket I would never see his body again, and I had never told Leonard that I loved him and needed him. Now it was too late. He would never hear me say the words that he so longed to hear.

- When my daughter died, as deeply as I loved her, I was haunted by her often asking me to *"not work so hard so that we could spend more time together"*. I was consumed with a need to provide for my only child all of the *things* that other children had ... *all the things I did not have while growing up*. I spent valuable and irreplaceable time in pursuing the financial means to *"give her things"* rather than spending that time in *"building more precious memories together"*. I thought we would have years to spend a lot of time together. Susan died at fourteen-years of age, and ... *our time "together" as mother and daughter had run out*.

- *Lessons learned from deep personal losses and haunting regrets deeply changed me*. When my mother grew old and ill she was terrified of being put into a nursing home, and she asked me repeatedly not to let that happen to her. So when she became too ill to live alone and to take care of herself, I quit my job in Houston to go back to Missouri to take care of her. It cost me a lot financially and emotionally. While I felt a deep personal loss standing there beside Mother's grave ... *I had no haunting regrets*.

To my dying day, I will thank God for giving me the ability, the opportunity, and the help of my dear friend that made it possible for me to be there for Mama during those months. Thank you, Jackie, for being there for me and for Mom even though doing so was at great sacrifice to you.

- Over the years that Carl spent as an invalid in their Oklahoma home and often in various hospitals ... *I chose to spend what time I could in visiting him and his wife, Jackie.* Likewise, I chose to use part of the financial blessings that God provided me through my job to make their physical and financial life a little easier. At Carl's funeral, while it was another deep personal loss, I had no *haunting regrets* of precious time wasted while he was still alive.

I say all of this about the *lessons I have learned* to urge you to give those whom you love your time, your attention, your help, and your love while they are still alive and able to appreciate it. This poem says it better than I ever could ...

** IF I KNEW **
{Author Unknown}

If I knew it would be the last time
that I'd see you fall asleep,
I would tuck you in more tightly,
and pray the Lord your soul to keep.

If I knew it would be the last time
that I see you walk out the door,
I would give you a hug and kiss
and call you back for one more.

If I knew it would be the last time
I'd hear your voice lifted in praise,
I would videotape each action and word
so I could play them back day after day.

If I knew it would be the last time
I could spare an extra minute
To stop and say, "I love you",
instead of assuming you would know I do.

If I knew it would be the last time
I would be there to share your day,
Well I'm sure you'll have many more,
so I can let just this one slip away.
For surely there's always tomorrow
to make up for the oversight,
And we'll always get a second chance
to make everything just right.
There will always be another day
to say, "I love you",
And certainly there's another chance
to say our, "Anything I can do?"

But just in case I might be wrong
and TODAY is all I get …
I'd like to say how much I love you
and I hope you never forget.

TOMORROW is not promised to anyone,
young or old alike,
And TODAY may be the last chance
you get to hold your loved one tight.

So if you're waiting for TOMORROW –
Why not do it TODAY?

For if tomorrow never comes,
you'll surely regret the day,
That you didn't take that extra time
for a smile, a hug, or a kiss.
And you were too busy to grant someone
What turned out to be their one last wish.

So hold your loved ones close today,
and whisper in their ear ...
Tell them how much you love them,
and that you'll always hold them dear.
Take the time to say, "I'm sorry",
"Please forgive me", or "That's okay".

THEN IF TOMORROW COMES ...

YOU'LL HAVE NO REGRETS ABOUT TODAY!

CHAPTER THIRTEEN

"FINDING HOPE"

Proverbs 13:12 ... *"Hope deferred makes the heart sick, but a longing fulfilled is a tree of life."*

HOPE (*Webster's New World Dictionary*) ... a feeling that what is wanted will happen; desire accompanied by expectation; a reason for hope; a person or thing on which one may base some hope.

HOPE (*The New Unger's Bible Dictionary*) ... in the New Testament the "expectation of good". The original Greek word *elpis* denotes a joyful and contented expectation of eternal salvation. Because of God's manifested salvation in Christ, and because He is the source of all the believer's expectations, He is called the "God of Hope". There are several Hebrew words used in reference to hope in the Old Testament meaning "safety, security, trust, refuge, shelter, deliverance". The believer's fountainhead of hope is the death, burial, and resurrection of Christ. "Christ in you" is the "hope of glory".

We are never without hope no matter how we may feel. We are never beyond the reach of God's grace and the touch of His love ... *no matter how distant these may seem at times.* Even when we are struggling, God brings people into our lives to encourage us and to help us. Then God wants us to use His Blessings by passing on to others tender touches, encouraging words, and expressions of their value to also bless them.

We have been given the privilege of *passing hope* along to others. We *pass hope* by telling others how we love them, how special they are to us, and how valuable they are to the Kingdom of God. We each have the ability to project into others the desire for a positive future by giving them hope and encouragement for their life's journey.

- **2 Corinthians 1: 3&4 ...** *"Blessed be the God and Father of our Lord Jesus Christ, the Father of mercies and God of all comfort, who comforts us in all our tribulation, that we may be able to comfort those who are in any trouble, with the comfort with which we ourselves are comforted by God."*

In times of trouble and difficulty, people long for comfort. God never wastes a wound. Through our suffering, we learn the ability to empathize with others who suffer, and we learn firsthand the comforting power of God. Only then can we come alongside the sufferer, knowing exactly how they feel and what they need from us, because *"we, too, have felt their pain"*. We can also assure them of God's comfort – *for we have experienced His comfort for ourselves.*

God comforts us so that *"we may be able to comfort those who are in any trouble, with the comfort with which we ourselves are comforted by God"*. What a glorious picture of the Body of Believers ... *comforting one another as difficult times arise!* When facing difficulty in our own life, we can trust God and rest in His compassionate arms. Then we will be ready to offer compassion – *to offer real hope* – to those in need.

God gives hope to us, His Children, as well. **Jeremiah 29: 11–13 ...** *"For I know the plans I have for you," saith the Lord, "Plans to prosper you and not to harm you, plans to give you hope and a future. Then you will call upon me and come and pray to me, and I will listen to you. You will seek me and find me when you seek me with all your heart."*

HOPE FOR THE FUTURE. If you are familiar with the prophecies of Jeremiah, you know that most of them were of impending judgment and messages of doom for a nation that had turned its back on God. But Jeremiah could also see beyond the immediate crisis to a day when God would deliver the captives of Judah.

Jeremiah told the people that God would limit their captivity in Babylon to seventy years. And he told them of God's Plans for them after that ... *they would indeed return to their homeland – Jerusalem.* Despite their present captivity and distress, God assured them that He had *"thoughts of peace ... to give them a future and a hope".*

Let's move forward now a few hundred years, and picture this scene. The Lord Jesus has been up all night. He has been scoffed at, lied about, and beaten for unfounded wrongs He was accused of doing. He has been shoved through the dark alleys and paraded through the rocky streets on His way from an unjustifiable and unfair trial to a hill of death in the cruelest possible manner ... death by crucifixion.

If anyone should have been *helpless* and *hopeless* in that circumstance, it would have been Him. But read again the Passages of His Crucifixion and look at the incredible power and *hope* that is found there. No person took Jesus' life ... *He voluntarily and purposefully laid it down for us* – so that we might live with *real hope* on this earth and for eternity!

Instead of hating, **Jesus prayed,** *"Father, forgive them"*, for the very soldiers who nailed Him to the Cross. When He could have been concerned only about the terrible agony He was suffering, He looked down instead at His mother and made arrangements for her to be taken care of. Just like He is right now, *seated at the right hand of His Father – and our Father,* looking down upon us and interceding for us ... *making arrangements for us to be taken care of.*

- As believers, our *hope* is in this Jesus who will never leave us and who will never forsake us no matter what we may be going through. **Matthew 28:20: *"... and lo, I am with you always, even to the end of the age".***

Things happen in this life. Painful separations happen constantly: friends move away, loved ones die, people betray our trust, and so life here on this earth goes. But when we trust Christ Jesus for salvation, nothing can separate us from the love of God. He is always with us. Even death cannot separate us from His love for we will be in God's Presence.

Nothing in life is powerful enough to take God away. Nothing in the unseen, nothing in time, and nothing in this entire vast universe can separate the Children of God from the love of their Heavenly Father. Satan, with all of his demonic forces, cannot tear us out of the Palm of the Hand of God our Father. When we feel alone, scared, or far from God, we must remember and hold on to His Promise ... *that He is with us always – even to the end of the world.*

- **Romans 8: 37–39 ...** *"yet in all these things we are more than conquerors through Him who loved us. For I am persuaded that neither death nor life, nor angels nor principalities nor powers, nor things present nor things to come, nor height nor depth,* *nor any other created thing, shall be able to sepa-rate us from the love of God which is in Christ Jesus our Lord".*

When Jesus cried out from the Cross, *"I thirst"*, it was not just from a parched throat, but was also in fulfillment of a well-known prophecy in the **Psalms** of what the suffering-servant Messiah would do. **Psalms 69:21 ...** *"They also gave me gall for my food, and for my thirst they gave me vinegar to drink."* And finally, Jesus completed His Work with the words *"It is finished"* ... not "I am finished".

Where would such confidence come from on this deadly Friday? From the assurance of a *hope-filled Sunday* three days ahead ... *a day when the Father had promised to raise Him, His Only Begotten Son, from the dead!* Jesus knew that there was no way of avoiding the Cross; no covering it up or hanging anything less on it than a sinless offering. But that knowledge did not make Him *helpless* or *hopeless*. Rather, He loved us so much and was so certain of God's Power to raise Him up from the dead, that He could face Gethsemane and not flinch from completing His Purpose.

Let me ask you this ... *what "Gethsemane" are you facing in your life, and will you place your hope and your trust in God's Power to raise you up and complete His Purpose for your life?* What habits and life-styles are you willing to *sacrifice on the cross* so that you can submit your life – *heart, mind, body, soul* – into the Hands of God, knowing that He will enable you to live your life victorious over death, hell, and the grave ... now and for eternity?

The *hope* that our Lord Jesus had lay beyond the pain in His immediate future; *it* lay within His place in heaven. Therefore, He could face the crown of thorns, the scorn, the horrible execution, and three days in a borrowed tomb ... all because He had *"a future and a hope"* and because of Him – *so do we.*

The next time something happens to make us feel hopeless, *and it will happen,* we need to remember how Jesus responded at His greatest time of need. His appearance before an unjust court was unfair. His being turned over for execution made escape impossible from a human viewpoint. His burial in a tomb left His disciples hopeless. But no matter what happens outside us, *from defamation of character to unfair death,* we can carry *hope inside* because we are under the loving care and guidance of the God of the Resurrection Morning!

While Jesus was born fully man, *He was also fully God,* which is a mystery unfathomable this side of heaven but a reflection of the untold strength He carried within Himself to build up and to bless others. And just think about this ... *the God of unsurpassed strength finds and invests tremendous value in us.* He saved us with His Blood, sealed us with His Holy Spirit, and will stand next to us one day when we approach the Father's Throne! We will never know the full measure of *God's Family Blessing* unless and until we have a *Personal Relationship with Jesus Christ.*

Without the Blessing that comes directly from our Heavenly Father to His Children, even an earthly parental blessing can't quite fill our cup. If you are one of those who didn't receive the *blessing of hope* from your earthly parents, you can get all the *hope* you need from the Heavenly Father by becoming His Child through Christ Jesus.

While it may be popular belief that every person created by God is a Member of God's Family ... this is simply not so. The *Blessing of God* is given only to those who believe in His Son.

- **John 5:24 ... Jesus said, *"Most assuredly, I say to you, he who hears my word and believes in Him who sent me has everlasting life, and shall not come into judgment, but has passed from death unto life."***

In addition to His own Blessing, God provides us with a Spiritual Family ... *other Believers who become like brothers and sisters, and fathers and mothers.* He uses these people to help meet our needs and *to give us hope.* So we need to be willing and eager to ask Him to use us to touch someone else for God ... *bringing hope to an all-too-often hopeless world.*

If you want to be blessed by my personal testimony of the hope and the strength I have found in God, read my book entitled, "Restoring & Rebuilding A HOUSE DIVIDED Healing From Abuse".

Many times I have found great encouragement by reading the story of the woman with the issue of blood found in **Mark 5: 25-34.** Alone, sick, and seemingly without hope, this woman with a *"flow of blood for twelve years"* and who *"had suffered many things from many physicians"* expected to live in pain and as an outcast until she died ... UNTIL SHE CAME TO JESUS!

This woman was not supposed to be in the crowd that day. Because of her condition of constant bleeding, she was in a continual state of uncleanness according to Jewish law. She was not supposed to be out in the public because others might touch her and become unclean themselves.

My friend, do you know how she must have been feeling? I sure do ... *a helpless and hopeless outcast* – alone, unwanted, unloved, and terrified. Have you ever been in a circumstance that made you feel the same way – *totally without hope?* Then do what this woman did ... *come to Jesus.*

When she heard that Jesus was coming to town, she *found hope* because she knew that He could heal her. She merely wanted to touch the hem of His garments, *knowing that if she could do so,* she would be made well. In her condition, *and as one of society's outcasts*, she probably wanted to come and get her healing and go away unnoticed so the crowd would not be angry that she had dared to come amongst them. But her very act of *reaching out to touch Jesus' garments* showed Him the depth of her faith.

Immediately the woman was healed. Jesus knew who had touched Him, of course, but He asked the question, *"Who touched me?"* Since He already knew who had touched Him, why did He ask this question? He asked so the woman could speak up and show her faith to others. **Then Jesus said to the woman, *"Your faith has made you well. Go in peace, and be healed of your affliction".***

What made that woman go against the law – *against all human odds* – to reach Jesus? She went out of her Faith in Him ... *Faith that He could do for her what He had already done for so many others.* Her *hope* was not the kind of hope that says, "Maybe it will happen. I sure hope so". Her *hope* said ... *"I KNOW THAT HE CAN HEAL ME."*

I now challenge you to take a few minutes to read the story for yourself and then apply it to your own life. Put your trust in Jesus and see what a real difference it will make for you in every aspect of your life. *Finding REAL HOPE comes through this kind of faith and determination;* no matter how impossible the circumstances you may be facing. Jesus is waiting to meet us at our greatest point-of-need ... however we come to Him and with whatever problem.

Our *only source of real and lasting hope* is in Him ... *not because we think He will help us, but because we know that He will help us.* Jesus always responds to those who *hope* in Him. No matter how great or how small we may be ... *He will always do far more than we can even begin to imagine!*

CHAPTER FOURTEEN

"GOD'S SIMPLE PLAN OF SALVATION"

To meet all the stresses, demands, and pressures of ordinary life, it takes an extraordinary person. Today so much is tearing at the very fiber of our hearts, competing with our affection for God and for others. The list is endless.

How often do we feel like saying, *"I don't really have anything left at the end of the day; I give, give, give - others take, take, take."* That's a common cry in our society. As a result, we feel empty, exhausted, yet still expecting – still hoping. Yearning for something more in their life; some turn to food, drugs, alcohol, sexual promiscuity, wrong relationships, work, or you can fill in the blank for yourself in your own life. We have seen it, *or lived it*, all before because it is all around us. BUT DO WE DARE LOOK INSIDE?

The truth is that no person, no position, no substance – nothing will meet the deepest longing of our soul. Only ONE can do that, and His Name is JESUS CHRIST. As God's "human" Son, Jesus does understand what you are going through because He has been there. He knows the pain of betrayal and severed relationships: His own disciple, Judas, sold Him for thirty pieces of silver; His own disciple, Peter, denied knowing Him repeatedly; His other disciples, afraid for their own lives, deserted Him; His own Father abandoned Him at His time of greatest need; and you and I – whom He suffered and died for – have ignored Him when we have needed Him the most.

Out of His tremendous love for us ... Jesus came, Jesus died, and Jesus rose again to bring us back to God in order to restore the one key relationship we were always designed to have. Our personal relationship with Jesus Christ is the ONLY RELATIONSHIP that will fill the GOD VOID within each and every one of us.

1. *God's Idea ... Together With Us Forever*: God loves us, and His original idea was for you and me to live in a close relationship with Him now and in heaven forever. Since God planned for us to live with Him forever, why are there so many broken and hurting people in our world? Why is there so much pain?

2. *The Problem ... Sin Gets In The Way*: God did not make us to be robots to mindlessly love and obey Him. Instead, He gave us a brain and freedom of choice. But, like Adam and Eve in the Garden of Eden, we often choose to disobey God and to go our own selfish ways. This choice is called sin and it separates us from God. That's where all of the problems begin. The bottom line is that our sin separates us from God.

3. *God's Answer ... Jesus And The Cross*: the good news is that God has provided the only answer to our problem of being cut off from God. That answer is JESUS CHRIST! Jesus died on the cross and rose from the grave to take the punishment for our sin. That is how He is able to reunite us with God.

4. *Our Part ... Accept Jesus*: it all starts when we accept Jesus Christ by believing His message and trusting in

Him alone to save us. It is like a footbridge crossing a great chasm. Belief in the bridge is one thing, but believing alone won't get you across the chasm. Only if you put your total trust in the bridge and apply your full weight upon it will you reach the other side.

When our broken relationship with God is restored, the path to healing and reconciliation in our own lives is opened. Only God can love you with a perfect love with no conditions attached. Once this love is accepted and understood, your life will be transformed ... made new and reborn.

The reality is that there are no extraordinary people, only ordinary men and women who are trusting in an Extraordinary God. But we can live an extraordinary life, with extraordinary peace during extraordinary circumstances, when we choose to trust JESUS CHRIST as our SAVIOR.

- **Hebrews 7:25 ...** *"He is able ... to save them to the uttermost that come unto God by him, seeing he ever liveth to make intercession for them."* I want to thank you, Jesus, for changing my life. Help me to share with others about the wonderful things you have done.
- **Jeremiah 6:16 ...** *"Stand ye in the ways, and see, and ask for the old paths, where is the good way, and walk therein, and ye shall find rest for your souls."* Thank you, God, for caring about the things of this world that need repair – like my life.
- **Psalm 55:22 ...** *"Cast thy burden upon the Lord, and he shall sustain thee: he shall never suffer the righteous to be moved."* Our trust is in Thee, O God. Let us never give in to discouragement.
- **Psalm 23:4 ...** *"Yea, though I walk through the valley of the shadow of death, I will fear no evil: for thou art with me."* Heavenly Father, when the

darkness comes over us and storms beat around us, shelter us under your wing.

- **Isaiah 65:24 ...** *"And it shall come to pass, that before they call, I will answer; and while they are yet speaking, I will hear."* Before I even prayed, Father, you answered. Thank You!
- **Psalm 145:18 ...** *"The Lord is nigh unto all them that call upon him, to all that call upon him in truth."* Lord, give me grace and strength to persevere and an obedient heart to do your will.

GOD'S SIMPLE PLAN OF SALVATION: I am asking you the most important question of life, and your joy or your sorrow for all eternity depends upon your answer ... ARE YOU SAVED? It is NOT a question of how good you are, nor if you are a church member, but <u>ARE YOU SAVED</u>? Are you sure you will go to Heaven when you die?

- God says in order to go to Heaven ... *you must be born again.* **John 3:7 ... Jesus said to Nicodemus, *"Ye must be born again."***
- First, *my friend,* you must realize you are a sinner. **Romans 3:23 ...** *"For all have sinned, and come short of the glory of God."*
- Because we are all born sinners, *we are condemned to death.* **Romans 6:23 ...** *"For the wages (payment) of sin is death."* This includes eternal separation from God in hell.
- We each will one day face the judgment of God Almighty. **Hebrews 9:27 ...** *"And as it is appointed for men to die once, but after this the judgment."*
- But God loved <u>YOU</u> so much He gave His Only Begotten Son – <u>JESUS</u> – to bear your sin and to die in your place. **2 Corinthians 5:21 ...** *"For He made*

Him who knew no sin to be sin for us, that we might become the righteousness of God in Him."

- Jesus had to shed His Blood and die. **Leviticus 17:11** ... *"For the life of the flesh is in the blood."* **Hebrews 9:22** ... *"And according to the law almost all things are purified with blood, and without shedding of blood is no remission."*
- Although we cannot understand how, God said that my sins and your sins were laid upon Jesus and He died in our place. Jesus became our substitute. It is true because God can not lie. **Romans 5:8** ... *"But God demonstrates His own love towards us, in that while we were yet sinners, Christ died for us."*
- True repentance is a change of mind that agrees with God that one is a sinner, and also agrees with what Jesus did for us on the Cross. **Acts 17: 30&31** ... *"Truly these times of ignorance God overlooked, but now commands all men everywhere to repent, because He has appointed a day on which He will judge the world in righteousness by the Man whom He has ordained. He has given assurance of this to all by raising Him from the dead."*
- **Acts 16: 30&31 ... the Philippian jailer asked Paul and Silas:** *"Sirs, what must I do to be saved?"* **So they said,** *"Believe on the Lord Jesus Christ, and you will be saved, you and your household."*

Can you really know that you are saved? YES! Simply believe on Jesus Christ as the One who bore your sin, died in your place, was buried, and whom God resurrected. His resurrection powerfully assures that the believer can claim everlasting life when Jesus is received as Savior.

- **John 1:12** ... *"But as many as received Him, to them gave He power to become the sons of God, even to them that believe on His name."*
- **Romans 10:13** ... *"For whosoever shall call upon the Name of the Lord shall be saved."* Whosoever includes you! Shall be saved means not maybe, *nor can*, but shall be saved.

Surely, you realize you are a sinner. Right now, wherever you are, repent and lift your heart to God in prayer. What does it mean *"To Repent"*?

- TO REPENT *(Webster's New World Dictionary):* to feel sorry for what one has done or has failed to do; to stop doing what one has been doing and to change one's mind about what one is doing or saying; to feel truly sorry and to ask forgiveness; to be contrite and *repentant.*
- REPENTANCE *(The New Unger's Bible Dictionary):* repentance contains a genuine sorrow toward God for our sins against Him and against others; an actual forsaking of our sins against God and against others; and humble self-surrender to the will and the service of God.

Repentance, it should be observed, *has different stages of development. Repentance* is the *Gift of God* made possible thru the *willing sacrifice of the Blood that Jesus shed for the sins of mankind.* Repentance and Salvation are a Gift from God through Christ Jesus ... *but the great decision of what we will do with this "gift" is up to each one of us as individuals.*

The first step in our *recovery process* is repentance. Genuine repentance involves several things. First of all, it involves confession. Confession acknowledges guilt. Not just, "Lord, I am sorry for my mistake," but *"Lord, I have sinned against you."* Repentance involves the recognition that the sin was against God. Repentance requires total honesty with God. We won't always be holy, but we can always be honest.

I believe God is looking for us to be honest about our sin … *honest about our weaknesses, our failures, our mistakes, and our frustrations.* Honesty promotes fellowship with God and in our relationships with others. As long as we continue to be open and honest with God, He can continue to work with us, even after we have committed our most grievous sin.

Do you want to be free of your past? Do you want to know the peace of Jesus in your life today right here in our crazy, mixed-up society? Do you want the assurance of an eternity with Jesus after your journey on this earth is finished? Don't fool yourself by thinking that your sins will be ignored. Confess your sins today and enjoy the freedom and the inner peace that God wants for you all the days of your life. **In Luke 18:13 the sinner prayed,** *"God be merciful to me a sinner."* Just pray …

Father God, I know I am a sinner. I believe Jesus was my substitute when He died on the Cross. I believe He shed blood, death, burial, and resurrection for me. I now receive Him as my Savior. I thank you, Father God, for the forgiveness of my sins, the gift of salvation, and everlasting life. I ask you to send the Holy Spirit to live within my heart from this day forward, and to help me to change those things in my life that are sinful. Help me to live each day in a way that is pleasing to you. I pray this in Jesus' Name and I believe I am saved. Amen

SALVATION RECEIVED! When we pray from our heart, God will hear our prayer, forgive our sins, and give us the Gift of Eternal Salvation.

The Hebrew term for "*salvation*" in the Old Testament is *yeshu'ah*, describing deliverance from distress as well as the state of well-being that results from being delivered. The New Testament uses the Greek word *soteria*, a term that includes not just deliverance but God's forgiveness of sins.

The Bible explains that *salvation* is based upon God's grace and accomplished by Christ's sacrificial death for sin. *Salvation* includes *justification - the act of being declared just or righteous by God;* and *redemption - being freed by the payment of Christ's blood for sin.*

SALVATION IS A GIFT OF GOD'S GRACE. We don't deserve it and we can't earn it. It must be received as a gift. As incredible as it sounds ... *Salvation is the Gift of God!* It can only be received by *faith.* When we believe that Jesus died for *our sin* and in *our place*, we can only respond in love and in gratitude.

The invitation of Scripture is clear. **Romans 10:13 says, "Whoever calls on the name of the Lord shall be saved."** So, what is *belief*, as defined by God? To be *saved*, people must *believe* in Jesus as Savior and Lord, but what exactly does that mean?

It isn't enough to say that we believe in God – even the demons believe that much. **James 2:19 ... "You believe that there is one God. You do well. Even the demons believe – and tremble!"**

It is not enough to believe that Jesus lived as some great teacher or miracle worker. *True belief* begins in the heart as the Holy Spirit opens a person to the *truth* of the *gospel message* that *God sent His Son, Jesus, who died for our sins and rose again.* Those who believe in Jesus simply move beyond intellectual assent that He lived to heartfelt gratitude that He cares for them personally.

Belief then reveals itself in actions. People who believe in what Christ has done for them will desire to live for Him. If we *confess with our mouths* that Jesus is Lord, and *believe in our hearts* that God raised Him from the dead ... *we will be saved.*

Take God at His Word and claim His Salvation by Faith. *Believe, and you will be saved.* No church, no denomination, and no good works can save you. Remember, it is God who does the saving ... ALL OF IT!

Charles Swindoll in "The Grace Awakening" talks about salvation in a simple and true manner. God's Word backs up his teachings all the way ... *there is no wage relationship with God. Spiritually speaking, you and I haven't earned anything but death. Everyone who hopes to be eternally justified must come to God the same way, on the basis of grace. It is a gift that comes to us absolutely free. Any other view of salvation, based on the Truth of God's Word, is heresy – plain and simple.*

We are justified by faith – not works. And having been justified by faith, we get the one thing we have always longed for – Peace with God. It is through Jesus Christ our Lord who paid the absolute and final payment for sin when He died in our place on the Cross. Sin against God required the payment of death. And Jesus Christ, the perfect Substitute, made the ultimate once and for all time payment on our behalf. Our salvation cost Jesus His very life. As a result, God gives the free gift of salvation to all who believe in His Son and accept Him as their Lord and Savior. JESUS LOVES EACH ONE OF US SO MUCH HE WAS WILLING TO DIE FOR US!

God's Simple Plan of Salvation ... *you are a sinner.* Therefore, unless you believe on Jesus Christ <u>WHO</u> died in your place, you will spend eternity in hell. If you believe on Him as your crucified, buried, and risen Savior, you receive forgiveness for all of your sins and His Gift of Eternal Salvation by Faith.

You say, *"Surely, it cannot be that simple."* YES – That Simple! It is Scriptural. It is God's Plan. My friend, believe on Jesus and receive Him as your Savior today. Your soul is worth more than the entire world. **Mark 8:36 ...** *"For what shall it profit a man, if he shall gain the whole world and lose his own soul?"* Be sure that you are saved. If you lose your soul, you will miss Heaven and you will lose all.

Please! Let God save you this very moment. Not only do we, *as Born Again Children of God,* have the assurance of eternity with Jesus Christ, but He will also lead you out of the sin and destruction your life is facing now to give you an abundant life here on this earth. HE will be the one friend who will never leave you nor forsake you ... the ONE PERSON who will never lie to you, betray you, or stop loving you. God's Power will save you, keep you saved, and enable you to live a victorious Christian life in Christ Jesus.

- **1 Corinthians 10:13 ...** *"There hath no temptation taken you but such as is common to man: but God is faithful, Who will not suffer you to be tempted (or tested) beyond what you can bear, but will always make a way of escape that you may be able to bear it."*

What Have You Got To Lose By Choosing Christ Jesus As Your Lord and Savior? You will *lose* the overwhelming fear and anxiety, you will be lifted out of the discouragement and/or depression, you will be forgiven and set free from years of guilt, and you will never have to walk all alone again.

What Have You Got To Gain By Choosing To Live Your Life For Christ Jesus? Eternity in Heaven with God *versus* Eternity in Hell with Satan. There is a HEAVEN, there is a HELL, and ETERNITY never ends! You, *my friend,* will spend your eternity in one place or the other.

God has given each person FREE WILL to CHOOSE whom they will follow ... Jesus Christ OR Satan. And by *"not making a choice to repent of your sins and to serve Jesus"*, you are in fact *"making the choice to deny God and to serve Satan."* There is NO in-between ... you can NOT serve both God and Satan!

By Choosing God's Plan Of Salvation, you will also find that your life is getting better and better day by day. Life is a *"journey"*, and even Christians will have their share of problems on this earth. The difference is that with God we have a friend and a Heavenly Father who will walk with us through the trouble to safely bring us out victorious on the other side!

Do not trust your feelings because feelings change. Stand on God's Promises because they never change. God is not man that He can lie. After you are saved, there are *three things* to practice daily for Spiritual Growth:

- *PRAY* ... you talk to God.
- *READ YOUR BIBLE* ... God talks to you.
- *WITNESS* ... you talk for God.

You should be *baptized in obedience to the Lord Jesus Christ* as a public testimony of your Salvation, and then get involved with a Bible-believing Body of Christ *(church)* without delay.

- **2 Timothy 1:8 ...** *"Be not thou therefore ashamed of the testimony of our Lord ..."*

- **Matthew 10:32 ...** *"Therefore whoever confesses Me before men, him will I also confess before My Father who is in heaven."*

LIVING WHAT WE BELIEVE: *knowing, believing,* and *applying Biblical Truths* are the *three key steps* toward having a renewed mind and experiencing the transforming power of a personal relationship with God. God's thoughts are perfectly true and He is more than willing to help us believe the truth.

Our emotions and actions will be transformed as we replace lies with truth. This is a difficult and lifelong process that involves challenges at every turn, but the rewards in our life now and the assurance of Eternal Salvation make all challenges we face and overcome worthwhile.

As we grow in our awareness of the unbiblical beliefs we hold, and we commit ourselves to take a Biblical view, our minds will be renewed and we can experience true freedom in Christ Jesus. Eternal Salvation and the more abundant life that Christ promised is ours if we will commit ourselves to a life found in His Truth.

Painful things happen constantly ... *friends betray us, people move away, loved ones die, marriages break up, we lose our jobs, our health fails, we are treated unfairly, justice doesn't always seem to prevail, and so life goes.*

When people have trusted Christ for salvation, *however*, nothing can separate them from the love of God. Death cannot separate - for we will all be in God's Presence. And nothing in life is powerful enough to take God away. Nothing in the realm of the unseen, nothing in time, and nothing in this vast universe can separate Believers from God's Love.

- **Romans 8:35 ...** *"Who shall separate us from the love of Christ? Shall tribulation, or distress, or persecution, or famine, or nakedness, or peril, or sword?"*

- **Romans 8: 38&39 ...** *"For I am persuaded that neither death nor life, nor things present nor things to come, nor height nor depth, nor any other created thing, shall be able to separate us from the love of God which is in Christ Jesus our Lord."*

When we feel alone or far from God; we must remember His promise that He is with us always, even to the end of the world. **Just read the promise of Jesus Himself found in Matthew 28:20:** *"... teaching them to observe all things that I have commanded you; and lo, I am with you always, even to the end of the age."*

When Jesus says *"Come to me,"* He doesn't say to come to religion, to come to a system, nor does He say to come to a certain doctrine. Jesus is giving each of us a *very personal invitation* to come to God ... *an invitation to a Savior.* Christianity is nothing more and nothing less than a desire and an effort to see Jesus ... *the man who called Himself the Son of God.*

Our God is not aloof. He's not so far above us that He can't see and understand our problems. Jesus is a Savior who came down and lived and worked and suffered with the people. The life of Jesus Christ is a message of hope, a message of mercy, a message of life in a dark world.

The message of a Savior who loved us so much that He was willing to suffer and to die for our sins ... *the Son of God who overcame death, hell, and the grave that we might have eternal life with Him as well as a more abundant life right here on this earth.*

Try Jesus ... He Never Fails!

CHAPTER FIFETEEN

"LIVING BY FAITH"

Maybe you have asked yourself, *or have had someone ask you*, this question … *"How do we get faith?"* Scripture tells us that God has given to each of us *"a measure of faith"*. What we need to realize is that we can have <u>*negative faith*</u> or we can develop <u>*positive faith*</u>. So let's take a look at the concept of <u>*developing positive faith*</u> and the blessings of doing so.

- **Hebrews 11: 1&3 … *"Now faith is the substance of things hoped for, the evidence of things not seen. By faith, we understand that the worlds were framed by the Word of God, so that the things which are seen were not made of things which are visible".***

The word <u>*substance*</u> used in the context of this Scripture means <u>*to take ownership of*</u>. I am going to ask you to keep *this word* and *its meaning* locked within your mind as we continue to seek knowledge of how we can have the real peace inside that only comes when we are "Living By Faith".

- **Romans 10:17 … *"So then faith comes by hearing, and hearing by the Word of God."***

We are all going to have faith in something or in someone. Whomever or whatever we choose to have faith in (*to believe in*) is where we will begin to place our energies. If you want to *develop a positive faith that can and does move mountains,* then your *starting point* is this ... *a personal relationship with Jesus Christ.* This is the kind of *positive mountain-moving faith* that we are going to be talking about here.

- The <u>first step</u> in *developing positive mountain-moving faith* is to search your own heart and to honestly answer this question ... *do you simply believe that there is a God – or do you have a personal relationship with Him?*
- The <u>second step</u> is to begin to read and to study God's Word. Ask the Holy Spirit for the wisdom and the knowledge to understand what you are reading, and to also know how to apply *these proven truths* to your own life. Be encouraged in *positive faith* as you read countless reports of God delivering, healing, restoring, and blessing His People as a result of their faith in Him.
- The <u>third step</u> is to begin to *speak these positive truths* over your own life. This is referred to as *your inner hearing.* We must *build ourselves up in our own faith* by reading and by hearing the Promises of God from His Word. When you are *Waiting on God* and becoming discouraged, begin to recall the supernatural help and miracles from your own past that He has given you or others in your life. God doesn't change ... *He is the same yesterday, today, and forever.*
- The <u>fourth step</u> is to *guard ourselves against the speakers of negative faith* in our daily associations. If you can not avoid being around negative people, *and we can't always do so,* we do NOT have to take

into ourselves the *negative lies of Satan* that he speaks through others to confuse and to weaken our own *positive faith* in the goodness and mercy of a Loving God.

- The <u>fifth step</u> is to stop taking into ourselves *unhealthy negative faith* by being very careful what types of materials we read, the teachings we choose to believe, the television shows or movies we choose to watch, and so forth. *Spiritual Well-Being and Positive Faith* grows in strength as we *feed on* the Word of God and positive influences just as our *Physical Well-Being* grows in strength as we feed on nutritious foods and get sufficient rest and physical exercise for our bodies.

- The <u>sixth step</u> is to belief that the *Age of Miracles* has never ended. We still serve the same God ... *the God of Abraham, Isaac, Jacob, David, Daniel, Abraham, Moses, Peter, Paul, John, and countless others.*

- The <u>final step</u> of living with *positive mountain-moving faith* lies in our willingness to remain *obedient to God* in our daily lives. God's Directives for our lives are not laid down as harsh arbitrary rules from a harsh arbitrary Heavenly Father. God's Directives are the *loving commands* from the *heart* of a *Loving Heavenly Father* laid down to protect us and to help us in much the same way that we, *as earthly parents*, have rules for our children to follow. As we discipline our children when they break the rules in order to protect them and to help them grow out of our love for them ... *even so does God discipline us, His Children, out of His love for us.*

Jesus tells us to **"come to Him with the faith of a little child"**, so let's talk about the ABC's of Faith ... {<u>A</u>} *absolute* {<u>B</u>} *belief* with *{<u>C</u>} confidence.*

To have faith means more than just to believe. FAITH involves ACTION based upon BELIEF sustained by CONFIDENCE that that which is believed is true. BIBLICAL FAITH is an ACT based upon a BELIEF sustained by CONFIDENCE that GOD'S WORD is forever settled in heaven.

- BELIEF involves the MIND.
- FAITH involves the MIND plus the WILL and ACTION.
- FAITH involves the EMOTIONS ... the CONFIDENCE to sustain FAITH.

When people have faith in God, they know without a doubt that He will keep His promises. We can live and make choices in this world based on the unseen reality of our future home in heaven. We can persevere in our faith despite pain, hardship, or persecution.

- **James 1: 2-4 & 12 ...** *"Consider it pure joy, my brothers, whenever you face trials of many kinds, because you know that the testing of your faith develops perseverance. Perseverance must finish its work so that you may be mature and complete, not lacking anything. Blessed is the man who perseveres under trial, because when he has stood the test, he will receive the crown of life that God has promised to those who love him."*

- **1 Peter 1: 6-8 ...** *"In this you greatly rejoice, though now for a little while you may have had to suffer grief in all kinds of trials. These have come so that your faith – of greater worth than gold, which perishes even though refined by fire – may*

*be proved genuine and may result in praise, glory,
and honor when Jesus Christ is revealed."*

By FAITH we can have ABSOLUTE BELIEF with
CONFIDENCE that the unseen God is with us. From this
FAITH in GOD we will find the POWER through GOD to
successfully and purposefully live our lives – both now and
for eternity.

So how do we reach the level of faith to generate such
levels of Power of God for our lives and for our God-Given
Purpose? We are each given a *"measure of faith"* by God,
and our Christian Walk is a *"journey of faith"*. As we *exercise our muscle of faith* it continues to grow in strength from
deep within us.

Don't grow discouraged when you stumble or even fall
on this journey, and you will stumble and sometimes fall.
But we have the Power in Jesus Christ to rise up again ...
moving forward and upward as wiser and stronger people.
Don't forget that *our emotions* play a major role in our *"walk
of faith"*.

The *Power of Faith* is so important that it is mentioned
over three hundred times in the Bible. The first reference
to believing in God is found in the story of Abraham. The
Scripture tells us in **Genesis 15:6 ... that Abraham** *"believed
in the Lord, and He accounted it to him for righteousness"*.
Abraham's *"Step of Faith in God"* is so significant that we
find it referred to three times in the New Testament:

- **Romans 4:3 ...** *For what does the Scripture say?
  "Abraham believed God, and it was accounted to
  him for righteousness".*

- **Galatians 3:6 ...** *just as Abraham "believed God,
  and it was accounted to him for righteousness".*

- **James 2:23 ...** *And the Scripture was fulfilled which says, "Abraham believed God, and it was accounted to him for righteousness". And he was called the friend of God.*

In **Hebrews 11:6 ...** we are told that *"without faith, it is impossible to please God"*. By his ABSOLUTE FAITH in GOD, his UNWAVERING BELIEF in GOD'S PROMISE and with his CONFIDENCE in GOD'S TRUTH and in GOD'S PROVISON; Abraham became the father of many nations.

But Abraham did not see the fulfillment of God's Promises in his life UNTIL he learned the POWER OF RELINQUISHMENT. Doing so did not happen overnight for Abraham, so what makes us think that just because we now live in a world of unbelievable technology that our desire for *"microwave faith"* will bring us to levels of true PEACE, FULFILLMENT, PURPOSE and POWER in GOD?

Are we willing to let God take us through His Divine Process Of Preparation? How willing are we to release, yield, resign, surrender, abandon, waive, or to give up something completely? Are we willing to totally surrender to God's Process in order for Him to reveal another facet of His Divinity and His Divine Will and Purpose to us? Are we willing to make the *journey* through the *Valley Of Relinquishment?*

In **Genesis 15:6 ...** the Scripture says that Abraham *"believed in the Lord, and He accounted it to him for righteousness"*. Abraham is without question one of the outstanding individuals of the Old Testament. God spoke to Abraham personally, actually visited him in his home, and even considered him a friend. Abraham loved God ... He obeyed Him, served Him, and was even willing to sacrifice his son to prove his faith.

Abraham is called the *"father of faith"*, but Abraham wasn't born that way. If we look more closely at some of the incidents in his life, we will see someone a whole lot like the rest of us – a person with many frailties and weaknesses.

Abraham had to grow and to learn by experience. His faith, his strength, and his power was a result of his willingness to accept *God's Process of Preparation* in his life as he gradually *learned to relinquish* his own desires to God's Will and Perfect Timing. Even Abraham, God's friend and the father of faith, didn't receive the *Power Of Relinquishment* until after he had walked thru the *Pain Of The Valley Of Relinquishment* ... making many mistakes along the way.

Genesis Chapter Twelve ... God told Abraham to uproot himself and his family from their familiar surroundings and to move to a new land. He invited them on a "FAITH-STRETCHING" journey. *By sheer faith* ... Abraham was asked to pack up his family, leave a lush river valley, and trust completely in God's Guidance, Protection, and Provision. God's Promise to Abraham included both a land and a legacy. God told Abraham He would give him a place and make from him a people.

- **Genesis 12: 1-3 ... God told Abraham, *"Get out of your country to a land that I will show you. I will make you a great nation; I will bless you and in you all the families of the earth shall be blessed"*.**

I can only imagine the thoughts and the questions that must have been going through Abraham's mind when God directed him to Canaan which was a hardscrabble land of warring tribes, but – *on this occasion* – Abraham trusted God. But you and I today need to remember that Abraham wasn't perfect in his faith. We need to read the whole story in **Genesis** of the life of Abraham in order to be strengthened during our own *Process Of Preparation and Relinquishment*.

Abraham's wife, Sarah, was a very beautiful and desirable woman. Abraham was so concerned that some might consider killing him over Sarah that he became afraid for his very life. Earlier we saw Abraham's awesome faith in trusting God with his entire life for himself and for his family. But now we see Abraham acting *first in faith – then in fear*. Why? Because Abraham was not only a man of God, but he was also "*a man – a human*" with human weaknesses.

- This <u>FEAR</u> caused Abraham to deceive Pharaoh into believing that his beautiful wife was his sister.
- This <u>FEAR</u> caused Abraham to sin against his wife whom he loved. Sarah, *as Abraham's wife*, had a God-Given right to expect her husband to not only provide for her but also to protect her ... *even if it meant laying down his own life.*
- This <u>FEAR</u> also caused Abraham to sin against his God whom he dearly loved and faithfully strived to serve.

Before we continue with the story of *Abraham's Journey of Faith*, I want to talk about three seemingly different words that are undeniably tied together in our Christian Walk, and even in our personal or professional lives ... <u>FAITH</u> – <u>RELINQUISHMENT</u> – <u>POWER</u>.

Let us focus our thoughts on how we can successfully move through the "*Pain of the Valley of Relinquishment*" to reach the "*Power of Total Relinquishment*" by "*Exercising our Muscle of Faith*".

What is the definition from Webster's New World Dictionary for the word relinquishment? To *relinquish:* {1}*to give up; abandon* {2}*to renounce or surrender* {3}*to let go.* To *relinquish* implies a *giving up* of something desirable and connotes compulsion or the force of necessity. To *abandon*, in this connection, implies a complete and final *relinquishment:* a voluntary *renouncing – surrender – and letting go* by refusing to insist on one's own personal rights or claim to something or to someone.

If we are going to walk in the *Power of God's Mountain-Moving Faith* in our daily lives, we will have to reach the *Point of Total Submission* to God's Plan of Salvation through Christ Jesus and to God's Perfect Will for our life.

Even though we are each given *"a measure of faith"* by God; we must do our part to exercise that faith and to develop a positive and life-changing faith that will literally rock our world! I can tell you from personal experience that nothing you give up to truly serve God will ever be as awesome as the incredible blessings you will know as a Child-of-God through a Personal Relationship with Christ Jesus!

Let's get back to Abraham. The promise God had made to Abraham of a land came true long before the promise of a child. When Abraham and Sarah were very old – *well past their childbearing years* – God promised them a son who would be the tangible evidence and living carrier of God's promise. Instead of waiting in faith, Abraham and Sarah took matters into their own hands. Their impatience and their actions produced much unhappiness for Abraham, Sarah, and Sarah's maid.

This is still true for us today. Instead of waiting in faith, I have taken matters into my own hands out of impatience or discouragement. When I did so, the result was the same every single time ... *a deep regret that I had not trusted God and His Promises enough to "wait for His answers".* But I have learned something very valuable from my mistakes. God's Delays do not mean God's Denials ... *many times I have found that what I was so desperately praying for at the time would not have been the best thing for me down the road.*

Here is a *personal example* of how I truly began to "*Let Go & Let God*" have total control of my life. God wants us to grow in our faith to trust in Him and in His Flawless Plan for our lives. I am sure we are all familiar with **Jeremiah 29:11** ... *"For I know the plans I have for you," saith the Lord, "Plans to prosper you and not to harm you"*. This translation is from the NIV Bible, but the King James Version gives us the same message ... God's Plans for our lives are for good – not for evil.

But I really struggled for years, *as a Christian – still sometimes do briefly*, with putting the matter into God's very capable hands and then not *"waiting upon Him"*. After a little while, with no obvious resolution in sight, I would begin to try and figure out a way to make things happen the way that I thought I wanted them to be. I firmly believe in praying God's Word out loud for a number of reasons ... *it strengthens our faith in God, and His Word is our weapon against the enemy.* When Jesus was hungry, tired, and tempted by Satan ... *His chosen weapon was the Word of God.*

One day as I was standing in front of my washer and dryer folding clothes – *telling God all about Jeremiah 29:11* – He answered me, but not the way I expected Him to do. In fact, He had to speak to me three times before I finally shut up to listen. Here is what God spoke to me that day, and it changed my life. He told me, *"That's right; I do know the plans I have for your life. When you are ready to stop trying to super-implant your plans over and above MY PLANS, then I will be able to change things for you."* God finally had my attention! Are you ready to give Him your attention and your plans in exchange for His Plans for your life?

As we continue to read the story of Abraham and Sarah in **Genesis Chapter Sixteen,** we can learn a very important lesson – one which we each need to apply to our individual life today. The story of Abraham and Sarah tells us much about God's compassion and His mercy, but we also learn from this story that God does not always spare us from the consequences of our lack of faith.

There is a lesson often repeated throughout the Bible ... *although sin is forgiven – the physical consequences are often still felt*. This was a lesson that even Abraham and Sarah had to learn the hard way. Despite their human imperfections, Abraham and Sarah were eventually blessed with the fulfillment of God's Promise to give them a son. When Abraham was one hundred years of age and Sarah was ninety years of age ... *the time for the fulfillment of God's Promise had finally come.*

- **Hebrews 11:11 ... *"By faith Abraham, even though he was past age – and Sarah herself was barren – was enabled to become a father because he considered Him faithful who had made the promise."***

Through Abraham and Sarah the Nation of Israel was born, the lineage of Jesus Christ was begun, and the PLAN to bless the world with a SAVIOR continued to develop. God's Plan rested on the shoulders of a man who practiced *"Inside-Out Mountain-Moving Faith"*. What Abraham *believed* within his mind and within his heart ... Abraham put into *action* with his *confidence* in God.

In the fullness of time ... God sent forth His Son – Jesus Christ. **John 3:16 ... *"For God so loved the world that He gave His only begotten Son, that whoever believes in Him should not perish but have everlasting life"*.**

Real *saving faith*, became *action* based upon a *belief* in God's faithfulness to His Word, sustained by *confidence* in God's own nature of faithfulness - that He is not a man to lie nor the Son of Man to repent ... what He says - He will do; what He speaks – He will make good; that God, as <u>Jeremiah</u> said, *"will hasten His Word to perform it"*.

We each have the choice of letting the stream of time and circumstances defy God's Promise, or we can reach up and grab hold of God's Word and know that ... *God's Word was, is and shall be - before and after the earth as we now know it.*

The Word of God, *forever settled in heaven*, is where we need to put our grasp, and no matter what any person or any circumstance says ... *hanging onto the Promises of God.* If we die, *still hanging on*, we'll be translated instantly into the realm where there is no friction or pain with *"Thus saith the Lord – Forever settled in Heaven".*

That is what God chose to identify as <u>Faith</u>: <u>Action</u> based upon <u>Belief</u> with <u>Confidence</u> that ... *Forever, O Lord, Thy Word is settled in Heaven.* To live our life by *walking in the Spirit* means *living a life of faith*: to walk in the Spirit, we must live according to God's Promise, trusting in the integrity of God Himself. Faith must have an object, and the object of our faith is God who is made known to us through His Word.

God has proven Himself to be worthy of our trust. There are literally thousands of promises for us contained within the context of God's Word, and no Christian has ever found even one of them to be untrue. When God says something, we can stake our very life on it because we can know with certainty that HE will not fail us.

- **Romans 8:28 ...** *"We know that in all things God works for the good of those who love Him, who have been called according to His Purpose".*

So what is faith and how does it differ from belief? I think the simplest explanation is that *saving faith* is *trust.* We trust God to take care of us, to do good for us rather than evil, to give us eternal life.

- Trust means knowing that God exists ... *knowing that He is good, knowing that He has the power to do what He wants, and trusting that He will use His Power to do what is best for us.*

- Trust means a willingness to put ourselves under God, to be willing to obey ... *not out of fear, but out of love.* When we trust in God it is because we love Him and we know He loves us.
- True faith is, *at its core*, trust in God and in His Son – Christ Jesus.
- We are forced to make a choice each day. Will we trust God – Or not?

Many people claim to know God, but do they really know Him? To truly know God requires faith ... a willingness to believe that though unseen – *God exists;* a willingness to trust that though unseen – *His rewards are certain.* When people have faith, they discover they can have a Personal Relationship with Jesus Christ – God's Only Begotten Son sent to save the world from the devastation of sin.

One does not learn to LIVE BY FAITH all at once, and it doesn't come naturally. We must learn, and as we are learning, we will make mistakes. But our mistakes need not cut us off from God because He is a patient, compassionate, and merciful teacher. He will work with us, encourage us, and sometimes He will allow us to be tried and tested, *"that your faith may be proved genuine and may result in praise, glory, and honor when Jesus Christ is revealed"*.

A life spent learning to obey God is like a journey ... *with a starting point, a route, and a destination.* For Abraham that journey began when he left his home to travel wherever God would lead him. He could not always know what route the journey would take, but he learned to trust God to direct his steps.

Our journey may not be as eventful as Abraham's, but we can be sure there will be tests and trials, ups and downs, success and failures along the way. Just remember that God hasn't left us all alone to make this journey. He will walk with us every step of the way. He will give us encouragement by the "EXAMPLES" in His Word from the life of not only Abraham, but many more ... Moses, Isaac, Jacob, Daniel, The Three Hebrew Children, David, Samson, Gideon, Ruth, Mary, Peter, Paul, John, and even Jesus Himself who was tempted and tested in every way during His time upon this earth.

- **Romans 10:17 ...** *"Faith comes from hearing the message, and the message is heard through the Word of Christ."*

The message is in the written word, **THE HOLY BIBLE**, and it is in the spoken word. *Jesus is the Author and Perfecter of our Faith,* but He does not work alone. Jesus does only what the Father desires and He works by the Holy Spirit within our hearts. The Holy Spirit teaches us, convicts us, encourages us, and strengthens our faith.

It is by faith that we have a fruitful relationship with God. It is by faith that we pray, by faith that we worship, by faith that we hear His Word in sermons and by fellowship. Faith enables us to participate in Fellowship with the Father, the Son, and the Holy Spirit. It is by faith that we are enabled to give our allegiance to God through our Savior Jesus Christ by means of the Holy Spirit working within our hearts to draw us to a relationship with God. It is by faith that we can love other people.

Faith frees us from the fear of ridicule and rejection. We can love others without worrying about what they will do to us because we trust in God to reward us generously. Through faith in God, we can be generous with others. Through faith in God, we can put Him first in our lives.

When we believe that God is as good as He says He is ... *then we will treasure Him above all else and be willing to make the sacrifices that He asks of us.* We will trust Him, and it is by that trust that we will begin to truly know and to experience the joys of our Salvation. Christian life is – *from first to last* – a matter of trusting God.

Faith is the *"key"* that unlocks the door of Heaven. Faith is also the *"key"* to getting our prayers answered.

- **Mark 5:34 ... we read the story of the woman who suffered with a severe issue of blood. When this desperate woman touched Jesus for healing, He responded ...** *"Daughter, your faith has made you well. Go in peace, and be healed of your affliction".*

- **Matthew 7:7 ... Jesus tells us,** *"Ask, and it will be given to you; Seek and you will find; Knock, and it will be opened to you".*

We can not make God answer our prayers because we don't always see His complete Will and Purpose in our lives. We just need to come to our Heavenly Father with a simple faith, *a childlike faith,* to just take Him at His Word and to believe in Him. We can always know that He will never leave us or forsake us, but that He will walk with us every step of our journey here on this earth. When our earthly journey is finished, *if we have lived by Faith in God through the Gift of Salvation by Christ Jesus,* we need have no fear of what lies beyond the door of death because death is but a passageway into an Eternity of Peace and Joy far beyond our human imagination.

Do you know that you know that you know that you have a Personal Relationship with God through Christ Jesus? Do you want to know the peace of knowing such a faith that will enable you to lie down each night and close your eyes in sleep never having to fear if you will awaken the next morning? Do you want the joy of waking up each morning and knowing that no matter what may happen during that day, everything will turn out okay because your life is in the Hands of your Heavenly Father who is both the Creator and the Keeper of the Universe and everything in it? Do you want the assurance deep within your mind and deep within your heart that nothing or nobody can separate you from the love and the care of God? Do you want to know, *beyond any shadow of a doubt,* that when your time on this earth is over you will be spending your eternity with God where there will be no more sickness or death, no more trials and temptations, no more loss and no more pain?

All it takes to begin your journey of *"Living By Faith"* is for you to acknowledge that Jesus Christ is the Son of God who died for our sins and arose again victorious over death, hell, and the grave; the courage to confess your sins and to ask God for His forgiveness; and the willingness to invite Jesus Christ to come into your heart and to be Lord of your life.

If you don't have a Personal Relationship with Jesus Christ, please don't turn Him away again. If you will accept Him as your Lord and Savior, together you will begin a new journey and you will find Him to be ... *the very bestest friend you can ever know!*

CHAPTER SIXTEEN

"WALKING IN CHRISTIAN LOVE"

WHAT IS LOVE? (Webster's New World Dictionary) *... to be fond of, desire; a deep and tender feeling of affection for or attachment or devotion to a person or persons; a feeling of brotherhood and good will toward other people.*

WHAT IS "CHRISTIAN" LOVE? Let's start with a definition found in The New Unger's Bible Dictionary ... *love is an attribute of God towards all of mankind. Love is a Christian virtue. The only word in the Bible translated "charity" means "love".*

- The absence of love invalidates all claims to the Christian name.
- Love is the antithesis of selfishness.
- Love is active, and dissatisfied, if not blessing others.

In love all human duty is summed up. Love is the first named element in the composite "Fruit Of The Spirit" found in the Bible.

- **Matthew 22: 36–40** ... *"Teacher, which is the greatest commandment in the Law?" Jesus replied, "Love the Lord your God with all your heart and with all your soul and with all your mind. This is the first and greatest commandment. And the second is like it: Love your neighbor as yourself. All the law and the Prophets hang on these two commandments."*

- **1 Corinthians 13: 1– 8a & 13** ... *"And now I will show you the most excellent way. If I speak in tongues of men and of angels, but have not love, I am only a resounding gong or a clanging cymbal. If I have the gift of prophecy and can fathom all mysteries and all knowledge, and if I have a faith that can move mountains, but have not love, I am nothing. If I give all I possess to the poor and surrender my body to the flames, but have not love, I gain nothing.*

  Love is patient, love is kind. It does not envy, it does not boast, it is not proud. It is not rude, it is not self-seeking, it is not easily angered, it keeps no record of wrongs. Love does not delight in evil but rejoices with the truth. It always protects, always trusts, always hopes, always perseveres. Love never fails. And now, these three remain: faith, hope and love. But the greatest of these is love."

- **Galatians 5:22** ... *"But the fruit of the Spirit is love, joy, peace, patience, kindness, goodness, faithfulness, gentleness, and self-control. Against such things there is no law".*

In the Greek language, *there are four distinct words for love*; however, it has been historically difficult to separate the meanings of these words. We are going to look at the senses in which these *"Greek words for love"* were generally used.

1. *Eros*: is passionate love with sensual desire and longing. The Modern Greek word *"erotas"* means *"romantic love"*, but *eros* does not have to be sexual in nature. *Eros* can be interpreted as a *love for someone* whom you love more than the *philia love of friendship*.

2. *Philia*: means *friendship* in Modern Greek. It includes loyalty to friends, family, and community. *Philia* requires virtue, equality, and familiarity. *Philia* is the only other word used for *"love"* in the ancient text of the New Testament besides *agape*, but even then *philia* is used less frequently.

3. *Agape*: means *"love"* in modern day Greek. The term *s'agapo* means *"I love you"* in Greek. The word *"agapo"* is the verb *"I love"*. This verb appears in the New Testament describing, amongst other things, the relationship between Jesus and the beloved disciples. In Biblical literature, its meaning and usage is illustrated by self-sacrificing, giving love to all ... both friends and enemies.

4. *Storge*: means *"affection"* in Modern Greek. It is a natural affection like that felt by parents for their offspring. Rarely used in ancient works, and then almost exclusively to describe relationships within the family.

Christian love is a selfless and giving love. Christian love is giving to others those things that you would want them to give to you if you were in their situation, and it is choosing to do so even when you know they can not pay you back. In fact, it is doing so especially when the other person can not pay you back. Christian love is respect for others. Christian love is mercy. Christian love is charity.

Naturally we care for our own physical, emotional, and spiritual needs. These needs, because they cause our desires, are the source of our *eros* love. But how natural is it for us to care for the needs of others? Another level of our nature seems to be involved in order to care about the needs of others. In this depth of ourselves, we are able to feel *empathy* with the needs of another person. When we reach this level of our being ... *me-centered eros* is surpassed by *you-oriented agape* as *desire* gives way to *charity*.

The greatest example of care for others is the Son of God hanging on a cross for our salvation. No greater love is there than laying down one's life for others. This is the ultimate in the *agape* kind of *love*.

- **John 3: 16&17 ...** *"For God so loved the world that He gave His only begotten Son, that whoever believes in Him should not perish but have everlasting life. For God did not send His Son into the world to condemn the world, but that the world through Him might be saved".*

Generally understood as charity, *agape is a selfless love for others*, even in their weakest and most needful conditions. Many would call this *love* supernatural – a grace from God beyond the power of our human nature. But we are able to receive the *gift of agape love*, and to respond to the needs of others. It is by our choice that we can become able to do so.

We are free to do what is either good or bad. This is where God's affirming love becomes the *divine agape love* that saves us. *Agape* is *redemptive love* that is immediately the result of *affirming love* for those who need to be saved. We have only to receive the *gift of agape love* with gratitude and to respond by changing our ways from the bad or selfish to the good and unselfish.

We are most like God when we, *consciously in attitude and action*, give ourselves to others in their time of need. Our *agape kind of love* helps to fulfill other kinds of love. *Affirming love* strengthens not only *storge* and *eros*, but also *agape* and *philia*.

- **I John 3: 1–3 ...** *"Behold what matter of love the Father has bestowed on us, that we should be called the children of God! Therefore the world does not know us, because it did not know Him. Beloved, now we are children of God; and it has not yet been revealed what we shall be, but we know that when He is revealed, we shall be like Him, for we shall see Him as He is. And everyone who has this hope in Him purifies himself, just as He is pure."*

No one can love more than God. The thought of God's astounding love bestowed on sinful humanity is beyond our understanding. It's incomprehensible that while we were still sinners in rebellion against God, Christ died for us. We sometimes struggle with loving, *which includes truly forgiving*, those who are important in our lives. Yet, throughout the Bible we read of God's patience and love as He longed to draw mankind to Himself.

Through the sacrifice of Jesus Christ, God brought His own to Himself, giving the title and relationship of *"children"* to everyone who accepts the Gift of Salvation through Christ Jesus. He allows us to call Him *"Father"*, and everyone who has faith in Christ is a beloved Child of God. So when we are struggling with loving someone who is being unlovable, just remember how deeply God loves us; even in our most unlovable moments! I have found that when I can't find love within myself towards a person, I can always love them with the love of Jesus!

- **1 John 3:18 ...** *"My little children, let us not love in word or in tongue, but in deed and in truth."*

To understand true love, we need only to look at the Cross where Christ performed the ultimate act of love. This fact alone should motivate us to love others. Loving others is not as simple as saying, *"I love you"*, but really loving others is shown through our actions every day. Loving actions reveal the truth and depth of our love.

1. We can love our families by showing respect, patience, and understanding in so many ways.
2. We can love our neighbors as we reach out in kindness and friendship.
3. We can love the needy of the world by sharing our time, our prayers, and our possessions with them.

- **1 John 4: 7–11 ...** *"Beloved, let us love one another, for love is of God; and everyone who loves is born of God and knows God. He who does not love does not know God, for God is love. In this the love of God was manifested toward us, that God has sent His only begotten Son into the world, that the world might live through Him. In this is love, not that we loved God, but that He loved us and sent His Son to be the propitiation for our sins. Beloved, if God so loved us, we also ought to love one another."*

GOD SHOWS HIS LOVE TO PEOPLE THROUGH PEOPLE! No one has ever seen God, but God reveals Himself to the world through His frail and imperfect people by perfecting His love in each of us. *As believers we go into the world living our faith*. By doing so, *in love*, we are revealing God to everyone we meet. By loving others we are revealing God's Presence in our lives.

When we, *as believers*, show love toward one another and to the unbelieving world, God makes Himself known and His love is "perfected" in us. God often shows His love through His People, and it is that *"love revealed"* that draws people to God in us. WHAT DOES YOUR LOVE FOR OTHERS SAY ON GOD'S BEHALF?

- **1 John 4: 20&21 ...** *If someone says, "I love God," and hates his brother, he is a liar; for he who does not love his brother whom he has seen, how can he love God whom he has not seen? And this command-ment we have from Him: that he who loves God must love his brother also.*

Too Many Critics: when believers hate one another, they certainly are not showing love. At times, a *critical spirit* will cause believer's relationships to become strained as they *judge* each other. Our *"job"*, according to Scripture, is not to assume the position of *"judge"*. God already has that posi-tion filled! And our judging and condemning of one another, *as believers*, is not going to draw unbelievers unto Christ. But loving one another through Christ Jesus will impact the lives of unbelievers. *Your testimony* is *your choice*.

Believers will disagree on some matters from time to time, *but even in their disagreement*, they should still be able to celebrate their unity in Christ. Those with critical spirits, however, are unable to truly love others. If we cannot love our fellow believers *whom we can see*, how can we possibly love the invisible God? Believers who claim to love God but hate others are lying ... *to themselves, to God, and to everyone else.*

Bold love is the courageous, unselfish, and often costly gift of doing good to those who sin against us. When we give that *gift*, we get a taste of the *true character of God. Bold love* is *forgiveness with feet* ... the kind of love that moves us toward the one who harmed us – not in anger or recrimination, but in a spirit of genuine forgiveness.

- **Romans 12: 9–21 ...** *Love must be sincere. Hate what is evil; cling to what is good. Be devoted to one another in brotherly love. Honor one another above yourselves. Never be lacking in zeal, but keep your spiritual fervor, serving the Lord. Be joyful in hope, patient in affliction, faithful in prayer. Share with God's people who are in need. Practice hospitality. Bless those who persecute you; bless and do not curse. Rejoice with those who rejoice; mourn with those who mourn. Live in harmony with one another. Do not be proud, but be willing to associate with people of low position. Do not be conceited. Do not repay anyone evil for evil. Be careful to do what is right in the eyes of everybody. If it is possible, as far as it depends on you, live at peace with everyone. Do not take revenge, my friends, but leave room for God's wrath, for it is written: "It is mine to avenge; I will repay," says the Lord. On the contrary: "If your enemy is hungry, feed him; if he is thirsty, give him something to drink. In doing this, you will heap burning coals on his head." Do not be overcome by evil, but overcome evil with good.*

We all need to take a hard look at the Bible's kind of love:

- It is realistic.
- It is tender.

- It is aggressive.
- It is tenacious.
- It is protective.
- It is forever.
- It is emotional.
- It is total.
- It is unspeakably sweet.
- It is tough.

God loves us with tough love and that is the way we need to learn to love each other. *"Bears all things"* simply means that love shelters or covers. *"Believes all things"* simply means that love never loses faith in others and is willing to think the best of them. *"Hopes all things"* simply means that love looks forward with optimism, knowing that God works all things together for good. *"Endures all things"* simply means that love holds on.

When we love, we take part in eternity. We can ask God *to perfect our love* for Him and for others.

- BOLD LOVE is fervent in spirit and service, strong and intense.
- BOLD LOVE is joyful, patient, prayerful, generous, and hospitable.
- BOLD LOVE blesses those who come against us unjustly, refusing to take personal revenge.
- BOLD LOVE is compassionate and humble.
- BOLD LOVE is peaceable.
- BOLD LOVE overcomes and destroys evil.

The above **Passage in Romans** tells us to love that which is good and to hate that which is evil. Hating evil does not give us license to hate the person who is doing evil. While we are not to allow ourselves to get caught up in the pollution of their actions, we are to release them to God and pray for them with Christian love because they, *too*, have a soul that needs the redemption of Christ.

We are not merely to forgive others by ignoring or letting go of the harm. We are called to serve those who have violated us as Jesus forgave us and died for us while we were still sinning against God. However, forgiving someone may not always lead to reconciliation. Forgiveness takes only one person - Reconciliation takes two or more people.

We are to provide others, *even those who hurt us,* with their most basic needs when we have occasion to do so. The whole context of BOLD GODLY LOVE implies that the *core basic need* is to be pursued in spite of our personal needs or emotions. We are to offer everyone a taste of passionate empathy, humble care, hospitality, and joyful generosity.

Please understand that forgiving and letting go does not mean that in offering Christian love to another person you are giving that individual the right to abuse you in any way. God does not condone abuse in any form, and neither does He ask you to stay in an abusive environment. If you are the abuser, get the help you need to stop. If you are the abused, get the help you need to leave and to rebuild a healthier life.

Love is God's weapon to destroy the power of darkness. While we need to be willing to stand up and share our faith in Christ, we are not going to win the battle over evil and darkness by becoming an advocate of violence. When we approach life with an adversarial attitude and take adversarial actions against others, we are not destroying evil. Instead, our attitudes and actions only incite violence and foster Christian self-righteousness.

Bold love destroys evil by empathy. Bold love destroys evil by hospitality. Bold love destroys evil by generously offering care for what is needed. Bold love is the very power we have from God *not* to become a part of the provocation of evil that surprises and shames those who harm us or others.

The Apostle Paul *ties doing good to pouring burning coals onto someone's head.* This means that we are not to flee from or to fight against those who have done wrong towards us. Instead, we are to unnerve them by disarming them with bold love. Their deep surprise that their evil has not been repaid by us with our own evil opens their heart to redemption.

Bold love offers a taste of the character of God. God is strong and tender. Our love is to be equal parts of strength and tenderness. Strength disarms false power, and tenderness invites the heart to rest when it is defenseless. Strength reveals that God is holy and hates sin, and tenderness reveals God's grace and reconciliation. What does *love* look like?

- Love ... *suffers long,* bearing annoyances and inconveniences, not losing its temper.
- Love ... *is kind,* taking the initiative to be considerate and helpful.
- Love ... *does not envy,* but rejoices when others succeed.
- Love ... *does not parade itself,* is not puffed up but instead draws others to it.
- Love ... *does not behave rudely or impolitely,* but acts in a manner worthy of Christ.
- Love ... *does not seek its own way,* but always seeks to benefit others.
- Love ... *is not easily provoked,* but will allow differences of opinion in matters.
- Love ... *thinks no evil,* but makes allowances for people's flaws.
- Love ... *does not rejoice in iniquity,* but always rejoices in the truth.

The goal of love is to give a taste of God. Bold love seeks reconciliation with all as far as it is possible for us to go. The Apostle Paul implicitly acknowledges that we will not be able to live at peace with everyone, but if there is any room for reconciliation, then we are to do so. The end result of receiving and of offering bold love is changed hearts ... ours and others.

CHAPTER SEVENTEEN

"LIVING A SUCCESSFUL LIFE"

What is a successful life? According to Webster's New World Dictionary ... *living a successful life means "having achieved success; specifically, having gained wealth, fame, etc."*

Let's take a moment to look at the world's definition of success *versus* God's definition of success. The world *(society)* bases success on outcomes ... *it is conditional, contingent upon achievement.* Our circumstances determine our success. On the other hand, God bases success on our Relationship with Him ... *it's unconditional – given freely in love – to be experienced in the present regardless of our circumstances.*

- **1 Samuel 16:7 ... *"The Lord does not look at the things man looks at. Man looks at the outward appearance, but the Lord looks at the heart."***

Each and every one of us will have to make a personal decision as to what the definition of "Living A Successful Life" will be within our own lives. The one specific question we all need to ponder within ourselves is this ... *"Are we willing to come to the end of ourselves - to let God drive?"*

In business, *as in so many facets of our lives*, we have been taught that *success* is often about outward appearance: *titles, achievements, mission statements, and posturing* – even if it means covering up the truth. We often deal with what so many refer to as *"the shades of gray"* or partial truths.

How often is the term *"It's Business – Anything Goes"* or *"It's Business – Do Whatever It Takes"* spoken in corporate boardrooms, on the playing fields of professional athletes, and even within our high school locker rooms? How often have we planted seeds of self-doubt, insecurity, fear and failure into the hearts and minds of innocent children, *as teachers and as parents*, by consistently dwelling on their weaknesses rather than applauding their efforts and their strengths? How often have the words spoken within our own lives by those in authority come back to haunt us, *making us afraid to try because we may fail again*, ... words that can leave devastating and long-term scars upon our very souls.

How often do we make the same mistake in the manner in which we teach and mentor those placed under our authority? An unwritten rule, *never show your fear – never show weakness*, runs strongly through the very foundational fibers of our life. Why have we been taught, *and why are we teaching others*, that in order to *be successful* we must hide the *truths* locked deep within us? We are taught that if we show any sign of *weakness* or *fear* that we will definitely pay a price for it.

Over time, *trying to live up to the impossible expectations of others*, we come to a *crossroads* and are forced to *choose the path* of our future. What is that choice? Do we begin to *"play within the shades of gray"*; do we begin to *"justify stepping over a line of acceptability"* until we feel that we have gone too far to go back – to feel that our only hope is to continue to cover up the truth?

288

If we are serious about building a relationship with God, with others, and to find *healing for the battle-scarred "land of our soul"*, we have to begin by truly *revealing our hearts*. We can't run, or hide, from God.

- **Psalm 139:23 ... "*Search me, O God, and know my heart. See if there is any offensive way in me, and lead me in the way everlasting.*"**

- **Psalm 139: 1-13, 15&16 ... "*O Lord, you have searched me and you know me. You know me when I sit and when I rise; you perceive my thoughts from afar. You discern my going out and my lying down; you are familiar with all my ways. Before a word is on my tongue you know it completely, O Lord. You hem me in – behind and before; you have laid your hand upon me. Such knowledge is too wonderful for me, too lofty for me to attain. Where can I go from your Spirit? Where can I flee from your presence? If I go up to the heavens, you are there; if I make my bed in the depths, you are there. If I rise on the wings of the dawn, if I settle on the far side of the sea, even there your hand will guide me, your right hand will hold me fast. If I say, 'Surely the darkness will hide me and the light become night around me,' even the darkness will not be dark to you; the night will shine like the day, for darkness is as light to you. For you created my inmost being; you knit me together in my mother's womb. My frame was not hidden from you when I was made in the secret place. When I was woven together in the depths of the earth, your eyes saw my unformed body. All the days ordained for me were written in your book before one of them came to be.*"**

- **Jeremiah 1: 4&5 ...** *The Word of the Lord came to me saying, "Before I formed you in the womb I knew you, before you were born I set you apart; I appointed you as a prophet to the nations".*

As a teenager in an unstable emotional, physical, and spiritual environment, my only focus was to get an education that would enable me to get a good job to provide the finances for me to *get out of there* and *to live my own life.* I did so, and ended up being quite *successful* by the *world's definition* of *success.* No one meeting me would have known the kind of background I had come from. I lived behind a facade of strong self-confidence and independence. I told myself, and others, that *"I don't need anyone"* and that if a person is strong enough *"they can get through anything".* I had no use for *signs of weakness* in anyone, and no tolerance for *signs of incompetence* in anyone.

Only much later in my life, *after these "lies of Satan" and "my personal choices" had cost me every thing – including the lives of my husband and my daughter,* did I finally learn that we all need others. I now understand, *because I have come to truthfully search my own heart,* that I have many strengths and I have many weaknesses. I am truly grateful for the *strengths* that God has placed within me, and I now look for and applaud the *strengths* in others. I have also learned to accept my *human weaknesses* and have chosen to invite the help of God in becoming a better person because of them. Furthermore, I have developed far more understanding and tolerance of the *human weaknesses* in others.

My mother told me often as I was growing up, *when I was faced with making a difficult decision,* something that has stuck with me all the days of my life. She would say, *"Sweetheart, before you decide what you are going to do about this, I want you to stand in front of a mirror and ask yourself this question ... 'Can I live with the consequences of*

*my choice?' Then she would tell me, 'You can always leave
any place or any person if it becomes impossible to stay, but
never forget that you will never be able to run far enough or
fast enough to get away from yourself.'"*

Mama didn't tell me that I also could never run far
enough or fast enough to get away from God. Mama was
one of the strongest women of Simplistic Faith in God that I
have ever known. So why didn't she *verbally* bring God into
her advice? Because she knew that I was not ready to hear
anything positive about God. I would not have taken the *fact*
of an *all-knowing God* as a *concept* to be comforted by – *as
I deeply now understand to be true.* I would have taken it as
just one more reason to be afraid of God and to become even
more embittered towards Him.

Through the *wisdom* God placed within my mother, she
knew what to say that would make me listen because I loved
her with all of my heart and I respected her more than anyone
I have ever known. I listened to Mama because I knew that
she loved and respected me.

As we are ministering to the needs in others, we need to
always ask God to enable us to *meet them at their level* in
order to *minister to their hearts with compassion and understanding* rather than to bombard them with *well-intentioned*
platitudes or doctrines. We need to be very careful to *not
jump to conclusions* and to *not point a finger of judgment at
another* in our daily lives and in our respective ministries.
Instead, *with a humble and grateful heart for His mercies
towards us*, we need to ask God to direct our every word and
our every action in our relationships with others.

To truly know God and to begin to comprehend the depth
of His love for mankind, we need to totally accept that He
created each of us and He knows our every thought. There
is nowhere to run and no place to hide from ourselves, nor
from God. *God has every hair on our head numbered – Not
one tiny bird falls to the ground without His knowledge.*

Accepting this *truth* makes us feel very vulnerable and is sometimes difficult and often painful within the *humanness* of ourselves. However, *as a Beloved Child of God*, we can find great strength and comfort in this truth.

On the other hand, *when we ask Jesus Christ to become Lord and Savior of our life – we receive a "new heart" and the Holy Spirit begins a new work within us.* Out of His endless love for us, God gives us a new heart – *a discerning heart* – to teach us and to guide us in His Truth. Within our *new heart* God places the power and the ability for us to hear His Guidance and to enable us to overcome any obstacle we face.

By accepting Jesus Christ into our hearts and into our lives we have taken the first important step on our *"journey of true success"*. However, we need to remember that God gave to all mankind free will – *the individual right of choice*. He will not force us to follow Him or to live our lives founded upon the *Proven Truths* found within *His Word*. That is why our *acceptance of Jesus* is only the *first important step* on our *journey to real success*.

Now we begin to *build our relationship* with God and to change how we *handle our relationships* with others. God did not send His Only Begotten Son, *Jesus Christ*, to suffer and to die for our sins so that we can go right back to our old destructive and deceitful way of living. Just like all good positive relationships, our relationship with God is a two-way street. God gives us the gifts needed *to succeed* in this world, but we have to do the work. God will not twist our arms to follow His Truths, but He does give us the choice. And depending upon our choices, we will either *"reap the rewards"* or we will *"suffer the consequences"*.

Whenever we become afraid or self-serving, and we make *selfish* or *unwise* decisions, we can not truthfully blame God when it all blows up in our face! When we make a mistake and truly come before God with a sincere confession of said mistake *(or sin)*, God is quick to forgive us and to help us to right the wrongs of our mistakes. But never doubt, *in order for us to learn from our mistakes,* God will allow us to walk through the consequences of wrong or dishonest choices. But, *even in our human error and weakness,* we don't have to walk through these consequences all alone. Jesus will walk every step of the way with us, and He will bring us to the other side ... *far stronger and wiser – far more humble within our own strengths – a "vessel" more valuable in God's Kingdom.*

So how do we become truly successful by God's Definition of Success? First, we are given *a new heart* by accepting Jesus Christ as our personal Lord and Savior. Then we ask God to *search our hearts* and to enable us to change those things within us that are not of His Will. It is up to *each individual person* to renew their mind ... to change their *"stinking thinking"* into *"righteous thinking"*, to amend their habits, and to make new choices.

A heart specialist can repair a heart to save a person's life, but only temporarily. A doctor can repair our *physical heart,* but they can't change our behavior or our environment. As a heart patient, if we *choose* to return to an unhealthy environment or to fall back into unhealthy habits, we will suffer the consequences as our hearts grow weaker over time. Our *spiritual hearts* are the same. God does not give us a *new heart* so that we can revert back to our previous way of living. He gives us *new hearts* so we can see through deception, to have the strength we find in our relationship with Him to choose to do the right thing, and to ultimately find *our path* and *our purpose* in this life.

Change never comes easily and it doesn't come overnight ... *it requires honesty within one's self, perseverance, and much hard work.* We will need to exercise our hearts and our minds every day by being faithful in obedience to the *Truths of the Teachings of God.* We will stumble on this journey; *sometimes we will fall,* but don't allow the *lies of*

Satan to cause you to give up or to stay down. God will forgive our mistakes, *with our confession and repentance*, and Jesus will always walk with you. He is truly the one friend who will never leave you, betray you, ridicule you, or ask you to do it all by yourself.

King Solomon became the wisest and the richest man who has ever lived. HOW? Because King Solomon chose to *"Partnership with God"*. The foundation of King Solomon's *great success* was what lay within his heart. King Solomon asked for a *discerning heart* ... not to promote his own gain, but to help him to serve others. King Solomon didn't ask God to solve his problems for him ... *he asked for the ability to discern between right and wrong - the ability to make the right choices and decisions for his own life and in his relationships with others.*

- **1 Kings 3: 9-12 ...** *"Give your servant a discerning heart to govern your people and to distinguish between right and wrong. For who is able to govern this great people of yours?" The Lord was pleased that Solomon had asked for this. So God said to him, "Since you have asked for this and not for long life or wealth for yourself, nor have you asked for the death of your enemies but for discernment in administering justice, I will do what you have asked. I will give you a wise and discerning heart."*

The Lord was pleased with King Solomon's desire to use God's wisdom for His purpose rather than for his own gain, and for this reason ... *God richly rewarded Solomon.* I do want to urge you to read the entire Story of Solomon in your Bible because it teaches us so many of *life's lessons.*

King Solomon started off right, *in his relationship with God and in how he dealt with others*, but he didn't always persevere in the wisdom that God had imparted to him in his most intimate personal relationships. Even the wisest and richest man who ever lived upon this earth had to learn one simple truth ... *just as he "reaped the rewards of obedience to God" – he also "suffered the consequences of disobedience to God".*

I want to get a little personal here with regards to my own success. As a teenager I knew that I had to develop focus on getting an education in order to find a job that would enable me to earn the monies to be free of my past and to build a new life for myself. *Years later I finally learned that I had not become free of my past. I had only buried it deep within and kept covering it up with layer upon layer of "positive-thinking veneer".*

Please understand that there is absolutely nothing inappropriate in the desire to get a good education or with the power of positive-thinking. I strongly applaud and my life reflects my commitment to both of these principles. I continue to study in order to learn every day ... *personally, physically, mentally, professionally, and spiritually.* And *positive thinking* combined with a *pure heart* and a *Godly mind* is imperative to *living a successful life.*

I became very successful based on the *world's concept* of success. By my mid-thirties I was very well known and respected professionally *(often resented secretly)* as *a woman of authority* in a man's world. I was enjoying the *"fruits of my labor"* both professionally and financially. In spite of two miscarriages and the doctor's very strong advice against my continuing to try and carry a child to term, I became a mother at nineteen years of age. Another reason for me to continue to push myself beyond the limits of human endurance ... my child was going to have everything all the other kids had – she would never suffer the pain of being laughed at or rejected because of my financial lack. I missed out on so many opportunities for sharing *quality time* with my child because my focus was on obtaining the *world's version* of success. And underneath all those layers of veneer there still lay the shame and the pain of my own childhood ... *deeply out of sight of everyone except me and God.*

In 1982, I met and began to love my third husband, Leonard Hobbs. After five short months, Leonard was murdered. I learned much later that he had been murdered because he was with me. I grew harder and colder within ... *so bitter towards God that I refused to even allow His Name to be spoken in my presence.* Once again, I swallowed my emotions and hid my riveting pain. I needed no one. I had my precious daughter and I had my professional success. I didn't need anything more or anyone else in my life. I was happy and successful ... Right? Wrong!

May 1984, without warning, my daughter was also murdered ... this time by mistake - it was supposed to have been me. By the time I cried out to God in 1987, and accepted Jesus Christ as my personal Lord and Savior, I had lost it all ... *professional position, financial security, family, and was running desperately in order to try and protect my own life.*

When I gave my life to Jesus, I was given a brand new heart. Things didn't change for me overnight. It took years for me to work through the consequences of my earlier years and to truly heal from my past. But what did change for me, *upon receiving Jesus Christ into my heart and into my life,* was the *"knowing"* that I was no longer all alone. I had Jesus, and He has walked with me every single step of the way ... *out of darkness into the Light of His Love.*

Now I live everyday immersed in the *rewards* that come from *choosing to seek* God's Will and Purpose for my life ... *knowing real peace and success is in Him.*

I was told that I would never be able to use my own name, Vel Hobbs, again because doing so would be far too dangerous. *But I serve a God of Restoration!* In business, and in ministry, I am known by many throughout the United States and even in other nations. I go to bed each night, *secure in God and at peace within my heart*, free from guilt and free from fear. I wake up each morning, *no matter what I am facing in my life*, without fear or worry because I *know* that God holds my life within His Hands. I know that because of His great love for me, everything is going to be all right. That, my friends, is *Living A Successful Life* by anyone's definition!

I found the success that I was so desperately seeking was God Himself. He is both the Giver of Life and the Reward all in one. In my *"Partnership With God"* I have found my true self and my true purpose. This is what I love the most about God ... *He Is The God Of Second Chances.* No matter how many times we mess up, no matter how many times we fail, no matter how much we struggle with our fears and insecurities ... *we can fulfill God's Call on our lives and become the success that He intended us to be.*

Among presidents, Abraham Lincoln stands head and shoulders above the rest. He once said, *"I desire to so conduct the affairs of this administration that if, at the end, when I come to lay down the reins of power, I have lost every other friend on earth, I shall at least have one friend left, and that friend shall be deep down inside me. I am not bound to succeed, but I am bound to live up to the light I have. Let us have the faith that right makes might, and in that faith, let us, to the end, dare to do our duty as we understand it."*

The difficulties of President Lincoln's day were hard, but no harder than the present difficulties of our day. The Power that President Lincoln knew a faithful God could supply is still available. But we, *as Christians*, also have the same responsibility that Abraham Lincoln had ... *to stand for the right*. It will often be a lonely and risky position, *but as we stand for the right*, God will supply the might. If you have never studied the life and history of Abraham Lincoln's climb to the highest political office in this land, you have no idea of how many times he failed – *in the eyes of others*. But he didn't see it as a failure, *but as a stepping stone*, and he always got back up, dusted himself off, and kept on going ... *all of the way to the top!*

How are you, my friend, going to answer this question within your own heart ... *"What does it mean to live a successful life?"*

"Father God, I want to thank you for the access I have to you through Jesus Christ, my High Priest. I choose in this moment to draw near to you. According to your promise, draw near to me as I seek your presence. I acknowledge my need for greater grace. I ask you to touch my heart and to fan into a burning flame the ember of love that I have for you. Stir up the spark of commitment to your kingdom that already burns within me. Abba Father, give fresh light to my mind in understanding your truth. Give courage to my heart in following your ways.

Dear Lord, I acknowledge my dependence upon you. Open the eyes of your servant to see as you see. Anoint my lips to speak as you would speak. Grant your servant the authority of your Son to stand against Satan and his works of evil, and to speak triumph over them in Jesus' Name. Impart unto me your graces and gifts to fight and to prevail in the battle for lost souls. Let nothing hinder the high and holy purpose you have for my life. Speak afresh to me ... I long to hear your voice. Train my hands for battle and assign me my place in your army. Teach me the ways of your Spirit, and lead me in the path of understanding for Jesus' sake and for the cause of His Kingdom. Amen"

EPILOGUE

"IT'S TOUGH & IT TAKES TIME"

We can lose our perspective while we are dealing with what is wrong with us. So we need to remember that it is not God's desire that we live in perpetual pain, morbidly focused on what is wrong with us. That tactic is the enemy's … not God's. God convicts us of sin, *through His Word and by the Holy Spirit*, only so we may be forgiven and enabled to walk in freedom.

- **1 John 1:9 … *"If we confess our sins, He is faithful and just and will forgive us our sins and purify us from all unrighteousness."***

Confession is not a list of petty blemishes drawn up grudgingly for the sake of an overbearing God. Confession is facing up to those cancerous vices that sap vitality, cripple freedom, and eventually kill. We are the ones who suffer if we sin. That is exactly why Satan, *the father of lies and deception*, does everything in his power to lure us with the momentary and fleeting pleasures of sin. Satan hates God and he hates God's Ultimate Creation … all mankind. If we fall prey to his cunning deceitful lies about God and about the temporary pleasures of sin, Satan will win and we will lose because in the end we are the ones who will suffer his destruction.

To see the victory of God's grace over sin is not something we can knock off in a weekend. Though we live in a culture that is always in a hurry, *demanding instant results*, the Bible admonishes us to wait, to work at it, and never to lose heart. I have discovered no magic key that will enable us to lock out suffering or the painful and often slow process of growth. I have found no shortcuts or gimmicks to becoming the person God desires for us to become. Evil never has the last word ... GOD DOES! But while we wait, we need to ask for the grace of tenacity, so that we can hang on – and on and on – while He works His excellent purpose in us.

We shouldn't underestimate the pain that will be involved. But neither must we forget what is happening to us as we are being changed into the likeness of God. Our pain in our journey is not only for us to become the men and women God created us to be. We are being refined and molded into a living testimony for a living and loving God that can shine with the love of Jesus in a world made dark with sin.

- **2 Corinthians 1: 3–8** ... *"Praise be to the God and Father of our Lord Jesus Christ, the Father of compassion and the God of all comfort, who comforts us in all our troubles, so that we can comfort those in any trouble with the comfort we ourselves have received from God. For just as the sufferings of Christ flow over into our lives, so also through Christ our comfort overflows. If we are distressed, it is for your comfort and salvation; if we are comforted, it is for your comfort, which produces in you patient endurance of the same sufferings we suffer. And our hope for you is firm, because we* *know that just as you share in our sufferings, so you also share in our comfort."*

In my relationship with Christ, I am taking a lifetime class in the art of being Christ like. As He teaches me, I keep one eye glued on Him. I try to imitate Him. Studying His Word helps me know His thoughts and actions in different situations. Jesus painted the whole New Testament with a broad sweep of love, forgiveness, and mercy. My prayer is that my life will be the same as His.

- **1 John 2: 5–6 ...** *"But if anyone obeys His Word, God's love is truly made complete in him. This is how we know we are in Him: Whoever claims to live in Him must walk as Jesus did."*

The greatest, *and toughest*, lesson that we can learn from Jesus is to surrender our complete life to God, to trust in His love for us, but also to grow in Faith to know that God has a Plan and a Purpose for our life. However, the journey to becoming the person that God created us to be will require daily sacrifice ... *the sacrifice to His Will over our will.* As Jesus did in the Garden of Gethsemane, we must become willing to trust in God's Love and God's Plan so much that – *once we have expressed our desires and have made our requests for what we want to happen in our lives known* – we can then say, *"Not my will but Thine be done".*

"WHY?" Because our self-will has brought us down a road of pain and self-destruction already so why would we want to continue to do the same old destructive things? We are not strong enough, *within ourselves,* to rebuild a life of freedom from sin and self-destruction. And every single choice we make, *every decision right or wrong,* will touch the lives of others either in a positive way or in a negative and destructive way.

When we begin to groan and complain because we think that God is keeping us in the *fiery furnace of refinement and change* too long, we need to remember the very simple TRUTH that God loves us more than anyone else ever can. Furthermore, God knows our *true hearts* far more intimately than anyone else ever will, and He knows what it is going to take for us to become all that He knows we can be.

God knows what it is going to take for us to grow in Him to become strong enough to make the choices and decisions for our lives that lie on the road ahead – *the long road hidden from us* – that will be positive and constructive for us and for those whom we touch daily with our influence.

While you are still in the *fiery furnace of refinement and change,* stop fighting what God wants to do in your life. Surrender to His Wisdom; grow strong in His Knowledge, lean upon His Love, and trust in His Perfect Plan and His Perfect Timing for you.

The word *hopeless* has no place in a Believer's vocabulary. If the Lord is present, so is *hope.* God's Word offers *hope* for all.

- Regardless of how dark or desperate a situation seems, *hope* abides. This means that we should hold tightly to our *hope.*
- Our *hope* is anchored in Jesus Christ; thus it is able to withstand any attack.
- Nothing can separate us from the love of God and the *hope* He brings. Any problem, situation, or affliction we face pales in comparison with the Power of the Lord who can help us to overcome it.

We must learn to look beyond our immediate circumstances, beyond the worry and despair that so easily grip us, and look toward the proverbial light at the end of the tunnel.

That light is the *hope* that God gives us in His Word. That *hope,* that confident expectation, can carry us through.

GOD HAS A POSITIVE ANSWER. Ladies ... when I read these promises from the Word of God, I know that there are no gender issues with my Heavenly Father. I change the *"him/he"* to *"her/she"* and make the promises my own! Enjoy and be strengthened in Christ Jesus!

- WHEN WE SAY ... *"It's impossible"*. GOD SAYS ... *"All things are possible"*. **Luke 18:27 ...** *Jesus replied, "What is impossible with men is possible with God."*
- WHEN WE SAY ... *"I'm too tired"*. GOD SAYS ... *"I will give you rest"*. **Matthew 11: 28–30 ...** *"Come to me, all you who are weary and burdened, and I will give you rest. Take my yoke upon you and learn from me, for I am gentle and humble in heart, and you will find rest for your souls. For my yoke is easy and my burden is light."*
- WHEN WE SAY ... *"Nobody really loves me"*. GOD SAYS ... *"I love you"*. **John 3: 16 ...** *"For God so loved the world that he gave his one and only Son, that whoever believes in him shall not perish but have eternal life."*
- WHEN WE SAY ... *"I can't go on"*. GOD SAYS ... *"My Grace Is Sufficient"*. **2 Corinthians 12:9 ...** *But he said to me, "My grace is sufficient for you, for my power is made perfect in weakness."* **Psalms 91:14–16 ...** *"Because he loves me," says the Lord, "I will rescue him, for he acknowledges my name. He will call upon me, and I will answer him; I will be with him in trouble, I will deliver him and honor him. With long life will I satisfy him and show him my salvation."*

- WHEN WE SAY ... *"I can't figure things out"*. GOD SAYS ... *"I will direct your steps"*. **Proverbs 4: 11&12** ... *"I guide you in the way of salvation and lead you along straight paths. When you walk, your steps will not be hampered; when you run, you will not stumble."* **Jeremiah 29:11** ... *"For I know the plans I have for you," declares the Lord, "Plans to prosper you and not to harm you, plans to give you hope and a future."*
- WHEN WE SAY ... *"I can't do it"*. GOD SAYS ... *"You can do all things"*. **Philippians 4:13** ... *"I can do all things through Christ who strengthens me."*
- WHEN WE SAY ... *"I'm not able"*. GOD SAYS ... *"I am able"*. **2 Corinthians 9:8** ... *"And God is able to make all grace abound to you, so that in all things at all times, having all that you need, you will abound in every good work."*
- WHEN WE SAY ... *"It's not worth it"*. GOD SAYS ... *"It will be worth it"*. **Romans 8:28** ... *"And we know that in all things God works for the good of those who love him, who have been called according to his purpose."*
- WHEN WE SAY ... *"I can't forgive myself"*. GOD SAYS ... *"I forgive you"*. **1 John 1:9** ... *"If we confess our sins, he is faithful and just and will forgive us our sins and purify us from all unrighteousness."* **Romans 8: 1&2** ... *"Therefore, there is now no condemnation for those who are in Christ Jesus, because through Christ Jesus the law of the Spirit of life set me free from the law of sin and death."*
- WHEN WE SAY ... *"I can't manage"*. GOD SAYS ... *"I will supply all your needs"*. **Philippians 4:19** ... *"And my God will meet all your needs according to his glorious riches in Christ Jesus."*

- WHEN WE SAY … *"I'm afraid"*. GOD SAYS … *"I have not given you a spirit of fear"*. **2 Timothy 1:7** *… "For God did not give us a spirit of timidity, but a spirit of power, of love and of self-discipline."*
- WHEN WE SAY … *"I'm always worried"*. GOD SAYS … *"Cast all your cares on me"*. **1 Peter 5:7** *… Cast all your anxiety on him because he cares for you."*
- WHEN WE SAY … *"I'm not smart enough"*. GOD SAYS … *"I will give you wisdom"*. **1 Corinthians 1: 26–31** *… "Think of what you were when you were called. Not many or you were wise by human standards; not many were influential; not many were of noble birth. But God chose the foolish things of the world to shame the wise; God chose the weak things of the world to shame the strong. He chose the lowly things of this world and the despised things – and the things that are not – to nullify the things that are, so that no one may boast before him. It is because of him that you are in Christ Jesus, who has become for us wisdom from God – that is, our righteousness, holiness and redemption. Therefore, as it is written: 'Let him who boasts boast in the Lord.'"*
- WHEN WE SAY … *"I feel all alone"*. GOD SAYS … *"I will never leave you or forsake you"*. **Hebrews 13:5** *… "Never will I leave you; never will I forsake you."* **Hebrew13:6** *… So we say with confidence, "The Lord is my helper; I will not be afraid. What can man do to me?"*

So once said Sophie Kerr, *"The future is now!"* We shape our future by how we *choose* to handle the present. In each moment the real future for me is now. Life is a personal journey for each and every individual. We each have the opportunity and the privilege to *choose* what value our life is going to have. The wonderful part of life's journey is this ... we can start fresh, *no matter where we are or where we may have come from*, and choose to go forward towards a rich and fulfilling future.

Are you ready to start a new way of life? Are you ready to *dare to dream?* Dreams make the difference between living your life and *really living your life*. Some of us get so caught up in the busyness of life, or become so lost in the struggle of life, that we have forgotten how to dream. Even if we once had a dream – were excited by our dream – we have let it all slip away from us somehow. When we *lose our dream*, we will also *lose our joy* for life and all that it offers.

Without a dream, you will find the journey of life to indeed be a very long and tough journey. If you have lost your dreams, here are a few suggestions:

- Find a quiet spot to just sit back and let your thoughts roam ... *what has God already done in your life - What might he still do?* Consider, just for a moment, what isn't but could be. Dream beyond where you are.
- Dreams begin with asking yourself some questions, such as ... *"If you could do anything you wanted with an extra hour today, what would it be?"*
- Sometimes dreams have their roots in the past ... *"When you think back over your childhood, what did you do with your spare time?"*
- Dreams can also peer around the corners of our everyday life and come right into the places where we live or work ... *thoughts and ideas to give us clues as to how we can grow – if we will pay attention to our heart.*
- Identify where and how you want to grow ... *then start dreaming a dream for your life and make a plan.*
- Ask God for insight into what he has designed for you to become in your life ... *seek out the true*

God-Given "desires of your heart". **Psalms 37: 3–5 ... "Trust in the Lord and do good; dwell in the land and enjoy safe pasture. Delight yourself in the Lord and he will give you the desires of your heart. Commit your way to the Lord; trust in him and he will do this."**

I can personally attest to one fact ... *our life becomes in reality what we choose to make of it under all circumstances.* My *journey* has been filled with many different and life-changing choices. I *chose* to not only endure some circumstances that would have defeated many, but I made a *choice* long ago to overcome the obstacles that popped up along the road... to *overcome* and to *succeed* at life!

I will be eternally grateful for *my choices to survive and to overcome*, and I will be eternally grateful that MY BESTEST FRIEND has walked with me every single step of the way from the depths of destruction to unbelievable victory since I invited HIM into my life in 1987.

What about your personal circumstances, and ... *what about your personal choices?* You will move through numerous "SEASONS OF THE HEART" on your *life journey*, and ultimately you will be the only one who can *choose* the *path* you walk ... *will it be a positive path, or will it be a negative and self-destructive path?* The *privilege to choose* your *path* and your *destination* is in your hands. It is not in the hands of anyone else ... not even God.

God loves you and offers to help you choose life over death, but He also gave you free will to make your own choices. He will always help you if you ask, but He will not force or coerce you against your will. I pray that you choose to walk a pathway of recovery and success.

OTHER BOOKS BY VEL HOBBS: the proceeds from my book sales are primarily used toward purchasing Bibles and other materials to be used in a Volunteer Counseling Ministry at the Women's Quarters of the Montgomery County Jail. My books can be purchased online at **www.amazon.com**; **www.christianbook.com**; **www.barnesandnoble.com**; and other websites.

1. "Restoring & Rebuilding A HOUSE DIVIDED Healing From Abuse": Abraham Lincoln once wrote, "A house divided against itself cannot stand". Even so, it seems that a prison cell can be built out of rubble, as described by author Vel Hobbs in **"A House Divided"**.

   For years, Ms. Hobbs was imprisoned by memories of childhood abuse, resentment, damaging relationships, and a growing lack of trust in other people. And yet, miraculously, the author was able to escape and to begin "a remarkable life-changing journey" to true freedom. Traveling from emotional and physical illness to spiritual health on a journey of self-discovery, Ms. Hobbs also embraced the friendship of Jesus Christ and the protecting love of God.

   This is a true story of a wonderfully spiritual journey, which built and continues to nurture a dwelling place for the Holy Spirit. GOD LOVES US, and there is life after abuse.

   If you are scarred by abuse of any type, please read this book. WHY? It is one thing to counsel others from what has been learned through intellectual studies, but it is quite another matter to receive counsel from *someone who has walked the same path in their life.*

This is my story and it has helped many across this country and overseas to make the emotional, mental, and physical transition from living their lives as *"victims"* by understanding they are not to blame for their past ... *how to not only be survivors but to also be over-comers!*

2. "Angels, Visions & Dreams, Prophecies": "God works in mysterious ways" ... throughout the Bible we read of supernatural intervention in so many people's lives: visitations by angels, visions, dreams, and words of prophecy. God is still the same God "yesterday, today, and forever". While we, as humans, have the gift of free will and learned knowledge, there are times when only supernatural intervention can help us.

This book will give astounding and true accounts of supernatural intervention upon and within the lives of people at a time when their very lives depended upon more help than even the strongest mortal could have provided. These are REAL-LIFE people with REAL-LIFE stories of SUPERNATURAL deliverance, protection, guidance, and provision in today's world!

If you are a skeptic, I understand. But do yourself a favor. Keep an open heart and a seeking mind. I promise that you will not regret doing so. God Bless.

3. "Deceptive Seduction": *"The Devil made me do it!"* Although we have all heard someone make this statement at least once in our lives, it still carries a very real truth. Have you ever ventured into the teachings of the *New Age Movement?* Have you ever dabbled in the adventure of *occult practices?* Have you ever visited a *psychic?* Are you seeking answers to spiritual questions or running from the concept of

God because of *spiritual confusion?* Or maybe you are just one of those people who are fascinated by anything having to do with the *supernatural?*

How could a young woman go from merely talking to a *psychic* in 1984, to finding herself being ordered to murder an innocent woman and her unborn child a few short years later? Read her story in this book, **"Deceptive Seduction"**, and then you choose who will be the MASTER you follow in your own life.

4. The FATHER and the SON and the HOLY SPIRIT "OR" Oneness – Jesus Only: this book strives to provide Biblically-Based answers to very important questions. Do we serve a Triune God who is ONE GOD and is seen in the three distinct persons of the Father and the Son and the Holy Spirit, as Jesus Himself taught in Matthew 28:19? Or do we adhere to the teachings of the "Oneness-Jesus Only" doctrines that contradict the *Directives of Jesus Himself* as given by *Him* to *His Disciples?*

This book also focuses on other doctrines within the "Oneness-Jesus Only" teachings that are in direct contradiction to the Word of God. Is *water baptism in the Name of Jesus Only* required for salvation? Is *speaking in tongues* a requirement of salvation as taught by Oneness believers, or is *speaking in tongues* one of the *Gifts of the Holy Spirit* as we read in 1 Corinthians Chapter Twelve? Are we *saved by grace through faith in Jesus Christ* as the Scriptures teach, "OR" are we saved *through faith and works* as set forth by some denominations? Who are we to follow ... God or man?

From Pastors, Ministers, Evangelists, Bible Teachers, Christian Radio Talk Show Host, and other people within the Body-of-Christ; I have been told that this book provides *Biblical Answers* to the question of *"The Trinity"* versus the *"Oneness-Jesus Only"* theology from many angles.

Ministry Of New Hope
Vel Hobbs
Ordained Minister / Non-Denominational
Associate of Theology in Christian Counseling
Board Certified Biblical Counselor
Christian Author
Business Woman
God's Child & Your Friend

Feel Free To Contact Me:
PO Box 1662 Conroe, Texas 77305
Email: ministryofnewhope@consolidated.net
Website: www.ministryofnewhope.com

Printed in the United States
140390LV00004B/22/P

9 781606 472095